BEYOND THE FRONTIER

Beyond the Frontier

THE MIDWESTERN VOICE IN
AMERICAN HISTORICAL WRITING

David S. Brown

The University of Chicago Press   Chicago and London

DAVID S. BROWN is professor of history at Elizabethtown College. He is the author of *Richard Hofstadter: An Intellectual Biography.*

The University of Chicago Press, Chicago 60637
The University of Chicago Press, Ltd., London
© 2009 by The University of Chicago
All rights reserved. Published 2009
Printed in the United States of America

18 17 16 15 14 13 12 11 10 09   1 2 3 4 5

ISBN-13: 978-0-226-07651-5 (cloth)
ISBN-10: 0-226-07651-2 (cloth)

Library of Congress Cataloging-in-Publication Data
Brown, David S. (David Scott), 1966–
Beyond the frontier : the midwestern voice in American
historical writing / David S. Brown.
p. cm.
Includes bibliographical references and index.
ISBN-13: 978-0-226-07651-5 (cloth : alk. paper)
ISBN-10: 0-226-07651-2 (cloth : alk. paper)   1. United States—
Historiography.   2. Historians—Middle West—Biography.
3. Beard, Charles Austin, 1874–1948.   4. Lasch, Christopher.
5. Turner, Frederick Jackson, 1861–1932.
6. Williams, William Appleman.   I. Title.
E175.45.B76 2009
973—dc22
2008040818

In Memory
Edmond Miller Brown
True

There is a separate Middle Western culture.
And I think everyone who knows it, and who knows the
nation, is profoundly aware that it is in the process of
becoming the dominant American culture.

BERNARD DEVOTO

Contents

Acknowledgments

A thousand collaborations made this book. Most especially, I'm pleased to identify in its closing pages the many and patient historians who sat—in Philadelphia diners, Madison coffeehouses, and wintry Ithaca offices—for gentle interrogations. Their labors, one and all, are deeply appreciated. Of the nearer constellations, my colleague, friend, and first reader Paul Gottfried offered commentary and conversation—the source of endless instruction. His impress traces lightly but distinctly across this project. In a later permutation, the manuscript received the collective wisdom of several thoughtful critics. Michael Brown, the late David Cronon, James Gilbert, Jeff Ludwig, Wilfred McClay, Kevin Mattson, and Robert Westbrook offered insights and suggestions that improved this book in ways both large and small; I am doubly in debt to Professor Westbrook for his kind permission to quote from the Christopher Lasch Papers. As the project progressed, Allan Bogue helped me to fill in fragments of the history of the modern historical profession germane to his experiences and not to be found in the written records. Each Bogue reply arrived like a piece to a puzzle. At the University of Chicago Press, Robert Devens improved each chapter, each page. While I had my eye fixed on a particular interpretive path, he saw another, broader and better one. Essential in every meaningful respect, Robert's good and varied editorial contributions, along with those of his associates at the Press, are here happily acknowledged. And lastly, Elizabethtown College granted me a timely sabbatical with this as yet a book unborn. For that, and other considerations, it has my gratitude.

The Golden Meridian

*If all the world were Wisconsin, the twentieth century might have been an
age of the golden meridian in which small producers and industrial craftsman
used republican ideals of equal rights to moderate the special privileges that
had been granted to big business under laissez-faire liberalism.*

ALAN DAWLEY, 2003

The Midwest is a state of mind. Close your eyes and think college football,
county fairs, and family picnics; think heartland, breadbasket, Dubuque
farms and Des Moines factories; think Pleasantville (IA), Pleasant Hill
(OH), New Haven (MI), New Hope (MN), and New Harmony (IN). The
most "American" of all American places, the Midwest is the spiritual soil of
resident sons and daughters Gatsby, Babbitt, Sula, and Carol Kennicott.
Home of the five-and-dime underdog and habitat to second cities, it lives
in four seasons, farms on flat lands, and swims in Great Lakes. In a nation
forever faithful to its redemptive rendezvous with destiny, the Midwest
imagines itself the country's indispensable karmic balance—the village reply to the epic "Bosnywash" megalopolis, the humble yeoman contrast to
a doomed southern hierarchy, and the commonsense salvation to coastal
California's fever dream for the new.[1]

And think history—made and written. Actors in the long age of reform
bookended by the Reconstruction 1870s and the New Deal 1930s, many
of the nation's great industrialists, most of its presidents, and a striking
number of influential historians shared midwestern roots. In the years after
this ascendancy, an interior-minded historical consciousness has continued to engage a diverse and critical public readership. It is distinguished
by a typology of progressive thought and politics—democratic, populistic, isolationist—different from the liberal typology of thought and
politics—elite, urban, interventionist—favored by the cosmopolitans. At
times these visions have clashed. Secure in their identities as Wasp insiders,
the middle-westerners in these pages never doubted their section's unique

contributions to national life, nor their own roles as regional interpreters. "Perhaps we of the West are only children who believe in Santa Claus," Wisconsin historian John Hicks wrote in the troubled 1930s. "But perhaps western belief that the disorders of the world can yet be righted will help to right them, perhaps even the naïve western assumption that the American experiment in democracy cannot possibly fail will help to keep it from failing."[2]

The peculiar strain of geographic fate advanced by Hicks found its most suggestive expression in the works of Frederick Jackson Turner, Charles Beard, William Appleman Williams, and Christopher Lasch. Collectively, this group advanced a century of scholarship sympathetic to populistic politics, critical of America's swift drift toward empire, and unreconciled to unrestrained capitalism. All were children of the Middle West and all struggled with the multiple meanings of their regional inheritance, meshing sharp and searching intellects with a faint but unmistakable provincialism.

Taking into account their all-too-human strengths and weaknesses, it seems appropriate to ask by what reasoning we might consider this midwestern persuasion, with its romantic undercurrent and partisan historical vision, worth our critical reflection. The answer is impact. Iconic books, scholars, and schools have left a long and influential legacy on the academy and the culture. It is the "big idea" that usually moves debate forward, and these men most decidedly moved debate forward. They labored productively in a profession dedicated to objectivity yet produced a wide stream of studies that combined the archivist's talent for research with the humanist's passion for the graceful grand narrative. In Turner's "The Significance of the Frontier in American History" (1893), Beard's *President Roosevelt and the Coming of the War* (1948), Williams's *The Tragedy of American Diplomacy* (1959), and Lasch's *The True and Only Heaven* (1991), the American metathemes of character, democracy, empire, and progress were addressed under the academic cover of footnotes. They, and others of their genus, allow us to reflect on the past in ways that go beyond raw and often isolated facts. They integrate memory with myth to comment on civic culture, shape public debate, and guide opinions. They speak not merely to our intellect but also to our sensibilities and sense of self. We look for our lives between their covers.

At its heart, mythology seeks to explain the nature and ways of the world. We use fables and folktales to understand our communities, our leaders, and our times. More generally, myths are mediums for conveying culture. The rise of the post–Civil War Middle West stirred regional pride and encouraged ways of reconceptualizing the section's people and its past, often in a language spiced with license, exaggeration, and allegory. Heroic dimensions were the order of the day as the likes of Paul Bunyan, Johnny Appleseed, and John Henry tickled the American imagination. In legends one could discover hidden truths and latent possibilities. An evocative midwestern architecture (farmer gothic), style of painting (the bucolic regionalism of Grant Wood and Thomas Hart Benton), literature (the elegiac F. Scott Fitzgerald), and poetry (Carl Sandburg's Chicago verses) moved interior thought and expression beyond the literal.

The region's historians had their say as well. To speak of a Midwestern School is to shorthand the collectors of creation myths, a group of pastmasters who internalized and revealed with clarity and rare insight the faiths and fears of their neighbors. Turner's frontier thesis encapsulated both the promise and the perils of American expansion; Beard placed the virtues of social democracy above the old property-rights conservatism, while both Williams and Lasch panned a capitalist elite in favor of a revived populism. As critics of an emergent military-industrial complex, they reflected their region's suspicion of the new order and responded sympathetically to its psychological needs. Thus, while I take quite seriously their remarkable and indeed canonical contributions to "objective" historical scholarship, I respect as well the curative value of their work. Books can be like medicine.

As intellectuals rooted in a middle-western frame of reference, Turner and his successors were vulnerable to the region's uneven fortunes. This uncertainty encouraged a body of research that ranged from the confident and expansive to the cautious and narrow. In the period 1890–1930, the interior claimed a special status among the nation's sections. A long train of recent Ohio Valley presidents testified to its political arrival, while the persistence of Anglo/rural folkways in an increasingly ethnic/urbanized country gave heartlanders the hereditary high ground. As an editorialist put it in 1912, "One finds in the Middle West today a larger proportion of men and women whose ideas, habits, and institutions are essentially those of Colonial America and of England, than can be found now in the East."[3]

This regional vanity suffered successive blows in the 1930s and 1940s. FDR's vigorous response to the Depression ushered in a fresh political dynamic that reoriented the party system from parochial to metropolitan. Soon thereafter, World War II ratified the new alignment by shattering the old isolationism. In a 1941 essay, *Life* magazine publisher Henry Luce explained where all of this was heading—he called it "The American Century." The son of missionaries, Luce urged his countrymen to abandon their continental solitude and aggressively push democracy around the globe. If liberal nations failed to expand, he argued, they would surely succumb to the authoritarian likes of Nazi Germany and Soviet Russia. "We are *not* in a war to defend American territory," he wrote. "We are in a war to defend and even to promote, encourage and incite so-called democratic principles throughout the world." Taking a long view of matters, we might find it appropriate to anoint 1898 rather than 1941 as year one of the American Century. Luce was born 3 April of that year—less than three weeks before William McKinley signed a congressional joint resolution proclaiming Cuba's independence from Spain. This document authorized the president to use military force if necessary to guarantee the island's "freedom." The resulting "splendid little war" made the United States an imperial power and christened its problematic engagement with internationalism.[4]

Luce belonged to a generation that, despite its rhetorical support for representative government, had lost faith in popular politics. Too deliberate, divided, and idealistic, the Western democracies had failed to stem German and Japanese marches across Europe and Asia. In reply, America's postwar globalists created fresh military, bureaucratic, and academic structures of power to contain a rising threat—Soviet influence. The new policy experts hoped to save democracy from itself, and they abandoned the old Jeffersonian fantasy of an empire of liberty for a leviathan strong enough to shore up Western civilization. As one historian recently observed, "The American Century reflected a turn away from democratic idealism and a turn toward the 'realism' of strong authoritative 'statesmen.' . . . The language of democracy proliferated, but the practice of democracy narrowed."[5] At its critical best, the Middle West thoughtfully addressed the deficiencies and dangers of the American Century. Imperial presidencies, covert wars, and a bourgeoning fiscal-military state were the high prices paid, its more skeptical reviewers warned, for enlarging the sphere of "secretive" power in a people's republic.

It might be helpful at this point to place the Midwestern School of historians in context. It once stood among a handful of sectionally centered intellectual movements that included the Vanderbilt "Fugitives," a notable collection of prewar southern writers, poets, and historians inveighing against America's hastily constructed liberal-industrial regime. In *I'll Take My Stand: The South and the Agrarian Tradition* (1930), Allen Tate, John Crowe Ransom, Robert Penn Warren, et al. composed an elaborate statement on the superiority of Dixie civilization in a nation spiraling, they complained, toward a soulless, unreflective worship of machines and technology. The market crash and subsequent Depression won their work a respectful hearing, yet in the 1940s America moved quickly to create a vast consumer-containment culture predicated on speed, flux, and conversion. The fading hope among some conservatives for a useful southern break from late modernity had already passed.

A second school, the Columbia University social scientists, captured the imagination of the postwar academy and played a key role in liberalism's rapid rise to ideological predominance. These scholars, comprised in the main of men of Eastern European and Russian Jewish background, including Daniel Bell, Seymour Martin Lipset, and Robert K. Merton, watched the disturbing growth of McCarthyism with great concern. They felt certain that a toxic mixture of mass society and mass democracy energized the Far Right, and in its place they pushed a tough-minded liberalism, one open enough to create opportunities for reform at home while vigorously fighting a cold war abroad. In accordance with this vision, they warmly embraced an expert-based culture: experts to oversee the New Deal state's vast social welfare programs, experts to operate the industrial might of the U.S. economy, and experts to run a greatly expanded and increasingly complex military. In this devotion to anointed intellectual authority resided a central premise that cut against the grain of the nation's egalitarian conventions—the few were to command the many.

For all their differences, the Vanderbilt and Columbia schools shared a common prejudice: each privileged a collection of particular regional values embedded in specific cultural traditions. And in their own ways, each betrayed an antidemocratic preference for American development in the twentieth century. The southern vision longed for a return to *local* elite control in the nation's regional centers; the eastern vision imagined a *national* elite running a top-down meritocracy.

The midwestern historians took a different tack. Unburdened by the quasi-aristocratic culture that stalked the southern imagination or the minority "otherness" familiar to many in the ethnically tinged liberal intelligentsia, they were passionate about the possibilities of democracy and unafraid of popular protest, which both their scholarship and their teaching recognized as a vital part of the American political tradition.

Three historical schools, three historical contexts. The Vanderbilt vision understood democracy and mass culture to mean the welter of force and power that smashed southern nationhood to bits in the 1860s and had subsequently made deep assaults on southern cultural practices. The Columbia social scientists understood the underside of democracy and mass culture to mean the unleashing of popular resentments by majority Anglos on minority immigrants—anti-Semitism passing as respectable cold war red-baiting. The Midwestern School, by contrast, embraced a frankly egalitarian identity. Its members basked in the regional inheritance of a great democratic tradition, the Populist/Progressive age of change. And more, they enjoyed the status of "insiders," Wasps whose patriarchs had crossed the Appalachians, won the Free-Soil war to reunite the nation, and established a slew of democratic state universities to counter the eastern grip on intellect. They saw themselves as a chosen people.

Exploring the life and times of the Midwestern School of historical writing allows us to observe the rise and fall—and rise and fall—of the last century's two great reform movements, progressivism (1890–1945) and liberalism (1945–1970). The distance between the Midwest's Protestant, populistic historians and their by turns Brahmin and Jewish counterparts at Harvard and Columbia encapsulates in the academy a larger cultural struggle played out in American politics between isolationists and internationalists, egalitarians and experts, provincials and cosmopolitans.

Unlike the electorally solid South and Northeast, the Midwest is a fluid political creature. No reform candidate—and no conservative candidate—has walked into the White House without first winning its allegiance. The progressive Republican Theodore Roosevelt won the region in 1904; the progressive Democrat Woodrow Wilson took most of it in 1912; Franklin Roosevelt swept the Midwest in 1932 as did Lyndon Johnson in 1964, Bill Clinton (excepting Indiana) in 1992, and Barack Obama in 2008. These states also went unanimously for McKinley in 1896, Harding in 1920, Eisenhower in 1952, Nixon in 1972, and Reagan (excepting Minnesota) in 1980. In the postwar push for civil rights, a recalcitrant South shifted its loyalties from the Democratic to the Republican Party. During these decades the Midwest has held, and still holds, the balance—when it joins the South, conservative candidates tend to win; when it ballots with the Northeast, liberals have their best chance of victory.

As a political player, the Midwest came of age in the shadow of Appomattox. A commitment to Reconstruction and Populist era platforms propelled the region's reform heritage into the next century. Throughout these later days, the Wisconsin Idea—an experiment combining university expertise and political power to improve the lives of the state's citizens—sought to make corporate influence defer to a democratic polity. It did so by encouraging professors in the social sciences to pioneer relationships with the statehouse that laid the foundations for fairer and more equitable tax, labor, and utility laws. In many respects, this melding of intellect and legislative power foreshadowed the regulatory state later crafted by Woodrow Wilson and still more completely by FDR.

It was at this point that a number of factors combined to split the East-Midwest political consensus that had, beginning with Lincoln, dominated American presidential politics. Much of the power once wielded by the Gilded Age interior ebbed back to the coast, the maturation of immigrant populations in eastern cities created a fresh ideological dynamic, and the new postwar liberalism seemed intent—following the destruction of the popular dictatorships in Germany and Italy—to clip the old reform tradition's ties to its populist roots.

A similar tearing of allegiances took place in the American historical profession. Certain sectional pressures had always informed relations between the new state schools and their elder Ivy brethren, yet these differences rarely rippled beyond the prewar academy. As progressivism gave way to liberalism, however, and liberalism bent toward advancing an elite rather than egalitarian vision of national life, the Midwestern School questioned the direction and sentiment of the new politics. It promoted, they insisted, an autocratic meritocracy culminating in presidential "courts," intellectually compromised multiversities, and highbrow attacks on those segments of the population (generally middle-western and Sunbelt right-wingers) that remained enamored with a pre–New Deal political culture. Many historians today lament the lack of an overarching synthesis in their profession and point to the pluralistic social history pioneered in the 1960s as the reason. There is some truth to this, yet it explains only part of the story. Ideologically, the grand synthesis began to split at the seams a generation earlier in the unquiet commotion of the progressive-liberal quarrel.

While writing a biography of the liberal historian Richard Hofstadter, I found myself interested in exploring the broader historiographical context in which his scholarship—and that of his critics—surfaced. I tend to think of that book and this one as constituting a cohesive work, an exploration of the ideological conflicts and ethno-cultural pressures that shaped American historical writing in the American Century. I cannot, of course, stake a claim to comprehensiveness. For there are other schools of history—southern, social, New Left, etc.—that are only glancingly reviewed in my contributions. But it seemed to me in sizing up the history of the historical profession—its impact on intellectual and political life, its evolution from a simple Waspish sensibility to one increasingly complex and diverse—that its major lines of confrontation, development, and growth were reflected in the progressive-liberal dichotomy.

I hope not to have favored one school over the other. There is, after all, much to appreciate all around, for the collective achievements of both have yielded a rich and enduring literature. The midwestern historians initially wrote from within the main currents of a native reform tradition. In the postwar years, by contrast, they composed in opposition to a consensus historicism that quickly came to dominate their increasingly conservative profession. As both majority and minority, these scholars discovered a mission for their historical imagination that spanned the century and touches us still.

Today, in the age of the Near Eastern wars, the postindustrial economy, and the divisive politics of family values, once subterranean concerns about empire, equality, and morality have returned in force. Opponents of imperialism and deregulated capitalism may or may not come from the Middle West, but they often convey their protest in a populist idiom and frame of reference that recalls the "history as conflict" worldview that absorbed Charles Beard's generation. This continuity should come as no surprise. A broad view of historical writing urges us recognize just how recently our modern midwestern universities and scholars emerged.

In 1889, Francis Parkman congratulated Frederick Jackson Turner on his study *The Fur Trade in Wisconsin*, "which," he reported, "I have examined with much interest." In 1922, Merle Curti began writing a Harvard dissertation under Turner's direction, and in 1948 David Cronon arrived in Madison to commence his graduate studies in Curti's department. Nearly sixty years later, in 2005, Cronon discussed with me his recollections of practicing history in the Midwest. The strikingly small degree of separation between Parkman and us underlines the familylike nature of the interpretive debates carried on among cross-country colleagues in what used to be a rather small and intimate profession. Today, deeply worn grooves on the marble stairs at the Wisconsin Historical Society connect the modern researcher to the century and more of historians and history seekers who came before. Here one walks, literally, in Turner's steps.[6]

The social/political singularity of the Madison experience made it at one time and for a long time something of a mythical destination for intellectually curious young people. In its heyday, Wisconsin's enrollments were replenished by UW history grads teaching in the big-city universities and small-town colleges of the Midwest, excited to send their best and brightest "home" to the eternal city of midwestern historical writing for an education that might change their lives.[7]

That education came in a distinctly "American" dialect. Suspicious of eastern power, many interior historians embraced a frankly provincial and populistic vision of the past. The frontier (not the cities) promoted democracy, common citizens (rather than intellectuals) best understood the national interest, and open-door imperialism (advanced under the aegis of "liberal internationalism") endangered republican government at home. Of course some of these deeply internalized "truths" have held up better than others. George Mosse, a German Jewish émigré who spent the balance of his academic career at Wisconsin, understood well the sentimental regionalism that seduced his colleagues: "I believe that a feeling of a lost utopia—disappointment with the lack of effectiveness of their midwestern vision of America—determined to a large extent their outlook upon the past."[8] To understand the depths of this vision and its impact on our culture and our country, we must approach the historians of the Middle West critically but with some degree of kinship. Their American Century, after all, has become our own.

Chicago, 1893

*Chicago was the first expression of American
thought as a unity; one must start there.*

HENRY ADAMS

In the late afternoon of a typically hot early July day in 1893, Frederick
Jackson Turner walked into what is today the Art Institute of Chicago
and proceeded to Hall 3, the great room housing the Columbian Exposition Congress of History. Ignoring the assorted attractions of the Midway
Plaisance six miles to the south—a mélange of elegantly housed exhibits
framed by Frederick Law Olmstead's heroic landscaping—the thirty-one-
year-old University of Wisconsin historian had toiled in the heat to hastily complete the essay on the American frontier he had promised nearly
five months earlier to deliver. "I am," he assured fellow historian and future
president Woodrow Wilson, "in the final agonies of getting out a belated
paper."[1]

Last on a five-person panel, Turner sat through an eclectic offering of
recitations ranging from "English Popular Uprisings in the Middle Ages"
to "Early Lead Mining in Illinois and Wisconsin." His own contribution,
"The Significance of the Frontier in American History," fell stillborn.
"One young historian who was present," wrote Turner's first biographer,
"remembered that the audience reacted with the bored indifference normally shown a young instructor from a backwater college reading his first
professional paper." Eager to exit into the downtown night, members of
the Congress of History had missed the meaning of the moment. But as
the climactic sentence of Turner's address cut through the hall—"and now,
four centuries from the discovery of America, at the end of a hundred years
of life under the Constitution, the frontier has gone, and with its going has
closed the first period of American history"—the seeds were sown for a

fundamental rethinking of the nation's past. That night, in Chicago, a new school of midwestern historical writing was born.[2]

Strange circumstances had brought Turner and his colleagues to the interior's flagship city. Four hundred years earlier a forty-one-year-old Genoan, sailing from Palos under the Spanish flag, made landfall in the Bahamas. Now, in celebration of this initial Christian encounter with the Western Hemisphere, a Columbian Exposition—the greatest of the world's great public pageants—had set up shop on the reclaimed marshlands of the Lake Michigan shoreline. In the minds of many locals, the fair afforded yet another opportunity for exploration—the East's discovery of the Ohio Valley's growth, power, and cultural ambitions.

Chicago proved to be a particularly potent symbol of middle-western ascendancy. A year before the exposition opened, its population surpassed one million—a modern phoenix fast rising from the ashes of the terrible 1871 fire. Along the way, it had developed into one of the nation's most ethnically spliced urban centers (three-quarters of residents claimed foreign-born parentage in 1890), experienced sharp labor disputes (the Haymarket Riot of 1886), and become a prominent center for social reform (Jane Addams established Hull House in 1889). The founding of the University of Chicago in this period gave the city a major intellectual resource in a region not typically noted for its idea culture. And then came a successful proposal (among bids from New York, St. Louis, and Washington) to host the exposition. On the cusp of the American Century, Chicago—and the broader Midwest—had come into its own.

Still, inconvenient questions of identity persisted. What exactly *was* Chicago? Mixed meanings abounded. Katherine Lee Bates gloriously referenced the coming Miracle Mile commercial district as a kind of urban utopia ("thine alabaster cities gleam") in her poem (and later song) "America the Beautiful." Carl Sandburg touched upon a truth no less telling when he praised Chicago as the world's "Hog Butcher"—a tribute to the grisly cutting business daily conducted at the Union Stock Yards. In countless ways, this city of contrasts swayed between agrarian simplicity and industrial complexity, between a defensive parochialism and an emergent cosmopolitanism. On the metaphorical level, this struggle for self-image fittingly pitted the pedestrian "Porkopolis" against the soaring "White City."

In 1893, the returns were hardly decisive. One Indian Brahmin visiting the exposition gushed that its success had the potential to usher in a new era in global harmony: "From the peaceful and contented behavior of the various nations and States that have made, on the Fair grounds, their common abode for a time, one is led to hope that a day may come when civilized communities will enlist themselves as members of a Universal Confederacy." A few years later, Rudyard Kipling declared Chicago a menace to civilization. "Having seen it," he sniffed in 1906, "I urgently desire never to see it again." The famed Palmer House struck the English author-poet as a remarkable house of horrors. "I have found a huge hall of tessellated marble, crammed with people talking about money and spitting about everywhere." As an instrument of a new and restless American energy, the city became for Kipling a cultural wasteland, a portent of misplaced power. In a speed and dream setting where "money is progress," he complained, "the grotesque ferocity of Chicago" threatened to cast the rest of the country in its hyper-opportunistic image.[3]

As a prelude to the American Century, 1893 left a lasting imprint on our nation's history. While nostalgia tugged at the heartstrings of the expo faithful—crowds flocked to see a lock of Thomas Jefferson's hair—the steam-powered steel machines dominating the exhibition halls anticipated a future far more complex than that of Jefferson's day. "Chicago," Henry Adams wrote, "asked in 1893 for the first time the question whether the American people knew where they were driving." He thought not. The nation, of course, seemed hardly to care. Aside from a few naysayers, Adams continued, "the whole mechanical consolidation of force" visible in the exposition building had tapped into "the new energies that America adored." A modern religion had found a responsive congregation. Motion, exuberance, and strength were worshiped in the White City and elsewhere.[4]

James J. Hill's Great Northern railway connected Seattle to the East in 1893, while Queen Liliuokalani's Hawaiian kingdom fell before the economic might of the McKinley Tariff. The appetite for expansion found a domestic windfall that year among the legions of land seekers taking part in the Cherokee Strip race, the greatest territorial run in American history. Fifty thousand claims were staked across eight million weathered northern Oklahoma acres. A few months earlier the old republic had lost an ancient warrior; P. G. T. Beauregard, the first distinguished officer in the armed forces of the Confederacy and commander of the Charleston defenses that fired on Fort Sumter, died in New Orleans. Thirteen hundred miles to the north, Thomas Edison opened the world's first film production studio in West Orange, New Jersey, a technological harbinger of entertainment and popular culture in the century ahead. Without Edison's invention of the moving camera the world might never have seen the likes of Mary Pickford, Mae West, and Lillian Gish—all born in 1893.

Beyond fairs, land runs, and the normal human cycle of christenings and funerals lurked a less salutary reality. In 1893 the nation suffered its worst economic crisis to date. A combination of unprecedented currency and investment problems prefaced five hundred bank failures and the collapse of some fifteen thousand companies. The unemployment rate more than tripled, from a negligible 3 percent to a painful 10 percent plus. When the government, in a bid to keep dollars in the East, declared its intention to right the fiscal ship of state by suspending its monthly silver purchase, the advocates of inflation—western mine owners and farmers—launched into action. On the same day that Turner delivered his famous address in Chicago, Silverites attending a convention in Denver issued a sharply worded warning to the nation. The peoples of the West, they announced, stood "in the gloom of impending disaster" due to "daily . . . assaults upon the law by Eastern money brokers" who had "inaugurated a panic" in order to declare a state of fiscal emergency and consolidate their grip on the nation's economy. A mob of pitiless bankers, the Denver men declared, preferred a mono-metal system that kept money precious and rural debtors under the thumb of their New York creditors.[5]

The Denver conventioneers rued the closing of the silver frontier for many of the reasons that Turner mourned the passing of the territorial frontier. Absent a money supply large enough to meet the needs of a growing nation, they insisted, "our foundries . . . our machine shops . . . our railroads with freights" would smash. And in a country that equated property rights with democracy, this would surely spell the end of republican rule. The Denverites claimed in the name of sectional autonomy a kind of secessionary right to reject the marching orders of the Wall Street elite, who treated them as colonial subjects subservient to a greater metropolitan civilization: "Though you may do all in your power, whether in ignorance or through selfish greed, to destroy us, we will not submit to the destiny of poverty without a struggle." Could this condition be reversed? Could desperate internal financial pressures be diluted in a common quest for markets and possessions overseas? Might a living empire take the place of a dying frontier? That same night in Chicago, Turner said perhaps more than he knew in a declaration that suggestively tied the fate of prosperity at home to acquisition abroad: "He would be a rash prophet who should assert that the expansive character of American life has now entirely ceased."[6]

In many ways, the Columbian Exposition represented both the old and the new of American civilization. The pageant wonders of the great White City capped a period of rapid but erratic development in the country's history. Just one century earlier, Washington had presided over fifteen struggling states; a mere thirty years earlier, Lincoln had prosecuted a vast war across a broken nation. But in the carnival and machine mix of fin de siècle Chicago, Turner looked forward to a new century and new challenges—a new period of development. More, he laid the foundations for a bold re-interpretation of the past, one sympathetic to the plight and preferences of the middle-westerners he represented. Historical writing in America would never be the same again.

PART I

The Progressive Age
1890–1945

The democracies of the past have been small communities, under simple and primitive economic conditions. At bottom the problem is how to reconcile real greatness with bigness. It is important that the Middle West should accomplish this; the future of the republic is with her.

FREDERICK JACKSON TURNER, 1901

Midwestern Renaissance

*Before the Civil War was over, the Middle West had become
in a peculiar way the heart of the United States.*

FREDERIC LOGAN PAXSON, 1930

For many generations, the recording of American history openly reflected the regional impulses and attitudes of its leading lights. The idea of the detached intellectual had yet to take hold; the cult of custom still held sway in college towns big and small. As one 1942 study put it, university "presidents and deans usually insist that their teachers should be spiritually attuned to the region. They demand 'Southerners who understand Southern people,' men who 'understand the local situation' in the Middle West, or teachers who will not offend the delicate ears of New England students with the outlander's harsh accents."[1] Today we are less inclined to acknowledge the imprint of academic inbreeding. The historical profession, after all, prizes range, depth, and diversity. Yet, like anyone else, the historian clearly absorbs throughout his life a series of cultural references particular to precise places and precise moments. And more, that the sum of these experiences shapes the scholar's views and lingers as a latent, unspoken prelude to his work. On this score, it seems particularly useful to explore the role of region on the historical imagination in America. Our nation's social mapping, after all, has long reflected distinct and sometimes deep differences among its peoples. This has led to a plurality of cultures and a plurality of pasts.

Going back to the first generation of professional historians, New England's affiliation with the Free-Soil principles that triumphed in the Civil War seemed to preface a long and unchallenged preeminence. And yet, in some vital ways, the settlement secured at Appomattox left the old Northeast in a funk. Rather than build upon its unique inheritance of reform, intellect, and industry, the section experienced a discernible if temporary eclipse. Wasp Boston, once the dynamo of the New World, replied to the appearance of the Mediterranean, the Slav, and the Jew with an aggressive provincialism advanced in theories of racial purity and biological hierarchy that tilted, in their most uncompromising forms, toward the new science of eugenics. In the dawning campaign between Anglos and ethnics, many of New England's most distinguished political and intellectual lions, including Massachusetts Senator Henry Cabot Lodge, the philosopher/historian John Fiske, and Harvard president A. Lawrence Lowell, hit the barricades. "The colonial spirit and the English influence have alike disappeared," Lodge lamented. "The huge increase of immigration, drawing its armies no longer from the British Isles alone, but from all Europe, has so diluted the English element that it is no longer all important."[2] Through the offices of the Immigration Restriction League, the region's cultural hegemonists fought a fierce battle for survival against "elements undesirable for citizenship or injurious to our national character."

With the East in abeyance and the South defeated, the Ohio Valley emerged from behind the long historical shadow cast by the Puritan and the planter. It hoped now to assert its own cultural distinction. "Innocence was of the West," Alfred Kazin wrote of the rising power, "it was childhood, newness, the great legend of American beginnings."[3] The springtime of the Midwestern Renaissance was at hand.

Considering the war's role in upending the traditional sectional balance, it seems fitting that the Trans-Appalachia states were in the vanguard of the reversal. "The great interior," Lincoln avowed to Congress in 1862, " . . . is the great body of the republic. The other parts are but marginal borders to it." The staggering human sacrifice born by the region over the next three years more than matched Lincoln's rhetoric. Midwesterners suffered 140,000 casualties, significantly larger than the 85,000 mid-Atlantic (New York, Pennsylvania, New Jersey) soldiers lost and more than tripling New England's 40,000. Combined, the Northeast buried an average of about 14,000 men per state; in the Midwest the figure came closer to 20,000. These losses were not in vain. While the famed Army of the Potomac struggled to a defensive stalemate in Virginia, the Union Army of the Tennessee—made up predominantly of men from the eight midwestern states—cut the Confederacy in half, winning critical victories at Shiloh and Vicksburg before its most accomplished leaders were sent east. "This army," Civil War scholar James McPherson recently observed, "penetrated farther into Confederate territory, destroyed more enemy resources, and experienced more consistent success than any other Union army."[4]

Aside from its proficiency as a blunt fighting tool, the Midwest served as the Union's breadbasket and beef butcher, shipped critical raw materials to northern factories, and produced the cream of the Northern army's high command. Ulysses S. Grant, William Tecumseh Sherman, and Philip Sheridan all grew up in provincial Ohio towns. As Union officers, these men rode from the battlefield into the history books, their exploits in Atlanta, the Wilderness, and the Shenandoah Valley becoming the stuff of legend. Importantly, they balanced martial prowess with an earnest and easy provincialism. In his autobiographical novel *Tender Is the Night* (1934), F. Scott Fitzgerald created the doomed Dick Diver, a child of New World wonder and possibility wrecked by European dissipation in the fragile years that followed the Great War. Long before his deadly fall, Diver—imitating the old Civil War generals—had waited in the anxious, unknowing hours of youth to meet his unfolding fate. He, and generations of American boys, grew to maturity in sleepy villages and quiet hamlets waiting for the ghost of fortune to softly whisper his name; they were, Fitzgerald wrote, "like Grant, lolling in his general store in Galena . . . ready to be called to an intricate destiny."[5]

Midwestern economic and military power naturally influenced other areas; the postbellum political world in particular smiled on the Ohio Valley. Of the fifteen presidents who held office before 1860, only William Henry Harrison called the Old Northwest home. His one-month reign (death by pneumonia, the first president to perish in office) underlined the scant opportunities afforded western men on the national stage. But within a generation the sectional split destroyed the old politics and a fresh party system emerged. Between 1860 and 1912 every president-elect but two (New Yorkers Grover Cleveland and Theodore Roosevelt) hailed from Illinois, Ohio, or Indiana. These were critical swing states, vital to both parties' success and conscious of their growing significance in a nation politically balkanized by a solid Democratic South and a static Republican Northeast. In the grand maneuvering leading up to the 1884 presidential election, Roosevelt urged Lodge to abandon the incumbent Chester Arthur—and he did so with a nod toward stark sectional realities. A New Yorker with limited appeal in the Middle Mest, Arthur had claimed the presidency only upon the assassination of the Ohioan James Garfield. "Arthur could not carry . . . Ohio or Indiana," Roosevelt predicted; "he would be beaten out of sight."[6]

No special pleading—with the sole exception of Lincoln—will be made here for the greatness of the Ohio Valley presidents. While the top tiers of presidential polls are crammed with powder-wigged Virginians, the likes of Grant, Garfield, Hayes, Harrison, McKinley, and Taft inspire a collective yawn—a blur of mostly bearded caretakers occupying seats of honor at what the literary historian Vernon Parrington memorably called the "great barbecue" of a corrupted post–Civil War politics. The canny Brahmin Henry Adams wrote without pity of the overwhelmed Grant, "The intellect counted for nothing; only the energy counted. The type was preintellectual, archaic, and would have seemed so even to the cave dwellers." This depressing, descending path of presidential evolution that tumbled from Washington to his Gilded Age heirs, Adams cracked, was proof enough that Darwin had missed the mark.[7]

As the wizened emissary of an older America, Adams spoke for a caste in eclipse. While the interior states confidently awaited the future, the politics of memory absorbed the psychic energies of the older regions. For New England's cultural elite, the war had validated the antislavery crusade and restored the promise of representative government first glimpsed by their Revolutionary forefathers. It had also frozen the thinking of an entire generation. Intellectually and emotionally invested in the great struggle to subdue a problematic slaveholders' republic, missionaries of the Yankee way worshiped the past. Among them, the ancient abolitionist Wendell Phillips looked now to consolidate his section's conquest. He advised "carrying Massachusetts to Carolina" as part of a broader colonizing effort to spread "Northern civilization all over the South."[8]

For white southerners a war had been lost but a separate peace could still be won. Edward Pollard's curious 1866 manifesto *The Lost Cause* celebrated the arc of plantation civilization from colonial slavery to nineteenth-century secession and served as a useful if interpretively dubious preface to the monuments honoring the Confederate dead that had begun to dot the Dixie landscape. In the words of Pollard, a Virginia journalist and perhaps the most important southern commentator of the war, the past stood poised to redeem the future: "It is for the South to preserve every remnant of her rights, and even, though parting with the doctrine of secession, to beware of the extremity of surrendering State Rights in gross, and consenting to a 'National Government.'"[9]

Following Pollard's lead, the white South enlisted history to both defend the timeless virtues of its fallen civilization and commemorate the epic tragedy of its defeat. Where generals had failed, historians hoped to prevail. Robert E. Lee, the greatest southern icon of them all, recognized the high stakes at hand. He reminded Alfred T. Bledsoe, editor of the *Southern Review*, of his important mission: "Doctor, you . . . have a great work to do; we all look to you for our vindication." Bledsoe had considerable help. Before the century expired, the Southern Historical Society and the Southern History Association were founded as critical sources of regional pride and revitalization.[10]

While both North and South made an apologia of the past, the Midwest looked ahead. The war energized the region politically, advanced its cultural aspirations, and touched off its economic boom. Jesup Scott, an Ohio Valley land speculator, exemplified the booster ethic that rippled through the interior. The intimidating title of his 1868 opus on urban development—"A Presentation of Causes Tending to Fix the Position of the Future Great City of the World in the Central Plain of North America: Showing that the Centre of the World's Commerce, Now Represented by the City of London, Is Moving Westward to the City of New York, and Thence, within One Hundred Years, to the Best Position on the Great Lakes"—advertised his regional pride. "After mature reflection," wrote Scott, "*the* great natural rival[s] to become the greatest city" were Chicago, Cincinnati, Toledo, and Alton, Illinois.[11]

Despite the efforts of boosters like Scott, painful abstractions continued to torment the interior mind. In the afterglow of an enviable postwar optimism, midwesterners continued to battle long-standing territorial insecurities—the psychological burden of a section accustomed to siege. Hostile Indian confederations, treacherous European empires, and legions of American railroad barons, liberal internationalists, and culture vulture metropolitans constituted a centuries-spanning band of villains that haunted the rural imagination. Some might deduce in this vast "nemesis" profile the paranoid contractions of an overweening provincialism—but one must be sensitive to the context from which it came. Shortly after the Seven Years' War (1756–63), the Ottawa chief Pontiac concluded agreements among Ohio Valley Chippewas, Miamis, Hurons, and Potawatomies that unleashed Indian power on Anglo settlements in the region. Before the fighting concluded, nine British forts were taken, Fort Edward Augustus (modern Green Bay, Wisconsin) had been abandoned, and Fort Detroit lay on the edge of surrender. A half-century later, the great Shawnee warrior Tecumseh and his brother, the prophet Tenskwatawa, spearheaded a Native revitalization movement with the intention of creating a vast pan-Indian confederation to prevent future white settlements in the West. The Battles of Tippecanoe (near Lafayette, Indiana) and the Thames (near Moraviantown, Ontario) bookended a period of fierce conflict (1811–13) that culminated in the Midwest's last great Indian wars.

These bloody confrontations between Anglo Americans and Native Americans were fought within the broader web of European imperial rivalries. Britain and France had long claimed dominion over the Ohio Valley, ringed its forests with military posts, and, when suitable to their strategies, armed the western tribes. The British, in particular, contested American control of the region, illegally maintaining armies there well into the 1790s.

No doubt these "outside" instigators distressed the infant New World republic, yet a host of equally menacing conspiracies were hatched from within. The most famous involved Vice President Aaron Burr, territorial governor of Louisiana James Wilkinson, and General Harman Blennerhassett, an Anglo Irish aristocrat forced to leave Ireland after marrying his niece. In 1806, Burr embarked from Blennerhassett's Island on the Ohio River with some eighty lightly armed men, perhaps to detach parts of the recently acquired Louisiana Purchase Territory from the Union. Wilkinson had once supplied valuable reconnaissance for Burr but for unknown reasons now betrayed his partner's allegedly seditions activities to President Jefferson, who wrote that Burr's enterprise "is the most extraordinary since the days of Don Quixote.... He has meant to place himself on the throne of Montezuma and extend his empire to the Allegheny."[12] Captured, tried for treason, and acquitted, Burr remains a shadowy figure to this day. Supporters insisted that he planned to conquer Spanish territory and present it to the United States—anticipating by forty years the Mexican-American War settlement. Burr's critics, however, joined Jefferson in suspecting that he coveted both Spanish *and* American lands west of the Appalachians. With control of the lower Mississippi, the city and port of New Orleans, and the northern Gulf Coast, he would have ruled over a powerful southwest empire that threatened the United States' hemispheric ambitions.

Real or imagined, internal or external, a conspiratorial mentality conditioned nineteen-century midwestern minds. Over time, the list of enemies grew longer. Saloonkeepers, Jews, Darwinians, socialists, and secularists rubbed uneasily against the insular character of the region. Born on what had once been the nation's geographic fringe, it had never really lost its sense of existing on its own terms, a land apart, a people both pioneering and parochial, deep in the heart of the *real* America.

It seems clear to any close observer today that the Midwest's much exalted homogeneity was far more apparent than real. Great industrial feuds erupted between capital and labor; agricultural communities lived in tension with urban centers; and isolationists, Prohibitionists, and fundamentalists informed a civic culture that idled on discontent. Considering these differences, the Middle West might be more aptly defined as encompassing a number of closely linked but distinct micro regions. Ohio, for example, enjoyed a reputation as a state "balanced" by northern and southern migrations. An idealized Buckeye composite can be found in the novelist Booth Tarkington's assertion that "interior folk are a pleasant people to know; easy-going, yet not happy-go-lucky; possessing energy without rush, and gayety without extravagance. They have a way of being hospitable without exertion, which they inherit from half their ancestry, which was Southern, and a way of competently entertaining each other and their visitors without lavishness—a trait they inherit from the other half, which came from New England."[13] The lower halves of Illinois and particularly Indiana were shaped by a stronger southern resettlement than was southern Ohio, while the upper Midwest took in large numbers of Yankees and Scandinavians. Complex industrial centers like Chicago, by contrast, attracted a much larger population of other ethnicities.

In terms of economic development, a wide range of interests distinguished the Midwest. The southern parts of Michigan, Wisconsin, and Minnesota were largely agricultural, while their northern lands attracted miners and lumberjacks. Far below them, a wheat, corn, and soybean belt pushed out westward from the midlands of Ohio into Iowa and the plains states beyond. Interspersed throughout the region were a handful of metropolitan centers—Chicago, Detroit, Milwaukee, and Cleveland—that, in consideration of their sizable populations, economic investments, and immigrant compositions, had more in common with some areas in the Northeast than with, say, Terre Haute or Sheboygan. In the anxious decade succeeding World War I—an era of prohibition, a revived KKK, and the Scopes Monkey Trial—intrastate cultural disjunctions were to be expected. In 1926, a writer for the *American Mercury* detailed a not untypical city-country split in Ohio between modernists and traditionalists. The state's urban wing, he observed, is "preponderantly foreign, wet, unionized and pagan, whereas its rural communities are preponderantly Nordic, dry, anti-labor and Fundamentalist."[14] Ohio—along with Illinois and Michigan—had in the early twentieth century become a major industrial player, and its connections with states like Iowa, Indiana, and Wisconsin rested less on common economic grounds than on a shared territorial past and a sense of regional identity outside of eastern cosmopolitanism and southern exclusivity.

The most diverse American region in 1900, the Midwest produced a stunning number of gifted authors whose talent for local color, capacity for the sly muckraking of moral outrage, and ability to comment authoritatively on the "capital-labor" question obliterated the genteel tradition favored by the eastern literary establishment. The Chicago Writers ("the

57th Street Colony") both prized and criticized the achievements of the hinterland's mini-metropolises, respectfully observant of their struggle to reap a cultural harvest against the varied backdrop of agrarian solitude and industrial multitude. Finding outlets in Harriet Monroe's *Poetry* (1912) and Margaret Anderson's *Little Review* (1914), Carl Sandburg, Edgar Lee Masters, Vachel Lindsay, Sherwood Anderson, and Theodore Dreiser inaugurated a new and searching era in regional literary history. "I turn ... to those who sneer at this my city," Sandburg wrote, "and I give them back the sneer and say to them: come and show me another city with lifted head singing so proud to be alive and coarse and strong and cunning." The collective contributions of this talented group more than justified H. L. Mencken's ringing claim that the best writers of his era had emerged "from the Middle Empire that has Chicago as its capital."[15]

Chicago may have produced the cream of the interior's literary crop, but first-rate talents surfaced throughout the Ohio Valley. William Dean Howells (b. 1837, Martins Ferry, Ohio) anticipated in his many novels and autobiographical writings the taste for realism that bloomed in the works of Hamlin Garland (b. 1860, West Salem, Wisconsin) and Frank Norris (b. 1870, Chicago). Ambrose Bierce (b. 1842, Meigs County, Ohio) pioneered the complex art of psychological horror; his classic stream-of-consciousness fantasy "An Occurrence at Owls Creek Bridge" offers an ingenious excavation into the mind of a man marked for execution. Both Howells and Bierce were products of provincial backgrounds that established the "feel" and context of their work. Their achievements were instrumental in laying the foundation for a remarkable flowering of first-rate fiction writing in the 1920s. Ring Lardner (b. 1885, Niles, Michigan) emerged as the Midwest's master caricaturist; Sinclair Lewis (b. 1885, Sauk Center, Minnesota) studied the region's small towns and cities in devastating (and hilarious) anthropological detail; Ernest Hemingway (b. 1898, Oak Park, Illinois) became his generation's most popular serious writer; and F. Scott Fitzgerald (b. 1896, St Paul, Minnesota) created in *The Great Gatsby* a historically sensitive sectional morality play between the old moneyed East and a rising frontier. "I see now," Fitzgerald later wrote of *Gatsby*, "that this has been a story of the West, after all—Tom and Gatsby, Daisy and Jordan and I, were all westerners, and perhaps we possessed some deficiency in common which made us subtly unadaptable to Eastern life."[16]

Despite such "deficiencies," many among the Ohio Valley literati pulled up their native stakes and sought nourishment in the salons of New York, London, and Paris. In his classic 1921 essay "Revolt of the Village," critic and Pulitzer Prize–winning biographer Carl Van Doren remarked on the recent stream of "acidulous" writings on the Midwest by midwesterners. Taking Edgar Lee Masters's *Spoon River Anthology* (1915) and Sherwood Anderson's *Winesburg, Ohio* (1919) as representative texts on "yokel" culture, he wrote that "the simple provincialism of the older America no longer met the needs of the Younger Generation, which had come to think of the country as dusty and dull. They attacked fundamentalism in religion, capitalism in industry, commercialism in education, science and the arts, chauvinism in international affairs, reactionism in public opinion at large." The revolt described by Van Doren correctly characterized the new authors' efforts to seek out a liberal, "Europeanized" East. As a consequence, the expatriate writers of the "Middle Empire" did not worshiped "a land of dairy herds and exquisite lakes, of new automobiles and tar-paper shanties and silos like red towers," as Lewis had nimbly put it, but rather embraced complexity and cosmopolitanism as antipodes to the tribal instincts of the village.[17]

Yet the literary men and women of the Midwest, no matter their zip code, stressed in their writings a shared spirit of change born of a restless energy common to their region. They were joined in protest by the unemployed "soldiers" of Coxey's Army, by the perpetually suspicious remnants of various grange, co-ops, and farmer movements, and by the Haymarket and Pullman strikers who organized on the front lines of the industrial crisis. Weary of being treated as something of a corn and cow colony for the older metropolis, the intellectual and industrial classes of the Ohio Valley rebelled in a powerful wave of revision known as the Progressive Era. Spontaneous and fluid, it quickly received direction from the region's most gifted thinkers. Lester Ward (b. 1841, Joliet, Illinois) inaugurated the discipline of sociological theory in America; his influential textbook *Dynamic Sociology* (1883) rejected the nation's laissez-faire past and championed the promise of a civic-minded republic. Ward argued for the adoption in academic circles of a new curriculum to provide the intellectual tools—contra classical economics, contra survival-of-the-fittest ideology—to intervene and thus humanize the marketplace. His theories were bracing and harmonized with the demand for regulation and reform. They received their broadest exposure when advanced and expanded upon by William James under the title "pragmatism" and still later in John Dewey's experimental program of "progressive education."

Eugene V. Debs (b. 1855, Terre Haute, Indiana) is remembered today as the nation's most famous socialist—he ran for the presidency in 1920 from an Atlanta prison ("penance" for assailing the Wilson administration's woeful wartime record on civil liberties). More of a humanist than a politician,

Debs, the child of immigrant Alsatian parents, discovered in American history native arguments for opposing the depressing nationalization of factory culture. His criticisms of capitalism were drawn directly from the old Jeffersonianism. Though deeply concerned with the problems and prospects of labor across the nation, Debs evinced a particular concern for the impact of industrialization on midwestern working men and women. "They don't know anything about it and they are especially innocent in regard to it in the small western cities and states," he complained of the encroaching proletarianism. The region's beau ideal, the rail-splitter president Abraham Lincoln, had sprung gloriously, Debs wrote, from "this primitive state of society" in a fruitful comingling of political purity and economic opportunity that now tripped in retreat. "Had Lincoln been born in a sweatshop," Debs warned, "he would never have been heard of."[18]

An equally severe, if more sophisticated, critique of the Gilded Age state emerged from the brilliant mind of Thorstein Veblen (b. 1857, Manitowac County Wisconsin). The son of successful Norwegian immigrants, Veblen read voraciously in philosophy, anthropology, history, and economics. A Yale student of the arch–social Darwinist William Graham Sumner, he reconciled himself to the predominance of industrial capitalism but delighted in exposing the lightly camouflaged violence that made the system run. Whereas classical economic theory pushed for a rational interpretation of production and accumulation (the law of supply and demand), Veblen argued in *The Theory of the Leisure Class* (1899) that the "conspicuous consumption" of commodities and recreation touched upon the deeper and more primal needs of economic actors. To be emulated or merely envied provided, in many societies, a singular satisfaction. The predatory instincts of the caveman, the Viking, and the Japanese feudal shoganate, Veblen wrote, were updated in the swollen homes, automobiles, and bank accounts of the industrial elite. "Trophies of the chase or of the raid," he wrote, "come to be prized as evidence of preeminent force. Aggression becomes the accredited form of action, and booty serves as *prima facie* evidence of successful aggression."[19]

Veblen's imaginative dissection of American consumerism pointed to cracks in the proud edifice of liberal economics. His colorful criticism, however, did not carry the day. In an age of stunning industrial growth, the status of the great barons eclipsed all comers. Who, after all, wanted to be the next Grover Cleveland if he could be the next Andrew Carnegie? At one time or another, an astonishing number of titans called the Midwest home. Cyrus McCormick abandoned his native Virginia for Chicago in 1847 and began producing agricultural implements to meet the demands of the dawning farming frontier. In 1902, McCormick Harvesting Machine combined with Deering Harvester and several smaller competitors to create International Harvester—owner of a staggering 85 percent of the heavy farm-machinery market. Among the Wheat Belt states the McCormick kingdom reigned supreme.

In terms of global influence, however, International Harvester paled in comparison to John D. Rockefeller's oil oligarchy. A native New Yorker, Rockefeller commenced his rise to wealth on the flats of Cleveland refining crude petroleum. In 1855, at the age of sixteen, this country boy entered Lake Erie's second-largest city looking for employment: "I went to the railroads, to the banks, the wholesale merchants. I did not go to any small establishments. I did not guess what it would be, but I was after something big."[20] The world's first billionaire, Rockefeller created in the Standard Oil Company its largest and most powerful monopoly. In the nomenclature of the age, the "octopus" of interlocking deals uniting big money, big business, and big railroads attested to the will, reach, and menace of John D's vast empire.

Standard Oil's lieutenants towered over every other business interest, organization, and man, excepting the most important titan of all, Henry Ford. Born on a small farm a few miles east of Dearborn, Michigan, in 1863, Ford pioneered improvements in the art of mass production that literally changed the world. Yet as a symbol of the midwestern ascendancy, he has always been a problematic figure. His conspiratorial view of international Jewish interests and extreme hostility to labor unions were controversial even in his own day. The "inventor" of the modern weekend and the five-dollar-a-day program, Ford mixed progressive change with a benevolent autocrat's quest for power and paternalism. Paradoxically, he mourned the loss of small-town America and the erosion of cultural continuity with the rise of large multiethnic industrial cities like Detroit—cities built, of course, by men like Ford. In a studied devotion to loss and memory, late in life he erected an elaborate temple of his youth in the Detroit suburb of Dearborn. This quiet Potemkin village of farmhouses, workshops, and mills resides incongruously beside the massive Rouge automobile complex, a cultural mausoleum in honor of the horse-and-buggy Midwest that Ford, more than anyone else, had irretrievably altered.

The enterprising spirit of a people can be quantified not merely in dollars, contracts, and corporations but also in patent licenses—the commodification of inspiration. Before the Civil War, roughly 90 percent of U.S. patents were granted to northerners. This spoke of the enterprising spirit of the region, its forward-looking mentality and commitment to encouraging a profitable kind of dissent. In the postwar decades, the Middle West deeply internalized the ethic of entrepreneurship. A number of Ohio-born industrial designers—Charles Bush, Thomas Edison, Granville Woods, Charles Kettering, and Wilbur and Orville Wright—invented the twentieth century as we knew it. Edison's gifts to the world—electric light, motion pictures, and recorded music—were rivaled in the public imagination only by the Wrights' flying machine. Behind these dazzling accomplishments lurked the midwestern taste for modesty. Kettering, the father of the self-starting automobile engine (a health-preserving improvement over the arm-shattering crank starter) downplayed his role among the nation's most prominent practical scientists by giving a stock response to well-wishers: "I'm a pliers and screwdriver man, not a theory man." Edison's famously nonthreatening quip "Genius is 2 percent inspiration and 98 percent perspiration" conformed to the simple appreciations of a country suspicious of eggheads and helped make him an American hero.

In sum, the Midwestern renaissance had produced great advances in the arts, both aesthetic and industrial. Fortunes were created, armies of farmers and factory workers flooded into the region, and Detroit, Cleveland, and Chicago emerged as capital cities of an industrial empire the size of France. The rapid movement of money and power inspired a volatility and expansion on a scale never before experienced in American history. New traditions and new transactions were waiting to be made. Increasingly self-aware, the region had begun to respond to its own instincts, determined to discover a literature, social criticism, and history consistent with its rising influence.

Few observers dissected the patterns of American provincialism with a sharper blade than Henry Adams. From the sublime detachment that money, intellect, and conceit could create, he grew into a wonderfully articulate if caustic critic of the "Nunc Age." Raised to rule over men in the deferential republic of his ancestors, Adams found himself instead waging a losing campaign against modernity's erratic trinity: industry, democracy, and multiculturalism. His alienation cut deep and he knew just whom to blame. "The Trusts and Corporations stood for the larger part of the new power that had been created since 1840, and were obnoxious because of their vigorous and unscrupulous energy. They were revolutionary, troubling all the old conventions and values, as the screws of ocean steamers must trouble a school of herring. They tore society to pieces and trampled it underfoot."[21] The common indignities and desperations that accompanied the machine age may have been every bit as shameful as Adams made them out to be, but the dynamo fostered certain virtues that escaped his unforgiving eye. The industrial complex demanded for its own preservation an educated middle class. Scientists, engineers, architects, accountants, and managers, shock troops of the new capitalism, were called upon to design the factories, make them efficient, and serve as loyal consumers of the products manufactured in them. The sheer immensity of this task (cultivating in the span of a single generation an entire professional class) meant carving out a fresh educational frontier.

The modern university arose in the 1870s, a creature of industrial society, robber-baron philanthropy, and a curriculum revolution that arrived with a German accent. The new institutions barely resembled the old New England colleges. East Coast education historically stood for the transmission of a priceless cultural heritage that privileged ancient languages, rhetoric, philosophy, and religion. Western learning responded to more contemporary concerns and emphasized the social sciences, professional schools, and graduate training. It demanded that education be practical, dynamic, and democratic. And it proved a smashing success. Shortly after the Civil War, enrollments at the nation's colleges and universities had lingered at a stagnant sixty-seven thousand, but within twenty years registrations had more than doubled.

The expectations of industry were chiefly responsible for the sudden surge in higher learning. As corporations expanded first across the continent and then beyond, they required armies of trained technicians capable of delivering the goods to market. This unprecedented operation required unbroken advances in research, and the old college system simply could not meet the crying need for human expertise in the industrial fields. Moreover, the liberal arts' traditional emphasis on the *preservation* of knowledge meant little to the increasingly powerful interests looking to *enlarge* knowledge in practical and efficient ways. In response to this shift in priorities, two types of universities emerged in the late nineteenth century, private institutions endowed by the industrialists themselves and land-grant schools financed by the states. The former proved immensely important in the history of American education. The corporate kings created some of the nation's most distinguished centers of intellect—Cornell (1865), Vanderbilt (1873), Johns Hopkins (1876), Stanford (1891), and Chicago (1891)—and broke New England's ages-old educational monopoly. "It is the best investment I ever made in my life," UC benefactor Rockefeller once wryly remarked. "Why shouldn't people give to the University of Chicago money, time, their best efforts? Why not? . . . The good Lord gave me the money, and how could I withhold it from Chicago?"[22] In an expanding (and increasingly money-driven) academy, businessmen and bankers, industrialists and retailers were the new power brokers, with board of trustee memberships to prove it. The clergy and small-town merchants who for generations had confidently ruled the nation's college towns were forced to step aside, ghosts of a passing phase in higher education.

As important as the philanthropy universities were and remain today, the adoption of the land-grant system played an even greater role in the history of American learning. Designed to combine research with public service, the seventy-one colleges and universities that traced their origins to government sponsorship in the post–Civil War decades emphasized science, engineering, and agriculture. Their sheer number, combined with minimum enrollment requirements and low tuition rates, democratized academe and placed it firmly on the side of progressive change. In the race to create new centers of practical intellect, the Midwest took the lead. Between 1865 and 1900 it built more than thirty public universities—thrice as many as were established in New England and nearly thrice as many as the eleven inaugurated in the Mid-Atlantic states. Among its most important new institutions were the University of Illinois, Purdue University, and Ohio State University. The land-grant program did not create the Middle West's most dynamic educational center, the University of Wisconsin, which had been founded as a public institution in 1848, but it helped to finance and enlarge the school, thus guaranteeing its future as a leading regional center for higher learning. Under the Morrill Act of 1862, nearly a quarter-million acres were allotted to the state of Wisconsin, the funds from which were used by the fledgling university to reorganize its faculty, embellish its curriculum, and grow its enrollment.

Madison's primitive accommodations (the city resided on the frontier until 1840) did not presage educational distinction. This handicap proved less cumbersome than one might imagine, however, because of an unusually close relationship between the public UW and the private Johns Hopkins University. Put simply, Hopkins supplied Madison with its best early faculty—educators who demanded that this callow Midwest academic outpost develop into a center of serious intellectual work.

Johns Hopkins holds a special place in the history of American universities. The first institution in the country founded primarily as a graduate center, it initiated a stiff and altogether salutary competition in higher learning. Nineteenth-century Harvard, Yale, and Princeton ambled easily along as sleepy social clubs with mild intellectual aspirations until Hopkins money and the Hopkins mission got their attention.[23] This pattern repeated itself in the Midwest, where the University of Chicago pushed Wisconsin; in the South, where Duke prodded the Universities of North Carolina and Virginia; and in the West, where Stanford pressed the University of California. In many respects, Hopkins stood in the forefront of the new education. It favored advanced coursework over undergraduate instruction, appropriated the German style of objectivity, and popularized social scientific research in the academy. Serious young men coveted the training they could expect at Hopkins, whose early PhDs included the exemplary triumvirate of Woodrow Wilson, John Dewey, and Frederick Jackson Turner.

While Hopkins revolutionized the American university, its historians adopted original approaches to recovering the past. For generations, gentleman scholars had produced a mixed bag of serious history (including William Prescott's splendid *Conquest of Mexico*) and patriotic hagiography (see Parson Weems's epic, if apocryphal, tale of George Washington's cherry tree indiscretion). The Hopkins men were instrumental in advancing a system of peer-reviewed journals, university presses, and graduate seminars designed to sharpen the professional historian's skills. Under their leadership, a more systematic and "objective" style of historical analysis began to take shape. Herbert Baxter Adams, the major Hopkins historian, introduced both German historicism and the American talent for self-promotion to the profession. Described by his student Wilson as "a great Captain of Industry," Adams helped found the American Historical Association in 1884; five years later, he and his allies convinced Congress to incorporate the AHA and formalized a relationship between the association and the Smithsonian Institute for the advancement "of historical studies, the collection and preservation of historical manuscripts and for kindred purposes in the interest of American history and of history in America."[24] To establish credibility as a learned society, the AHA commenced publication of a flagship journal, the *American Historical Review*. During its crucial early years, the *Review* benefited from the editorial expertise of John Franklin Jameson, the first Hopkins PhD in history (also an Adams student) and a leading light in the professionalization movement. Due largely to Jameson's efforts, Congress created the National Archives in 1934.

In Baltimore, Adams pioneered the famous seminar method of instruction, modeled his own scholarship on the Germanic ideals of *Wissenschaft* and *Objektivitat*, and turned out a slew of newly minted doctorates. Largely through his efforts, the Hopkins method was fanned throughout American higher education. The early giants in the University of Wisconsin's history department, Charles Homer Haskins and Frederick Jackson Turner, and in the social sciences, John Commons and Edward Ross, all earned their academic stripes in Baltimore.

At Hopkins, Wisconsin, and other "progressive" centers of higher learning, the social sciences challenged the moral dilemma brought about by the impact of industrialization, secularism, and modernity. For generations, the nation had defined itself as a republic of small-scale producers, happily absent the sharp social gradations that afflicted a class-ridden Europe. But in the postbellum decades, this satisfying self-image lost much of its magic. The rise of great trusts, the rebellion of the farming class, and the dead hand of government corruption all conspired against the old Jeffersonianism. The public clamored for reform, but the free-enterprise system offered no relief.

In the end, classical economic theory surrendered before the industrial crisis. The disinterested market envisioned by Adam Smith devolved in Jay Gould's America into a cornered economy of railroad rebates, monopolies, cartels, trusts, and the wholesale transfer of public lands to private corporations. Into this great breach between rhetoric and reality leaped the new universities. In the name of preserving republican values, the social sciences created an intellectual argument both strong enough and *American* enough to take on the trusts while avoiding (for the most part) the stigma of socialism.

The new scholarship attained prominence under the guiding hand of Richard Ely. A self-described "son of New England, a Connecticut Yankee," he took his undergraduate degree at Columbia University and then followed the PhD trail to Europe. Under the tutelage of the Heidelberg economist Karl Knies, he wrote of his love affair with German scholarship, "You learn here, and only here, how to do independent, real scientific work."[25] Armed with a doctorate, Ely accepted a post at Johns Hopkins; there his efforts on behalf of organized labor became the stuff of legend.

A pioneer in the field of modern political economy, Ely helped found the American Economic Association and cowrote the classic *Labor Movement in America* (1886). The strident tone of the book ("I was full of enthusiasm and was fired with the thought that I was fulfilling a mission") led conservatives to accuse its authors of radicalism. The study, in fact, is full of friendly aphorisms not unlike the secular sermons found in Benjamin Franklin's *Poor Richard's Almanac*. In it, Ely counseled laboring men and women to trust in organized religion, "cast aside envy," and practice temperance and frugality. Far from glorifying the working class, he championed its rights precisely because he believed that most artisans, farmers,

FREDERICK J. TURNER.   CHARLES H. HASKINS.   RICHARD T. ELY, Director.   DAVID KINLEY.   JOHN B. PARKINSON.
WILLIAM A. SCOTT.   JOHN M. PARKINSON.

Figure 1. Social Science Superstar: Richard Ely.
Courtesy University of Wisconsin–Madison Archives.

machinists, and mechanics would never rise above their current station: "One of the elementary truths which we in this country specially need to grasp is that the average man is not a particularly gifted man."[26] Like his contemporary Theodore Roosevelt, Ely believed that muckrakers might foolishly incite the masses to rebellion. Rights for workers, he reasoned, would avert revolution.

In 1892 Frederick Jackson Turner, already a rising figure at Wisconsin, lobbied President Thomas C. Chamberlin to bring Ely to Madison. Dissatisfied with his low Hopkins salary and middling status amidst a constellation of faculty stars, Ely accepted and came west to organize a school of economics, history, and political science. His influence within the profession guaranteed Madison's reputation as the center for social scientific research in America. Just as important, Ely's Baltimore exodus marked the first time that a major East Coast scholar had crossed the Ohio River Rubicon. One year earlier, Herbert Baxter Adams had declined a lucrative offer to teach at the University of Chicago. In the midst of negotiations, he drew up a spare balance sheet and carefully weighed the consequences of leaving:

EAST	WEST
Quiet	Rush
Continuity	Broken
Society	New People
Conservatism	Boom
Duty	Advantage
Settled	Moving
Identification	Lost

He obviously stayed put. Ely proved to be made of more adventurous stuff—and presumably possessed a thicker skin than Adams. "When my eastern friends learned of my decision to leave the Johns Hopkins," he remembered, "they thought I must be losing my mind to go to the 'wild and woolly' country of Wisconsin."[27]

Born a frontier, the Midwest inherited in the crib a cold suspicion of metropolis from earlier east-west struggles. In the Declaration of Independence, Thomas Jefferson had denounced George III's determination to subdue his unruly North American colonies by making their representatives conduct legal affairs in remote Halifax and London—"places unusual, uncomfortable, and distant from the depository of their public records." Far from seeing the center-colonial split to a successful conclusion, the Revolution simply reprised this unequal relationship in the nation's backcountry. In 1787, a small-scale civil war erupted in Massachusetts's Pioneer Valley as subsistence farmers under Daniel Shays fought their coastal creditors in the Battle of Springfield. In 1794, an army of thirteen thousand commanded by George Washington marched into Pennsylvania to confront the "Whiskey Rebels" of the Monongahela Valley. These settlers opposed a federal tax on liquor that fell disproportionately on the people living in the Keystone state's hinterland.

Fast forward to the post–Civil War Ohio Valley and one finds a similar sectional power struggle, this time over the control of railroads, utilities, markets, and credit. The Illinois-born novelist Frank Norris emphasized the brutality of the industrial system in the vast, unforgiving apparatus of the nation's rail lines, which he called "the leviathan, with tentacles of steel clutching into the soil, the soulless Force, the iron hearted Power."[28] Conservatives mistook the new style of western protest—farmers' cooperatives, industrial strikes, and calls for currency inflation—for an American Marxism. But Petrograd hardly prefaced Peoria. Among the nation's most prominent reform governors, Wisconsin's Robert La Follette, Illinois's

John P. Altgeld, and Michigan's Hazen S. Pingree pitched their protest in a uniquely American key, seeking to carefully prune the advantages of producers in order to protect the rights of consumers. They accepted the main contours of the property-rights system and simply wished to see it operate more equitably.

Of all the midwestern states, Wisconsin advanced the progressive agenda most alertly and successfully. Peopled largely by Germans, Scandinavians, and New Englanders, it brought together various strands of reform politics that had censured slavery, supported public education, and believed passionately in Christian charity, workers' rights, and the efficacy of moral uplift. In his small gem *The Wisconsin Idea* (1912), Charles McCarthy portrayed Wisconsinites as a pioneer people in the forefront of a great campaign to redeem the promise of American life. The ethno-cultural dimensions of the crusade are fully evident in the author's sentimental dedication "to the Norse lumberjack and the 'forty-eight' German and the men of the 'Iron Brigade,' and all toilers who, by their sweat, made possible our schools, a great university, and all the good that is with us."[29]

Long before McCarthy's book appeared, observers made note of the Germanic character of the upper Midwest. The writer Franz Loher mused of Wisconsin in the 1840s, "They can have German schools and universities, German literature and art, German science and philosophy, German courts and assemblies; in short, they can form a German State, in which the German language shall be as much the popular and official language as the English is now, and in which the German spirit shall rule." Several of the University of Wisconsin's most prominent scholars had studied under the direction of the political economists who built the Bismarckian social welfare system. German thinkers dismissed the "dismal science" school of Anglo economists—David Ricardo, Thomas Malthus, and Herbert Spencer—and pointed to the powers of the universities and the state to combat social ills. The Teutonic model proved irresistible among the Madison illuminati. In Germany the most distinguished professors received fabulous salaries (upward of $30,000 as compared to the rather generous—in American terms—$5,000 paid to Hopkins's best), advised its government on a variety of pressing social and economic issues, and enjoyed a mandarinlike status in the German social hierarchy far beyond the reach of the typical American instructor. In the United States, the cult of "Herr Doktor Professor" created its own elaborate mythology. Following Leopold von Ranke's death in 1886, his library "including his portrait, study, tables, chairs, and pens . . . [was] set up as a shrine at Syracuse University."[30]

A star-struck academy may have worshiped its German fathers, but the

Germanic influence on American social institutions needed a bona fide crisis to set the wheels of reform in motion. In the spring of 1893, a financial panic rocked the nation's banking system and radicalized the Midwest. One-fifth of Wisconsin's lending institutions failed during this black year, while a third of its citizens were unable to find work. The threatened proletarianization of the laboring class and the postwar accumulation of private wealth and influence mocked the region's claims to having raised an egalitarian society. In Jefferson's day, the "citizen" was the source of political power, and the citizen's capacity for self improvement and self-denial were important foundations of civic strength. But in recent years the citizen had lost important ground to the "consumer." Vulnerable to market fluctuations, at the mercy of managers and landlords, the small laborer in the factory or on the farm could be wrecked by a single vicious spike in prices. The idea of a consumer republic had yet to congeal in the American mind, and progressives were determined to make it the rightful heir of the fading agrarian dream.

Ely's scholarship was immensely useful on this score. He produced numerous studies on Wisconsin land usage, drafted reports on irrigation and water rights for the U.S. Department of Agriculture, and helped found the American Bureau of Industrial Research and the American Association for Labor Legislation. Too, he groomed an impressive stable of talented protégés at the university. His brilliant student John Commons reveled in Madison's progressive milieu—"I was born again when I entered Wisconsin"—and proved a worthy successor to his mentor. Commons's seminars on economic theory drew great interest among graduate students, and his publications, including a jointly edited work with Ely, *Documentary History of American Industrial Society*, and the solo authored *Social Reform and the Church* and *Distribution of Wealth*, are classics in progressive thought. His civic services were further noteworthy. Commons drafted the Wisconsin civil service bill of 1905 and its public utilities law of 1907; his pioneering ideas on unemployment insurance were adopted by the Chicago clothing market. "What I was always trying to do, in my academic way," Commons once remarked of his career, "was to save Wisconsin and the nation from politics, socialism, or anarchism, in dealing with the momentous conflict of 'capital and labor.'"[31]

Commons's distinguished colleague Edward Ross enjoyed an equally auspicious career. A year at the University of Berlin produced the usual salutary impression—"they taught me what Science really is"—before the pilgrimage to Hopkins. Professional success came quickly, including appointments at Cornell and Stanford. The Palo Alto adventure nearly cost

Ross everything. There he coolly denounced the monopolistic powers of the region's railroad barons, particularly their practice of importing cheap labor to drive down wages. Considering that the university's principal benefactor, Leland Stanford Sr., had held the presidencies of the Central and Southern Pacific Rail Roads and hired Chinese immigrants to build his lines, such heresies were bound to antagonize. In 1901 Ross was fired. A five-year purgatory at the University of Nebraska followed; there his views on the still hotly debated currency question—"in the whole country I was the only professor speaking up for silver"—aligned with Lincoln's. Yet the backwardness of the institution worked against a longer stay. "It galled [me]," he later wrote, "that the 'ceiling' for professors' salaries was $2,000. The pay schedule had been fixed in law after the 'grasshopper years' of the seventies. The average merchant in a 'county-seat' had a better living than scholars of national reputation."[32] In 1906 Ely brought Ross to Wisconsin. Though he continued to champion unpopular causes—and earned a Board of Regents censure for sponsoring talks by Emma Goldman and the free love advocate Parker Sercombe—Ross found a congenial academic home at UW. He remained a Madison fixture until his 1951 death.

The progressivism favored by men like Ross—an advocate of eugenics and immigration restriction—was by its nature attuned to racial and hereditary implications of "improving" societies. Under the progressive canopy, the new social sciences presumed that discernible intellectual disparities separated the races, thus justifying segregation, ethnic quotas, and the recent American colonialism in Puerto Rico, Guam, the Philippines, and Hawaii. Turner's famous frontier thesis too adopted a social scientific bearing in its advancement of Anglo American exceptionalism. He saw the American West as a region destined for a Protestant civilization eager to abandon the country's increasingly ethnicized cities—the original white flight. Like his colleague, Ross, Turner's work suggested a hierarchy of intellect, talent, and character that could be maintained only through racial purity. He never went as far as Ross in these views—he never, that is, embraced eugenics, and his opinions on immigration were mixed. And yet, beyond these distinctions, we might note that the early progressive movement in Madison and throughout the Midwest contained within its search for order, stability, regulation, and reform a positive prejudice for the "professional" and little patience with "regressive" populations.

An overweening utilitarianism further compromised the educational pretensions of the University of Wisconsin. The advances in architecture, literature, and the sundry liberal fields of scholarship which had once distinguished the midwestern renaissance took a second seat to the pursuit of popular democracy and consumer rights. The departments of history, political science, economics, sociology, and agricultural science dominated a campus that produced no prodigies in the fine arts. In its race toward reform, Madison sacrificed other areas of discovery; thus an undercurrent of anti-intellectualism compromised the Wisconsin Idea and confirmed the East's sense of academic superiority.

More positively, Theodore Roosevelt once described Ely's empire as a "laboratory for wise experimental legislation" that produced "scientific popular self-help."[33] A presidential imprimatur is difficult to live up to, and once the crisis years had passed so did the heroic days of the social scientist as superstar and the university president and state governor as national celebrities. The legacy of this golden age, however, lingered long. The stellar cast of Ely, Commons, and Ross embodied a founding generation par excellence. These men shaped the debates and produced the studies that popularized a midwestern style of reform. No one in these early years of academic growth proved more important in communicating the progressive vision to the rest of the nation. No one, that is, except Frederick Jackson Turner.

TWO

Founding Father
Frederick Jackson Turner

Still trying to answer your question about the
frontier—perhaps it was in the blood.

FREDERICK JACKSON TURNER
TO CARL BECKER, 1925

In his 1902 short story "The Middle West," the Indiana expatriate Booth Tarkington good-naturedly mocked Easterners' reluctance to mix with their western kin. The setting: a luncheon on the south shore of Long Island. The principals: four New Yorkers, two Bostonians, and "a young man from the Middle West." The crisis: barbarians at the gate.

> One of the women from New York nodded pleasantly to the Westerner. "I am sure, Mr. McWhirter, that you are too broad-minded to resent what I am about to say," she remarked— a preface which of course braced the young man to receive with a winning smile any insult to his *alma mater* or to his section of the country. "It is only that I have decided that my sons must go to Harvard," she continued, turning to the Bostonians, "because at Princeton or Yale," (Mr. McWhirter's *alma mater* was Princeton) "they might be thrown in contact with Westerners."[1]

A few years earlier, John Franklin Jameson, a young Brown University historian, expressed a less varnished contempt for his interior colleagues. "The candid statement of fact is . . . Western history is stupid." The cut followed the 1888 meeting of the American Historical Association—a botched affair in Jameson's opinion. In respect to that year's centennial of the settlement of the Old Northwest by citizens of the United States, the AHA had planned to convene in Columbus. This proved an inspired if unwise move. A last-minute lack of accommodations sent the conventioneers to Washington—not enough time for the usually reliable eastern men (so put off by the prospects of an Ohio holiday that they had resolved to skip the gathering) to change their plans. "There were," Jameson groused, "more nobs [nonprofessionals] than usual in attendance . . . and of the New England historical professors, most interesting men, only one was present besides me."[2]

Jameson belonged to a rising generation of professional historians resentful of the bear-meat and saddlebag scholarship it associated with "Western history." Its representatives were university men, believers in building a "science" of the past predicated upon doctoral programs and peer review journals and presses. Enemies of amateurism, they found their initial returns less than promising. As Jameson complained, antiquarianism ruled the early days of the AHA, its annual meetings a long litany of dull and conventionally argued papers on battles and local history. In its first years of existence, perhaps only a quarter of association membership derived from college and university instructors—the "nobs" were still in charge. In a word, the profession craved legitimacy.[3]

How ironic that the first great idea to capture the high ground for professional historians came from the West. In his famous address, "The Significance of the Frontier in American History," Frederick Jackson Turner upended more than two centuries of historical interpretations that celebrated the nation's Puritan and Chesapeake roots. These Old World offshoots struck Turner as utterly incapable of explaining the astonishing transition of the European peasant into an American democrat. Optimistic, pragmatic, inventive, individualistic, and restless, the pioneer personality type that sustained republican government, Turner argued, bloomed most abundantly along frontier fault lines.

The "free-land" hypothesis received a particularly favorable review in the Midwest. It validated academic history in the region's new state universities, advanced the social scientific methodology then in vogue at Madison (Turner made use of census data), and forced men like Jameson to concede the importance of the hinterland in American life. It was a view long ignored by the AHA. In its first twenty years, the Association's annual meeting was held west of the Alleghenies on only five occasions. Even more tightly did eastern men grip the association's presidency. Between 1884 and 1909, every AHA president had either been born on the east side of the Appalachians or, in the case of Ohio native James Ford Rhodes (1899) and Edward Eggleston of Indiana (1900), lived there at the time of his selection. In 1910, Turner became the first AHA president to be affiliated with a western university in the year of his address.[4]

Turner's thesis placed the Ohio Valley firmly in the middle of the American story. In so doing, it raised the status and self-esteem of scholars long accustomed to falling in line behind their New England cousins. On occasion, Turner suffered the arrogance of the Brahmins first hand. Harvard president Charles W. Eliot, visiting Madison in 1891, had dismissed at every opportunity the Johns Hopkins PhDs earned by Turner and his colleague Charles Homer Haskins. "Didn't we know that Harvard was the place to study history, that they alone had the libraries and the instructors?" Haskins remembered Eliot's sneer. "It passed his power of comprehension that students in the West were so ignorant of the proper place to pursue graduate studies. He was quite discourteous in his manner and apparently created a reaction. Even in the West one is expected to be a gentleman."[5]

In time, of course, middle-western historiography came to dominate the profession, if only briefly. A great shift in population and power triggered the change. During the near century-long span that separated the Louisiana Purchase (1803) and Turner's frontier thesis (1893), twenty-eight new states entered the Union. By the end of this period, nearly twenty million Americans lived in the Midwest, exceeding by some two million the combined populations of New England, New York, New Jersey, and Pennsylvania. To what extent could the nation's history be told without an investigation of the influence of the new lands on the old settlements? The cumulative impact of this revolution in thought and demography inspired a moment of unsettlement, an opportunity in the arena of historical writing for the East to restore its dominance or for the West to discover fresh paths to the past.

Eastern and western schools both espoused "scientific" views to validate their section, but it was Turner's frontier hypothesis that captured the public mind. In 1895, Jameson invited both Turner and Henry Adams to contribute original essays to the inaugural edition of the *American Historical Review*. He made clear to Turner the regional implications of his request. "We wish to make it, obviously and from the first, an organ representative of the historical scholarship of all sections of the country alike. It is deemed essential that the first numbers ... shall contain an article by a representative historical scholar of the West, and, if he is willing, upon some topic in Western history or connected therewith. It was the unanimous vote of the Board, at its recent meeting, that I should urgently invite you to send me an article for this first number."[6] Turner did not disappoint. He composed "Western State-Making in the Revolutionary Era" as an offering from the interior.

A decade after Turner's article appeared, *The Education of Henry Adams* quietly arrived on the scene. This wry, remarkable, and incomplete autobiography argued in its late chapters for a "dynamic theory of history," a gloomy idea inspired by the second law of thermodynamics. In 1852, the British physicist William Thomson had explained that as energy could be generated only by the dispersal of energy, the universe would one day reach a stage of maximum expenditure, followed by entropy and finally death. Applied to human history, the "speed-up" of time from Neolithic hunting and gathering to the current age of modern industrial capitalism seemed analogous to the physical world's inevitable exhaustion—a case of too much energy moving too quickly. At his most pessimistic, Adams obsessed over human fate in a mechanical world where the cry of machines and crush of immigrants had overturned the America of his youth. "Resistance is its law," he wrote of the new power, "and resistance to superior mass is futile and fatal." A long lament, *The Education* was conceived by its author as a personal statement rather than a socially instructive text. Adams refused to have it widely distributed in his lifetime, presenting only one hundred privately published copies to friends and colleagues. And though it would later and justly be hailed for its deep insights and rich descriptive qualities, the work, if Turner's reaction to it is representative, initially failed to connect with a nation moving into an age of economic and imperial expansion, a nation still basking in youth, still imbued with a missionary impulse, and still confident of its role as a counterpoint to European hierarchy. Turner, who met Adams on two or three occasions, summed up his section's rejection of *The Education* as the case of an alien philosophy that had failed to connect with the native mind. "Henry Adams was the leader of American historians in his day," he wrote shortly after the old patrician's death. "His *Education* is a literary classic, an illumination and a tonic stimulant—but not normally American."[7]

Turner included among his favorite "American" writers a French expatriate and a Virginia aristocrat. Born into a cash poor line of the Norman gentry, J. Hector St. John de Crevecoeur arrived in New France in 1755, serving as a cartographer for the King's Army in the St. Lawrence Valley. Wounded on the Plains of Abraham in the epic battle for Québec, he changed his name, forgot his military past, and resurfaced in New York. "I never was but a simple surveyor of lands, a cultivator of my own grounds, or a wanderer through the forests of this country," he informed the Duke de la Rochefoucauld. Crevecoeur journeyed widely throughout the British colonies in the years preceding the Revolution, gathering material for his celebrated *Letters from an American Farmer* (1782). The War for Independence made his book into something more than just another travel account; in its aftermath Europeans were eager to understand the character of the people who had broken from the bonds of Old World custom. Crevecoeur offered them an epic and satisfying myth. "What, then, is the American, this new man?" he asked in the monograph's most famous line. "We have no princes for whom we toil, starve and bleed; we are the most perfect society now existing in the world. Here man is free as he ought to be."[8]

If Crevecoeur placed the "new man" in North America, Thomas Jefferson more specifically drew his destiny to the new West. Affiliating himself with a Trans-Appalachia he would never see, Jefferson was the nation's first public servant to take seriously the ideals of the backcountry. Long before Turner popularized the expression "safety valve," Jefferson had emphasized the soundness of siphoning congested eastern populations into the open lands. "When we shall be full on this side," he wrote in the year of the Louisiana Purchase, "we may lay off a range of States on the western bank from the head of the mouth [of the Mississippi River], and so range after range, advancing compactly as we multiply."[9] Jefferson's unshakable faith in the undeveloped territory's future was shared by Turner, who must have recognized in the Virginian's claim that human geography passed through stages of Savagery (Indians) to Civilization (Anglos) a convenient preface to his own generation's reliance on Darwinian theory.

Despite his reputation as a cosmopolitan in love with French wines, Italian architecture, and Philadelphia bookstores, Jefferson had never wavered in defense of the western ideal. As he grew older, his opinion of the region only increased—and so did his appraisal of its prospects. "I am eighty-one years of age, born where I now live, in the first range of mountains in the interior of our country. And I have observed this march of civilization advancing from the seacoast, passing over us like a cloud of light, increasing our knowledge and improving our condition, in so much as that we are at this time more advanced in civilization here than the seaports were when I was a boy. And where this progress will stop no one can say."[10] Naturally Turner saw in himself the embodiment of Jefferson's grand western revelation. He hailed from Wisconsin, a territory whose laws were influenced by Jefferson's "Report of a Plan of Government for the Western Territory" (1784); he grew up in Portage, an old traders' town just thirty miles north of Jefferson County; and he spent the most fruitful years of his life in a city named for the Virginian's chief political lieutenant. In sum, Jefferson initiated both Turner's West and an enduring discipleship of the imagination extending from the holy see of Monticello to the university city of Madison. There its people imbibed the frontier ethic in the crib.

"Is it strange that I saw the frontier as a real thing and experienced its changes?" Turner wrote late in his career. "My people were pioneers . . ." The Puritan Humphrey Turner abandoned England in 1634, and from a primitive decampment in Winthrop's Massachusetts his heirs and their heirs dispersed into Connecticut, Vermont, upstate New York, Michigan, Wisconsin—even Alaska. A ninth-generation American, Frederick Jackson Turner absorbed a family lore that connected his kinsmen to the nation's glorious past. A great-grandfather served in Washington's army at the Battle of White Plains, a grandfather fought in the War of 1812, and his own father, Andrew Jackson Turner, bore the name of the hero of New Orleans, the proto-populist slayer of the old aristocratic National Bank.[11]

"Jack" Turner edited the weekly *Wisconsin State Register*, the Republican newspaper in Portage, a prosperous village on the edge of the frontier. This print work left ample time for his two great passions: local politics and local history. Jack served as a delegate to national conventions, worked on census and redistricting committees, and maintained an active correspondence with historical societies in neighboring states as part of a lifelong interest in the territorial days of the Midwest. Young Fred took all of this in: "I spent my youth in a newspaper office in contact with practical politics, and in a little town at 'The Portage,' Wisc. over which Marquette had passed. There were still Indian (Winnebago) tepees where I hunted and fished, and Indians came into the stores to buy paints and trinkets and sell furs." Portage's human geography evolved before Turner's eyes, a path littered with the paraphernalia of rising and receding cultures that made him sensitive to the race and pace of historical change in the American West. His sense of self-possession and regional identification secure, he anointed himself an actor in the great transformation of the backcountry, "a son of Wisconsin, when the frontier was in the process of passing."[12]

In its wake, the backwoods left a raft of opportunities for the enterprising type. Jack Turner seized his share. "My father was . . . . a kind of Thurlow Weed in Wisconsin politics," Frederick proudly wrote. "He was a politician of considerable influence in the inner ranks of the Wisconsin Republicans, and not without influence in other states." A four-time member of the Wisconsin legislature and long-time editor of the *State Register*, Jack earned a reputation as a dependable dobbin for the midwestern wing of the G.O.P. He supported Lincoln's plans for southern reconstruction and later explained away the Credit Mobilier scandal in his paper as "a ruse of the Confederate press." Jack pined for a congressional seat, but more powerful Republicans stood in the way and he had to make do with an appointment as Wisconsin's railroad commissioner. He later served as mayor of Portage.[13]

Though Frederick dined with presidents, he never felt the pull of politics in quite the same way as his father. The historical profession's gain was the Wisconsin G.O.P.'s loss. A painfully reluctant writer, Turner acquitted himself as a gifted orator—the much coveted currency of the statesman. He won a copy of Macaulay's *History of England* for a high school oration on the power of the press and captured the junior and senior speech prizes in college. Carl Becker, a Wisconsin PhD and a major figure in American historiography, wrote of his initial meeting with Turner as a man writes of falling in love.

> There I stood, and presently he turned to me with the quick upward flash of blue eyes that seemed to lift and throw over and through me a shaft of live light. I seemed, dumb shy youth that I was, to stand fully revealed in the light of those extraordinary eyes—cool, steady, challenging, yet friendly too, and hoping for the best. Haltingly I asked my foolish question, and was answered. The answer was nothing, the words were nothing, but the voice—the voice was everything: a voice not deep but full, rich, vibrant, and musically cadenced; such a voice as you would never grow weary of, so warm and intimate and human it was. I cannot describe the voice. I know only that it laid on me a kind of magic spell which I could never break, and have never wanted to.[14]

If Frederick possessed forensic skills superior to his father's, the two men appeared to be on more equal footing in regard to a shared love of nature. In words that could easily have been written for his son, Jack was described in his 1905 obituary as a devotee of "the wholesome sport of out-of-doors. . . . He was an angler untiring and enthusiastic; few men in Wisconsin knew the game fish of the state as he did, not only as sportman but as naturalist." The younger Turner famously suffered from writer's block, and rather than face the agony of filling up empty pages, he devoted countless hours to hiking, fishing, and camping in the Wisconsin and Maine woods. He treasured these times and appeared out of place in a young profession hyper-sensitive of its shortcomings and eager to build a mountain of monographs. Turner, the first great twentieth-century model of the historian as social scientist, may in fact have been the last of the great nineteenth-century gentleman scholars in his devotion to research for its own sake. He could have cashed in by completing the numerous textbooks that Henry Holt and Company contracted him to write. But cranking out monographs never appealed to him. He preferred instead to collect data, pore over maps, and pass his leisure in the great outdoors. "If I ever longed for wealth," Turner sighed near the end of another long school year, "it was to be able to go fishing where and when I wanted, and in the real wilderness."[15]

Turner entered the University of Wisconsin in the fall of 1878. There he had the good fortune to encounter William Francis Allen, a polymath professor and early chronicler of slave songs and spirituals. The son of a Massachusetts Unitarian minister, Allen had graduated from Harvard in 1851 before continuing his studies at the Universities of Berlin and Gottingen. During the Civil War, he served as an instructor in the Freedman Aid Association in South Carolina and later as an agent of the Sanitary Commission in Arkansas. A specialist in ancient languages and history, he arrived in Madison in 1867. Turner once appreciatively described Allen—his first serious intellectual model—as "a Harvard man who began as a Latinist but changed to a historical scholar, of an ability and breadth of view not adequately recognized by students of historiography. . . . His breadth of interest in social classes, economics, and cultural factors, was ahead of his time in this country."[16]

Like his contemporaries, Allen piled on lots of German learning in the classroom. He introduced his students to constitutional history, the study of representative institutions, and a professional vocabulary steeped in scientific jargon. Turner's lecture notes in Allen's courses are peppered with the linguistic evidence of a culture-conscious academy—"evolution," "Teutonic," "Barbarian"—that stressed the importance of racial hierarchy in the Western world. Tracing the history of language, Allen taught his students that the Indo-European dialects broke sharply along descending "genetic" lines—"1 Teutonic Germany, 2 Slavonic Russians, 3 Celtic Irish, 4 Italian Romans, 5 Hellenic Greeks." Naturally, Allen's course on "Mediaeval Institutions" emphasized the Germanic character of early democracy. The Teutonic "Mark," a tract of shared public land, struck many American professors as a precursor to an egalitarian Jeffersonian state. Turner wrote in his notes for Allen's section that "the community inhabited the village [and] held the common Mark in mixed ownership." Over time, a complex system of feudal restrictions replaced "public lands," thus infringing upon the autonomy of the free-born sons and daughters of Germany—an ominous historical allegory of the growth of industrial power in Turner's America. "This theory then concludes," young Turner wrote, "that the community starts as a kind of democracy of freemen. This changed during later times

Figure 2. Frontier Father: Frederick Jackson Turner.
WHI-56683, Wisconsin Historical Society.

into serf communities—Manors." The German frontier, in other words, had closed.[17]

Allen's lectures offered Turner exciting lessons in social evolution, land transference, and political economy. They further suggested to the alert undergraduate that the recreational activities enjoyed by his father— amateur historian, outdoorsman—could be pursued at a respected professional level. What better way to chart the progress of democracy than by studying its migration from the German forest to the Wisconsin frontier? "My work really grew out of a preliminary training in Mediaeval history," Turner wrote near the end of his career, "where I learned to recognize the reactions between a people in the gristle, and their environment; and saw the interplay of economic, social and geographic factors in the politics, institutions, ideals and life of a nation and its relations with its neighbors."[18]

When Turner arrived in Baltimore in 1888 to pursue doctoral work, he entered the most intellectually stimulating setting that American higher education could offer. "The Johns Hopkins atmosphere was friendly to new ideas," he later remembered, "men like [John] Commons, Charley Andrews, [Charles Homer] Haskins . . . as well as [Woodrow] Wilson, called out one's best and challenged one's originality." Turner struck up lifelong friendships with both Haskins and Wilson, and it was probably the work and warm competition of his peers that excited him most at Hopkins. In many respects the university itself, with its casual prejudice against western institutions, generated a largely negative influence on Turner. His reflections on Herbert Baxter Adams were slight and unenthusiastic: "H. B. Adams told the seminary . . . while I was there, that American institutional history had been well *done*. That we would better turn next to European institutions. The frontier [thesis] was pretty much a *reaction* from that due to my indignation."[19]

A Massachusetts native, Adams, as I have noted, took a PhD in Germany and, like Allen, emphasized the Teutonic roots of democracy. The "germ" of participatory government emerged from the prehistorical folk and shire "Moots" (county courts) of the Black Forrest, he argued, and traveled in diasporic waves to England and finally New England. This clean, uncomplicated, and thoroughly Anglo-Saxon history explained in its sweeping connection of ideology, race, and politics everything from the Boston Tea Party to the need for immigration restriction. But Adams's thesis stunned Turner, who saw in the Trans-Allegheny region an unusually powerful expression of individualism, self-assertion, and intolerance for hierarchy and tradition. In reaction, he rethought the germ theory, questioned the primacy of political history, and turned his attention to the influence of environment on human development. The German Mark and Moot disappeared in Turner's bold reappraisal of the past, swallowed up in a fiercely nationalistic vision of American uniqueness. "This new democracy that captured the country and destroyed the ideals of statesmanship came from no theorist's dreams of the German forest," Turner boasted a few years after his Hopkins days. "It came stark and strong and full of life, from the American forest."[20]

When Turner returned to Madison in 1889, the writing of western history lay firmly in eastern hands. Francis Parkman (Boston), Theodore Roosevelt (New York), and Owen Wister (Philadelphia) offered imaginative and immensely popular appraisals of imperial clashes, the great Indian wars, and the romance of frontier expansion and frontier justice. The continuity in their views is difficult to miss. Roosevelt dedicated the first volume of *The Winning of the West* (1889) to Parkman; Wister dedicated his classic tale *The Virginian* (1902) to "my dear critic," Roosevelt. Together, these men combined to give western history its final classic narrative texts before the dominance of the PhDs set in.

Parkman was the descendant of Puritan divines (Cotton Mather on his mother's side), a product of Beacon Hill (his grandfather was a wealthy merchant and ship owner), and a son of Harvard College. His books, including the dramatic and vividly painted *The Oregon Trail* (1847) and the epic seven-volume *France and England in America* (1851–92) offered up western history in a style that clearly catered to eastern tastes. In these accounts New Englanders traveled deep into the hinterland, imprinting the region and its colorful cast of Indians, outlaws, and Europeans with Yankee values, institutions, and expectations. At bottom, Parkman described an inert interior whose destiny awaited definition by outsiders.

The titles of Parkman's books—*La Salle and the Discovery of the Great West*, *Count Frontenac and New France under Louis XIV*, and *Montcalm and Wolfe*—testified to their author's belief that great men and great empires shaped history. Parkman envisioned the New World as a contested ground between French Catholic absolutism and English Protestant constitutionalism. Here, larger-than-life figures clashed—not to create a new civilization but rather to export the customs and cultures of established powers into the backcountry. Parkman's aristocratic perspective guided his approach and shaped the questions he asked: To what extent did the court of Versailles influence river trade in Canada? Why were the Jesuits more successful missionaries than the Puritans? Did William Pitt the Elder or Louis XIV play the larger role in the Europeanization of North America?

The hero worship practiced by Parkman ignored the environmental point of view that drew Turner to the past. The Brahmin's cast of exceptionals—Champlain, Pontiac, La Salle—struck the Wisconsin historian as entertaining figures, but he wrote of the human West as a region defined by the impact of "nature" upon less reified actors—traders, trappers, and farmers. This emphasis ironically led Turner to celebrate (frontier) individualism while churning out historical studies nearly devoid of individuals. As a first-generation social scientist, he was determined to meet the academy's expectations for an "objective" style of exploration and expression. No doubt Turner's attention to demographics, market centers, and agricultural belts gave to western history a much needed complexity, though even his best students yearned for more stories, personalities, and narrative rhythm in his lectures. Too often the West became something of an abstraction in Turner's clinical telling. "There were no anecdotes," his student Merle Curti remembered,

> there were no concrete dramatic illustrations which would liven it up and give a sense of actual people. To be sure, on one occasion in the seminar when we asked whether he thought John Brown was deranged, Turner said that in his view, his mind was badly arranged! Occasionally he'd give us a little something about some personality, but he just wasn't interested.... There were lots of statistics. He would project statistical tables on the screen and comment on them. Lots of maps—maps that he had made, as well as others, and long commentaries and explanations of these figures.... He thought of himself as a social scientist.[21]

Certainly no one would have mistaken Turner's friend Theodore Roosevelt for a product of the seminar table or the lecture/lab. The romantic-minded soldier-statesman bore, rather, the superficial markings of the Parkman pedigree—a Harvard blueblood flush with family wealth. Though he lacked training in historical methodology and never held an academic post, Roosevelt enjoyed a solid reputation among professional historians perhaps overly impressed by his political success. He served in 1912 as president of the American Historical Association, and in 1937 the best appraisal of American historians to date, *The Marcus W. Jernegan Essays in American Historiography*, devoted a chapter to his work. Unlike his admirers in the ivory tower, TR seemed to possess the will-to-power to make history happen. His books emphasized the expansion of the English-speaking peoples across the frontier, serving as an eerily prescient guide to the imperialist spasms that seized the nation in 1898. The climax of that period—the Spanish-American War—made Roosevelt a national hero and prefaced the direction of his presidency, one dedicated to expanding U.S. influence in Latin America, Europe, and Asia. Despite the grandeur of a global vision, this cowboy king cut his imperial teeth at home. His *Winning of the West* glorified conquest and looked toward the capturing of future frontiers through honorable manly conflict.

Roosevelt consciously patterned *Winning* after Parkman's *France and England in America*. Dynamic leaders and defining events took center stage, with chapters devoted to battles, massacres, and wars. And like Parkman, Roosevelt rejoiced at the fate of Catholicism in North America, telling the Protestant-pleasing story of its violent rollback into snow-covered Canadian and sun-baked Mexican enclaves. In its wake, the Anglo-Saxons expanded across the globe. "The spread of the English-speaking peoples over the world's waste spaces has been not only the most striking feature in the world's history," he proclaimed, "but also the event of all others most far reaching, in its effects and its importance."[22]

More than any historian of his (and perhaps any) era, Roosevelt believed that violence served as a prologue to American greatness. The industrial process had yielded a handful of fortunes, yet it failed, TR insisted, to inspire a higher hope among his countrymen. He feared that too much technology made them machine-slack and machine-soft, idling away, as he imagined them to be, in artificial cities that denied the human craving for hunting, harvesting, and (noble) aggression. He saw history as something far greater and more important than a neatly cataloged accumulation of dead yesteryears. It became for him instead a living, breathing process of opposition and overcoming, a perpetual testing of strength sharpened by competition over a vast continent. No doubt such views owed much to the stark social Darwinism of his day, a set of attitudes seemingly validated in the blunt Bismarckian political realism that made the German nation-state in 1871. Thinking about the frontiersman's victory over his enemies and his environment, Roosevelt placed the Simon Kentons and the Davy Crocketts on the new lead line of conquering peoples—Romans, Teutons, and English. To emphasize the "correct" racial character of the western warrior archetype, he punctuated his work (as had the supposedly scientific Allen) with genetically exclusive terminology: "pure blood," "stock," "Saxon," "admixture," "half-breed," "half-savage." In Roosevelt's fated frontier, conflict is embraced for its regenerative powers; it is a compass by which Americans discover both their identity and their destiny. Turner, by contrast, believed that the pioneer process inspired an essentially peaceful dynamic; his examples— farming, clearing forests, and negotiating the daily demands of the land— were pacific means by which the European became an American.

Roosevelt's stress on the wars of the West personified precisely the type of "unscientific" history that Turner hoped to relegate to the dustbin. In correspondence, he drew sharp distinctions between their respective approaches to the frontier. "Mr. Roosevelt has written admirably on some phases of the history of this region, but his work is expressed in the title of his work. He studies the process of war, diplomacy, etc. by which the region was *won*. I should treat this aspect of the subject as incidental to the problem of how the West came to be what it was, and is, in American life." In another letter, he lightly complained that Roosevelt "was more concerned with *men* than with *institutions*, and especially with the strenuous life, and more particularly the fighting of the frontier."[23]

Despite their differences, Turner and Roosevelt occupied much common ground. Both agreed that the West was a human-changing region, that an evolutionary process brought civilization to it, and that a frontier mentality shaped the American mind and gave sanction to future expansion. Roosevelt doubtless believed that he and Turner were working toward the same ends. Shortly after "The Significance of the Frontier" appeared in print, he congratulated its author: "I have been greatly interested in your pamphlet, 'On the Frontier.' It comes at the right time for me, for I intend to make use of it in writing the third volume of my 'Winning of the West,' of course making full acknowledgment. I think you have struck some first class ideas, and have put into definite shape a good deal of thought which has been floating around rather loosely."[24]

Roosevelt's comment raises an interesting question. If the ideas that Turner "put into definite shape" had long circulated through his society, why did he receive such adulation? No doubt timing played a critical role. Turner's Chicago address appeared in a decade of great uncertainty for America. Populism, urbanism, immigration, war and empire overtook the republic; for a country reeling under a series of shocks, the frontier thesis both explained the source of its temporary eclipse (the enclosure of native arable lands) and its ultimate salvation (expanding the nation's democratic, capitalist institutions beyond North America). Additionally, in an age of Marx, Darwin, and Freud, the frontier idea came packaged in a scientific idiom rapidly replacing traditional appeals to providence. In a brief, evocative, and highly readable essay, Turner had crystallized the hopes and anxieties of his countrymen. He helped them to articulate their concerns, putting into new language old beliefs and old values.

While Roosevelt presumed that the frontier thesis embodied a currency of ideas common to scholars, Turner believed that most historians in fact misunderstood his work. "I have been so generally classified as limited in my scope to the West as a geographic area," he once objected to Carl Becker, "rather than as a factor and phase of American life."[25] The distinction is important. To Turner, the frontier reflected a dynamic *process* rather than a fixed *place*. At one time, he argued, the Atlantic coastal areas framed the colonial frontier; later, interior New England and upstate New York drew fresh generations into a wilderness republic. The western cowboy, trapper, and backwoodsman constituted only the latest phase in the Americanization of the European. The key was not so much where the open lands lay as what they did to the individual.

Eager to circulate these views, Turner worked hard to persuade, and his writing fell upon a rhythm and diction that appealed to both the public and the professors. "The Significance of the Frontier" mixed poetry—"this perennial rebirth, this fluidity of American life"—with the latest insights of the social sciences. Darwin's imprint was obvious. Turner wrote of "the process of evolution," "the study of European germs developing in an American environment," and he described the hinterland as "the melting point between savagery and civilization." It culminated in a curious and selective reading of the territorial record. As a matter of course, Turner emphasized the "uplift" qualities of the backcountry, its putatively happy mixture of education and politics in a pristine environment unspoiled by the dead weight of custom and corruption. "If the ideals of the pioneers shall survive the inundation of material success," he insisted, "we may expect to see in the Middle West the rise of a highly intelligent society where culture shall be reconciled with democracy in the large." Maybe. But what are we to make of the numbing isolation—in Turner's time and our own—of places like Sioux County, Nebraska? Or the grim catalog of crop failures, suicides, lynchings, foreclosures, ghost towns, and aggressions against Indian peoples that made up the darker chapters of the Yankee exodus? One could easily argue that the frontier process culminated in the *devolution* of the standards of living and morals of a good many who answered the siren call to "go West."[26]

Turner, of course, saw it all quite differently. Eastern life, he argued, constricted individualism, eroded equality, and demanded tighter concentrations of social control. The old New England settlements had once produced patriots eager to throw off British power, yet in Turner's day it was in the farmer movements that steered prairie politics that the pioneer spirit flourished. Grangers, Greenbackers, and Populists carried the covenant of frontier democracy into the West and proved worthy heirs to the revolutionary tradition in America. "Bryan Democracy, and Roosevelt Republicanism," Turner wrote approvingly, "all found their greatest strength in the Mississippi Valley."[27] Instead of producing, as Crevecoeur had put it, a "new man," Turner's frontier helped to restore the old man. Like Henry Ford's Greenfield Village, the Rockefellers' restoration of Colonial Williamsburg, and Walt Disney's famous "Main Street" theme parks, Turner selectively commemorated those characteristics of American life he found appealing and ossified them in a dream world of virtuous pioneers and brave frontiersmen.

For the modern reader, the conservative underpinnings in Turner's work are easy to identify. He lovingly portrayed a patriarchal Wasp frontier all but empty of Native Americans, women, and slaves. The index to *The Frontier in American* History (1920) has more citations for "Germans" than for "Indians"; there is an entry for "Slavery Question" (how the regions and states looked upon the peculiar institution) but not for "slavery"; 135 males are listed in the index, and there are only two women cited. Turner was hardly the first historian to portray the American past as an interplay of the universal Pilgrim, Patriot, Jeffersonian, and Jacksonian. His failure to include less studied historical actors, however, is notable on two accounts: first, it revealed a taste and talent for mythmaking, and second, it distorted the history of the West through omission. This last point is particularly ironic considering Turner's confidence that his scholarship gave a full and fair view of the frontier. "My work, whether good or bad," he wrote one student, "can only be correctly judged by noting what American historians and teachers of history . . . were doing when I began. . . . The attitude toward Western history was at the time largely antiquarian or of the romantic narrative type devoid of the conception of the West as a moving process— modifying the East, and involving economic, political, and social factors. The West seemed to me the most neglected part of our history."[28]

No doubt the romance of the West tugged at Turner's heart, even if he expressed this attachment in terms somewhat different from those of either Parkman or Roosevelt. While they focused in an engaging way on personalities, Turner's lyrical description of the landscape proved equally captivating for his readers. Considering his training, we should not be surprised that his adoring "American" conception of the past owed much to an earlier German romantic historicism. In *The Philosophy of History* (1832), Hegel had argued that a universal Spirit passed through the ages in readiness to rendezvous with humanity's final phase—universal freedom. Progress moved from East to West, he maintained, from the "despotic" Orient, to the democratic awakenings of the Classical world, and finally to a near-perfect Germanified Europe. The Spirit needed human hands to carry its cause, and Hegel, after observing a conquering Napoleon riding through the streets of his native Jena, gushed, "Today I saw the World-Spirit riding on horseback." Despite his reservations with the Johns Hopkins "germ" theory, Turner clearly believed that the liberalizing streak identified by Hegel was evident in the American character. Here, New World historical figures—George Washington, Daniel Boone, John C. Fremont—conducted the World-Spirit to the edge of the Ohio Valley, through the Cumberland Gap, and beyond the Mississippi. The spiritual dimensions of this new civilization were liberating. While Augustine's European City of God appealed (in Protestant eyes) to superstition, ignorance, and political autocracy, the American frontier seemed destined to spread the fire of global democracy. "The world," Turner promised, "is on the eve of a new religion."[29]

But what happens when the free lands disappear? Turner raised this suddenly palpable threat in "The Significance of the Frontier" without answering it: "And now, four centuries from the discovery of America, at the end of a hundred years of life under the Constitution, the frontier has gone, and with its going has closed the first period of American history." Was Turner suggesting that a "second" historical phase anticipated the collapse of America's democratic institutions? Such a terrible prospect seemed too awful a truth to tell. And so he didn't. But others noted the flaw. In a private communication Carl Becker acknowledged to Charles Beard that

> there was a fundamental inconsistency in Turner's general philosophy. His thesis was that the "peculiar" (how often he used the word) American ideas and institutions were essentially the result of the environment of a new country. If so, the conclusion would be that as these conditions of a new country disappeared and came to resemble those of older civilizations, the peculiar ideas and institutions would be modified and perhaps disappear altogether. But Turner, although never explicitly drawing this conclusion, never liked explicitly to admit it either. He was so in love with America and its ideas that he clung to the notion that our blessed liberty, equality, and fraternity was not only something new in the world, but that it would always somehow remain what it was.[30]

The interpretive sleight-of-hand noted by Becker eventually drew Turner's attention away from the frontier idea per se and toward the study of sectionalism. The shift is detectable in the titles of his books. Several of Turner's early essays were republished in 1920 as *The Frontier in American History*, while many of his late career writings were repackaged in 1932 as *The Significance of Sections in American History*. Their author discovered the relative ease with which he might defend the mystique of the frontier idea if he concentrated on its relationship to sections, which, unlike frontiers, do not disappear. He maintained, in a terrific leap of logic, that as the products of formerly unsettled areas, they retained the "peculiar" egalitarian character of the backcountry. The Wisconsin wilderness might have vanished, but old-timers like Andrew Jackson Turner had passed on the pioneer ethic to their children. The frontier had died only a physical death—its spirit lived on. "The frontier is and will be just as important a subject as ever for study in the era of its dominant importance," Turner assured a skeptical Becker. "The West which has already evolved from the frontier will continue to be fundamentally important, and there is much Western settlement, social and political construction still to follow. The end of the free land doesn't mean the end of creative activity in the West."[31]

In 1910 Turner left the University of Wisconsin for Harvard, the embodiment of patrician wealth and social conservatism—the anti-Midwest. This flight to the Ivy lands took on the dimensions of a regional tragedy, and letters of disappointment poured into Madison from dispirited Ohio Valley scholars. "I regard Wisconsin's loss as the greatest blow any western university has sustained within my lifetime," remarked the University of Michigan's Charles Van Tyne. At the University of Illinois, Clarence Alvord lamented Turner's "going to the 'effete East.' I can not yet readjust myself to the idea of your absence from Wisconsin. The loss of that institution is also a loss to the West, for your presence with us gave us western historians a standing which we can hardly hold with you across the mountains."[32]

What compelled Turner to cast his lot "across the mountains"? He assured Becker that ego played no role in the affair—"I am not leaving Wisconsin for greater prestige"—and his long-standing loyalty to the university bears this out. He had turned down an attractive proposal from Princeton in 1896 despite the prospect of joining his good friend Woodrow Wilson on the faculty. Four years later, the University of Chicago had offered to make Turner the head of its history department, pay him a salary far beyond Wisconsin's ability to match, and hire his friend Haskins to boot. Later, both Johns Hopkins and Stanford had failed to lure Turner out of Madison. In each case, Turner believed that the University of Wisconsin better embodied the promise and future of democratic education than the private schools that coveted his services. His rejection of the Princeton offer accentuates this point. "There is the atmosphere of creative activity in the West, and now that it has laid the economic foundations, I look for the West to turn its youthful and vigorous enthusiasm and initiative into University-lines. The men who rise with this uplift will have an influential and important place in American educational life."[33]

By 1910, Turner seemed convinced that the University of Wisconsin—and perhaps the West as a whole—had squandered its great potential. Specifically, the creeping utilitarianism of the state legislature and the UW Board of Regents combined to trouble Turner in his final Madison years. They discouraged, he believed, serious intellectual work outside the hard sciences; they exhausted "circuit riding" faculty, as professors were expected to participate in the statewide extension program; and they mistook academic excellence for academic privilege. For all his democratic sensibilities, Turner had become accustomed to the creature comforts a major scholar might expect at a major school; this included a hefty salary and one semester free of teaching each year. Shocked and hurt that his special arrangements had suddenly come under question, he accused the institution—in a fit of high sarcasm—of anti-intellectualism. "Here in Wisconsin where all our best students are engaged in saving the state and nation by studying political science, law, and economics—or are helping *on* the Wisconsin crusade for educating all the people, any time, any where, any how ... I feel the need for encouragement. Our regents are determined that our pork, poultry and cows shall have a great moral uplift, and as a loyal exponent of the economic interpretation of social development, I have every reason to rejoice. The University is the 'instrument of the State,' and the state is busily using it."[34] Discouraged by a statehouse determined to emphasize classroom teaching at the expense of research, Turner tendered his resignation in the late autumn of 1909 to take effect the following year.

How painful it must have been for Turner, a great champion of public university education, to withdraw to the epicenter of private university education. The move, he knew, would be "regarded by the public as a promotion. But I myself feel as though I were abandoning a very dear dream of helping build an independent center here." The meddling of the regents no doubt triggered the retreat, yet it seems plausible that Turner's crippling aversion to writing also played a part. He produced in his lifetime but a single monograph and a separate book of essays. Long at work on a major study that remained unpublished at his death, he frequently stressed the important research carried on by his students, implying, of course, that their scholarship must be counted as part of his own legacy. "I know it is hard for a busy man to produce," he counseled one of his PhDs, "but don't yield to the temptation of doing your duty as a teacher solely. Your growth and the stimulation of your teaching depends in part on your continuing to investigate and produce." Turner would have done well to take his own advice. He brooded much too long over the content of his courses, frequently taught summer sessions (in part to repay advances for aborted manuscripts), and mentored a large cohort of doctoral students. His Maine retreat served as a welcome respite from classroom duties, but it coaxed no books from him. "He is a glutton for data," a former colleague once remarked, "and years ago, yes decades, became overwhelmed by his accumulation." Teaching the frontier and playing frontiersman fulfilled Turner in ways that writing never did. He had one big idea that he worked over and over into ever finer increments—the next magical "Significance of . . ." never arrived. By going east he left behind old relationships, expectations, and failures. At least in New England Turner could recast his late professional days as a grand and valuable missionary service. "The west needs Eastern ideas," he once wrote Herbert Baxter Adams, "I think the West, too, has a word for the East."[35]

The circumstances that gave rise to the frontier thesis changed dramatically in the first decades of the new century. The Populist revolt, the influence of German historicism, and the rapid growth of midwestern economic and political power gave a certain coherency to Turner's work. But this eclectic center failed to hold, and few historians have ever seen their scholarship so thoroughly scrutinized. According to Curti, his last doctoral student, Turner accepted his critics with generosity and an open mind. "He just said 'I expect there will be revisions but I don't think its all going down the drain. Revisions are what scholarship is really all about.'"[36] And by the 1920s, the revisions were coming hard.

Historians pointed out that Turner had underestimated the impact of nongeographic forces in the making of democratic states while overestimating the frontier's power to produce representative government. A few examples will shed light on their claims: the European Renaissance and Enlightenment along with the Atlantic slave trade, rise of cities, industry, and organized labor, were critical factors in America's development that stood alongside—not behind—the frontier; the Protestant Reformation had a liberalizing influence on western Europe that promoted some of the same qualities—individualism, competition, opposition to centralized power— that Turner implied were unique to the pioneer lands; the development of a republican Parliament in England was accomplished on a small island nation that contained no sizable frontier, while the Russian and Chinese frontiers failed to generate democratic states; and finally, the idea of the West as a "safety valve" must be severely qualified—the poor rarely possessed the financial means to uproot and so remained in the cities.

A famous early criticism came in a tart 1921 *New Republic* review of Turner's collected essays by Charles Beard, who then stood supreme among

Americanists. The article signaled open season on the frontier thesis. In his own scholarship, Beard accentuated economic self-interest as the primary impulse behind historical activity, and he viewed Turner's geographic determinism with a deep skepticism. "The agrarian West, slavocracy, labor, and capitalism do largely *explain* American development up to 1893," he wrote, "but certainly free land and the westward advance of settlement alone do not." Point by point, Beard denied Turner's most salient claims, culminating with an assertion that while the frontier thesis "came like a breath of fresh air into a realm of provincialism and mythology," thirty years on it had little to say to an urban-industrial nation.[37]

Days after Beard's piece appeared, Turner wrote to his daughter:

> I enjoyed Beard's review, though I am writing him of some points of doubt about his microscope. He read the first essay at least, and that is more than can be expected of most reviewers, and his reactions are interesting and have a real point to them. Only, as you hint, there is something besides the urban side of the case. But at the present (30 years or so after the first essay) the capital and labor side has an importance which I think emphasizes the importance of the *ending* of the frontier, while he thinks the movement was all along more important than the frontier. The truth is both were related.... No—he's not a disgruntled American Historical Association member, but an ex Columbia professor, radical in tendency, but chiefly interested in urban problems and in the struggle of capital and labor. The review will do no harm.[38]

Turner's letter to Beard has never been recovered, but we know that Beard tried to make amends of sorts. Seven years after his review appeared, he addressed the following careful note to Merle Curti (knowing full well his words would reach Turner):

> In that Review I gave the grounds for my dissent from the extreme view that free land and the westward movement "explain American development." They partly explain it, but only partly. Mr. Turner felt somewhat wounded by my review, I fear, and perhaps it was sharper than I should have made it, in view of the great service he had rendered to American history. In my opinion (and you may quote this if you like), Mr. Turner deserves everlasting credit for his service as the leader in restoring the consideration of economic factors to historical writing in America.... Besides this, he is a scholar of fine talents and unwearying industry. His stamp is deep and indelible on historical writing in America.[39]

Beard's review anticipated a critical reappraisal over the next two decades of both Turner's scholarship and Turner's America. Much, after all, had changed since 1893. Immigration, urbanization, the market crash, and the New Deal suggested the centrality of cities, cooperation, and government aid in the American experience. For a generation weaned on Depression-era federal support, frontier individualism and its ideological underpinnings suddenly made no sense. Henry Steele Commager, a representative of the emergent urban-liberal wing of historical writing, tendered a respectfully negative review of Turner's final and posthumously published book, *The United States: 1830–1850*, that captured both the intellectual and political climate of the changing times. "Implicit in Turner's narrative is an abiding idealism, and a faith in democracy," Commager wrote. "And it is a faith, not an easy assumption, a faith to which Professor Turner clings in the face of evidence which he himself presents and which might lead other students to different conclusions. It is upon this note that he ended his book, and in this faith he ended his life."[40]

Turner died in Pasadena, California, on 14 March 1932. Six months later, Democratic presidential candidate Franklin Roosevelt delivered a eulogy of sorts. Addressing the Commonwealth Club in San Francisco, Roosevelt declared, as Turner had nearly forty years earlier in Chicago, the closing of the frontier. The great age of individualism, opportunity, and competition had smashed along with the bull market. Americans faced new challenges and sought fresh solutions. FDR stated the bad news: their pioneer heritage was a dead end, a handicap to be overcome rather than a precious resource to be mined. "A glance at the situation today only too clearly indicates that equality of opportunity as we have known it no longer exists," the candidate reported. "Our last frontier has long since been reached, and there is practically no more free land. More than half our people do not live on the farms or on the lands and cannot derive a living cultivating their own property. There is no safety valve in the form of a Western prairie to which those thrown out of work by the Eastern economic machines can go for a new start."[41]

In 1968, the historian Richard Hofstadter wrote of Turner's work, "From the early nineteenth-century to the First World War thirty million Europeans were added to the American population. By what process were the ideas of the frontiersmen and the frontier experience transmitted to them and their children?" To Hofstadter, himself the son of an immigrant, the Turner thesis struck a sour note. It drew a divisive and seemingly uncrossable line between rural Anglos and the Slavs, Italians, and Jews who clustered in the cities. He had a point. While Turner insisted in a 1922 letter that the frontier in his own Wisconsin served as a melting pot that united diverse populations, the groups he named—Irish, Pomeranian, Scotch, Welsh, Norwegians, Swiss, and English—were conspicuously of northern European or British Isles ancestry. As a young man, Turner rarely came into contact with non-Anglos (outside of Baltimore's black population), and what few encounters he experienced provoked a reaction. Touring Boston for the first time in 1887, he exhibited a genteel Victorian anti-Semitism not uncommon for its time. "Hardly had I turned aside from the noise of Hanover Street when an entirely different atmosphere was entered. The word atmosphere is well chosen. In a moment I saw what had happened. I was in Jewry, the street consecrated to 'old clothes,' pawn brokers, and similar followers of Abraham. It was a narrow *alley*, we would say in the west—and was fairly packed with swarthy sons and daughters of the tribe of Israel—such noises, such smells, such sights. . . . At last, after much elbowing, I came upon the Old North [Church] rising out of this mass of Oriental noise and squalor like a haven or rest."[42]

Despite his great respect for the talents and work ethic of the Jewish people, Turner's published work occasionally trafficked in stereotypes. A 1901 essay printed in a Chicago newspaper worried over the large numbers of Jews entering the country each year. "There has always been, of course, a considerable immigration of inferior immigrants. But the more recent immigration of the Jews in startling proportions from congested and miserable regions in Eastern Europe constitutes a new phenomenon." The disinclination of most Jewish Americans to retreat into the interior and find good Christian husbands and wives caused Turner additional concern. "The very poverty and consequent congregation of the Russian and Polish Jews into restricted areas of our great cities, and especially of New York, prevents them from assimilating with Americans. Intermarriages with gentiles are so rare that they need to be considered. Religion and language operate powerfully to perpetuate their isolation."[43]

What did recent trends in immigration mean for America? "It is obvious," Turner soberly reported, "that the replacement of the German and British immigration by southern Italians, Poles, Russian Jews and Slovaks, is a loss to the social organism of the United States." These latter groups defied the frontier's magic by refusing to replicate the pioneer persistence of their Anglo elders and create new lives. They were, by his definition, *less* American. In the cities, they remained a people of tightly knit clans, suspicious of the dominant democratic culture and hostile to the system of free enterprise, individualism, and social mobility. Turner argued that many of the bloody clashes between Gilded Age barons and their striking workers were at heart ethnic rather than economic confrontations. "During the past fifteen years," he wrote in 1903, "the labor class has been so recruited by a tide of foreign immigration that this new class is now largely made up of persons of foreign parentage, and the lines of cleavage which begin to appear in this country between capital and labor have been accentuated by distinctions of nationality."[44] The new immigrants' steady resistance of "Americanization" frustrated Turner. They refused to join the centuries-long procession of foraging, farming, and frontiersmanship that melded the dissonant voices of individual groups into a single people. E Pluribus Unum—but apparently only west of the Hudson River.

And yet despite these ethno-cultural tensions, lasting relationships were made. In 1909, Selig Perlman, a Russian Jewish student soon to become an influential economist, found himself sitting in Turner's course on the West, making insightful historical connections between his teacher's frontier and his own.

> As Turner lectured on the frontier there kept going through my mind the following idea. Now that's your American frontier, but that was a soft frontier; after all, the few Indians couldn't hold the white settlers back. So that an individual could negotiate a frontier, he could enter the wilderness, as it were, and he stood a pretty good chance of making a success of it. . . . Now, the Russian frontier was a hard frontier and for that reason Russia had to work itself up into a hard battering ram to continue battling away at that frontier. . . . I couldn't help but feel that a good deal of the basic characteristics of the American society and of the Russian society respectively, were influenced by its political or geographical situation.[45]

Beyond encouraging historical models of geopolitical development, Turner offered to the men in Perlman's circle—Jewish immigrants on the political left—a salutary representative of the American progressive mind. Ever the correct gentleman, his soft anti-Semitism never clouded his personal relations. "What attracted our group to Turner (we were all socialists, yet we knew that he was *not*), and especially what drew me, a 'greenhorn,' in this country, to him," Perlman explained, "was his liberal and democratic nationalism, a nationalism which knew no 'betters,' either on the grounds of wealth or culturo-ethnic origin and background, but was a nationalism with the 'welcome sign' out to all who were capable of being infected with his own inspiring enthusiasm for America."[46]

A myth has the power to explain the past, clarify the present, and foretell the future. Turner set forth in the frontier thesis such an epic impression of America's democratic origins and prospects, on such a startling scale, that it remains a popular totem to conceptualize both the meaning and the mission of the country. Politicians in particular have long been drawn to the frontier theme. In his 1960 address to the Democratic National Convention in Los Angeles' Memorial Coliseum, John F. Kennedy signed Turner up for duty on the front line of liberal activism. "I stand tonight facing West on what was once the last frontier. From the lands that stretch three thousand miles behind me, the pioneers of old gave up their safety, their comfort and sometimes their lives to build a new world in the West. . . . Today some would say that those struggles are all over—that there is no longer an American frontier. But I trust no one in this vast assemblage will agree with these sentiments. For the problems are not all solved and the battles are not all won—and we stand today on the edge of a New Frontier."[47]

As things turned out, the East Coast liberalism exemplified by Kennedy failed to master the frontier motif. Power and population migrated to the Sunbelt, and a revived Republican Party connected with a public frustrated with the cultural shift of the 1960s. If American democracy could be revitalized on the "frontier," than millions of Americans might believe that their own pilgrimage out of the postindustrial cityscapes of the northeast—and Midwest—had put them into closer contact with the nation's *true* values of freedom, individualism, and opportunity. In the 1980s Ronald Reagan became the dominant symbol for this persuasion.

In his own day, Turner wrestled the meaning of the West from the poets, novelists, and politicians who observed the hand of God behind every fallen Indian and every cleared acre cut by the plow, and he gave back their myth cloaked in a respectable "scientific" shell that took critics a generation to crack. By that time, Turner had established not only the significance of the Middle West but its uniqueness, vitality, and historical importance. In an age of unprecedented industrial development, the American pastoral appeared to be on the verge of extinction. Complexity, bigness, and proletarianization threatened the dream of a republic based on competition and mobility. Yet Turner assured his readers that as long as frontier ethics persisted, the spirit of democratic citizenship would continue. In 1930, as the Great Depression began to clutch at the country's confidence, Turner's successor at Wisconsin, Frederick Logan Paxson, looked for hope in the nation's rural roots rather than in its looming, uncertain urban future. "I move with hesitation. . . . I may be wrong. . . . [but] I cannot believe the democracy is done for, or that on the whole there is any superior foundation for government and the social order than that of the common people who live within them . . . . My confidence is grounded upon testimony that seems to me to be derived from an examination of our frontier past."[48]

As the architect of Paxson's trust, Turner had dismissed a historiography of southern and New England exceptionalism to make space for a mystical Trans-Appalachia frontier. His motives are easily understood. Coming of age in a section made newly important, he ardently, provocatively read its prospects across the landscape of the American past and projected its influence into the distant future. As a representative of a developing interior intellectual tradition, he came to symbolize for the general public the aspirations and potential of the midwestern mind. Across several generations, the nation's children had memorized a patriotic catechism thick with the adventures of men named Bradford, Winthrop, Washington, and Jefferson. Now, new circumstances called for fresh heroes. The Civil War had pushed Ohio Valley presidents and generals into the forefront of the American scene for the first time, and Turner rode that momentum into Chicago in 1893. There, he emerged as the founding father of modern professional historical writing—and more, the popular symbol of a middle-western historical consciousness.

THREE

Progressive Maximus
Charles Beard

I don't know how you feel about Beard, but after reading everything I could get my hands on ... I have come to a pretty definite conclusion that he is one of the ... most dangerous propagandists for socialism that we have in this country.

DOCUMENT IN CHARLES BEARD'S FBI FILE, 1940

Like no other public intellectual, the iconic Charles Beard popularized the pool of ideas that characterized midwestern resistance to the American Century. Born of interior moods and attitudes, the will and weight of his work captured the uneasy climate of the times by pleading for the improbable survival of the old republic. To the millions of rural and small-town folk uncertain about their prospects in a brave new liberal internationalist world, Beard spoke plainly and with felt conviction to their concerns. For this reason, as the Indian summer of progressivism approached, he briefly won their hearts. "There was a time," marveled one astute observer, "when all American history seemed to dance to Beard's tune."[1]

If Turner's frontier thesis introduced the public to a distinctive vision of America, Beard offered an equally fresh and far more controversial trinity of ideas: he risked running with the Marxists by applying economic self-interest to historical change, he flirted with professional heresy by deserting the objectivist dream for a modern and skeptical relativism, and he assailed Franklin Roosevelt's foreign policy, to the delight of interwar isolationists. More than merely questioning the wisdom of Roosevelt's decisions, Beard hinted strongly that the president—hoping to unite a nation badly divided between continentalists and interventionists—provoked the Axis powers into striking the United States. No doubt reflecting on the Great War, he believed this new crusade would end for his country in a wave of regret, with a Soviet-dominated Eastern Europe giving strength and succor to a reform-killing anticommunism in America. In essence, he anticipated both the cold war and the McCarthyite fears it fed.

Beard's rebuke of Roosevelt infuriated postwar liberals, some of whom tarnished his reputation by surrendering to the Star Chamber tactics of gossip and poisonous book reviews. Their comeuppance came quickly enough. Many of the professors who later decried the narrowing of intellectual freedom in the 1950s were among those who had once refused to give Beard's foreign policy studies a fair hearing. During the scrum, several of the Midwest's most important historians broke ranks and made their stand with the old man. They believed that in an era of escalating defense budgets, imperial presidencies, and undeclared wars, his scholarship offered the key to constructing a respectable critique of cold war liberalism. With flags flying and armor shining they marched together, partners on the last great progressive crusade.

Born in 1874 on a small farm near Knightstown, Indiana, the young Beard embraced the right-leaning parlor politics of his father, William Henry. "That is a great tradition," he insisted in later years, referring to the Federalist-Whig-Republican strain. "I was brought up in it myself and did not discover that any other tradition was possible until I reached early manhood." Despite these conservative roots, a congenital nonconformity seemed to motivate the Beard men. Charles's Quaker grandfather, Nathan, lost worship privileges in his church after breaking denominational ranks and marrying a Methodist; William Henry abandoned the family's ancestral home in the tiny Guilford County village of Beardstown, North Carolina, to avoid Confederate military service. And Charles may have inherited his father's politics, but filial piety only went so far. He turned his back on the GOP around 1900, insisting that a mongrel mix of industrialists, imperialists, and spoilsmen had pirated the free-labor party of Lincoln. In search of honest government in an era of honest graft, Beard's remarkable career as a political maverick had begun.[2]

As with Turner, it is tempting to see in Beard's formative years the cultural imprinting of the small-town values and references that later shaped his intellectual work. Yet too close an identification would threaten to reduce either man to a formula. While Beard playfully fancied himself "an American from the wilds of Indiana," his "frontier" looked much different from Turner's. Unlike rural Portage, Knightstown enjoyed important connections to the region's metropolitan centers. It sat on busy Route 40, the old National Road; thirty-five miles to the west rose Indianapolis, the booming capital city in the state's largest county. Mutual aid rather than rugged individualism colored Beard's boyhood. "I knew in my youth pioneers in Indiana who had gone into the country of my birth when it was a wilderness. My early memories are filled with the stories of log-cabin days—of community helpfulness, of cooperation in building houses and barns, in harvesting crops, in building schools, in constructing roads and bridges, in nursing the sick, in caring for widows, orphans and the aged. Of individuals I heard much, of individualism little." To Beard, the frontier, or at least the settled farming lands that he knew, offered an attractive mixture of personal liberty and social support. These twin strengths proved critical when he later quit Columbia University in a fight over academic freedom. The details of that resignation, as remembered by one of his students, capture the simple and morally uncomplicated universe of its subject. "Beard came to class ... and he made a speech which I have remembered all my life. In this speech, Beard told about his farm in Indiana and said: 'As long as there is corn in Indiana and hogs to eat the corn, Charlie Beard will bow to no man.'" After leaving Columbia at the relatively young age of forty-three, Beard refused to accept another permanent post in the academy. He made his living, rather, writing history books and operating dairy farms in Connecticut.[3]

One can make too much of Beard's Hoosier roots—much happened, of course, after he left Indiana. A Columbia PhD, study at Oxford, and trips to Asia and Europe brought him in touch with a world beyond the Midwest. More generally, Beard's reputation as the nation's most controversial historian put him into daily contact (depending on what arrived in his rural Connecticut mailbox) with any number of intellectuals, politicians, economists, and cranks. And yet for all of these post-Indiana engagements and experiences, the fundamental ideas that moved Beard—suspicion of centralized power, belief in the corruptibility of the industrial state, and hostility to imperialist diversions—were firmly in place by the time he left the Midwest. A curious mixture of Quaker pacifism, Lincoln Republicanism, and progressive idealism guided Beard like a polestar. His sepia-tinted memory of nineteenth-century Knightstown, he wrote at the age of fifty-five, "seems beautiful against the wars, hatred and intolerance of this age; and all the best of the old days I should like to recover, for America and for the world."[4]

Beard's most important book, *An Economic Interpretation of the Constitution of the United States* (1913), came out of the progressive politics that shook the Midwest. The founding fathers, Beard famously argued, drafted the Constitution in order to secure their considerable personal fortunes against a swelling debtor class and to open untapped commercial opportunities for future investment. By introducing the idea that self-interest influenced the framers, Beard forced students of the American past to consider the Constitution as an economic rather than a merely legal, let alone divinely inspired, text. He performed this exercise in exposure with a particular end in mind. If an eighteenth-century propertied elite could produce a document responsive to its pocketbook interests, a twentieth-century middle class could amend that document to reflect its disenchantment with monopolies, cartels, and growing concentrations of wealth.

Critics hated the book, many of them dismissing it as an odd piece of Marxist propaganda. Beard countered that *An Economic Interpretation* reflected the musings of an open American mind mixing "more or less [with] the 'spirit of the times.'" Looking for cover, he added that James Madison's celebrated "Federalist #10" had actually pioneered the materialist approach by drawing attention to the sharp income disparities generated in the early republic. "The most common and durable source of factions has been the various and unequal distribution of property," Madison wrote. A host of economic interests—agriculture, mercantile, manufacturing, creditors and debtors—"grow up of necessity in civilized nations, and divide them into different classes, actuated by different sentiments and views." At a 1926 conference of the Social Science Research Council, Beard tactfully traced his debt to Madison's celebrated circle: "It is from a study of the American fathers that I derive such ideas as I have on the subject, although a great many people seem to think it came from Russia." At other times, Beard credited—with a half-smile—William Henry's shrewd Yankee insights on the power of property: "People ask me why I emphasize economic questions so much. They should have been present . . . when my father and his friends gathered to discuss public affairs."[5]

Crowning James Madison and Beard *pater* as the silent partners of *An Economic Interpretation* acknowledged certain influences, but not all. The two scholars whose work, more than any other's, shaped Beard's thinking came from Wisconsin—Frederick Jackson Turner and Turner's student Orin G. Libby.

At the time of his death, Turner's files literally overflowed with fraying maps and self-sketched charts on population, voting patterns, and agricultural production. A trailblazer in regional economic analysis, Turner expected his students to employ statistical evidence to strengthen and polish their work. In this vein, Libby produced his groundbreaking 1894 study *The Geographical Distribution of the Vote of the Thirteen States on the Federal Constitution, 1787–8*. Formerly a dissertation prepared under Turner's eye, the volume assessed Federalist and anti-Federalist economic power prior to the state conventions called to ratify the Constitution. At the time Libby's book appeared, the thirty-three-year-old Turner—still a relatively little known figure in the historical profession—was eager to assert his claim as the nation's preeminent scholar of sectionalism. In the "Editor's Note" to *The Geographical Distribution*, he wrote that Libby had produced merely "one of a series of studies carried on in my seminary in American history" and that "a preliminary paper" by Turner himself ("The Significance of the Frontier in American History") anticipated important aspects of his protégé's work. What aspects? Principally the impact of complex economic forces on local politics. Myriad commercial interest groups, Libby demonstrated, vied for power and influence *within* each state; to argue for a simplistic regional approach to the Constitution-making era hardly did justice to the rich mosaic of early American republican culture. "It is believed that many phases of our political history have been obscured by the attention paid to state boundaries, and to the sectional lines of North and South," Turner wrote, nearly twenty years before Beard published his famous book on the Constitution. "At the same time the economic interpretation of our history has been neglected."[6]

With good reason, Turner believed that his frontier essays had earned their author a prominent place in the emerging field of economic history. He assumed more credit for Libby's work, however, than was his due. "Although not devoid of error," Allan Bogue has written, "Libby's dissertation was a more important substantive and methodological contribution to American historiography than Turner's own thesis." Unable to gain a secure position at Wisconsin, and certain that Turner had appropriated his research, Libby cooled on his mentor. A particularly painful episode in 1899 may have sealed the breach. Hoping to marry his fiancée, Eva Cory, Libby needed a promotion in order to secure sufficient income. Turner had other plans. "He said," Libby reported, that

> my line of investigation was too much like his for us both to stay in the department. That I never could be more than an instructor unless I would teach and work in another line. If I would do that I could have $1500 and chance of a steady rise. You can imagine my fix. To see the wished for prize attached to such hard conditions. Of course in the end I had to refuse because I am pledged to carry out the line of work I have begun. It is too late to change—it is what I am fitted for and nothing else. It was dastardly of him to ask me to leave my work for pay and do what I am not fitted to do.[7]

In the spring of 1902, Turner, without informing Libby, recommended his unhappy junior colleague for a position at the University of North Dakota. With some reluctance, Libby accepted the isolated post.

Turner may have staked an overly proprietary claim to Libby's scholarship, yet it is difficult to imagine Libby producing a study on the regional roots of the Constitution anywhere other than Madison or under the direction of anyone but Turner. It is difficult, as well, to imagine Beard's own work on the Constitution appearing without the earlier Wisconsin studies. While his evaluation of the economic status of convention delegates eclipsed Libby's more general analysis in scope and sophistication, Beard essentially followed the same methodological strategy—charting Federalist and anti-Federalist strength in the individual states in relation to their "interest" holdings. Far from drawing attention to his own unique contribution to American historical writing, Beard generously acknowledged his Madison predecessors. "It is not without significance," he wrote in the opening pages of *An Economic Interpretation*, " . . . that almost the only work in economic interpretation which has been done in the United States seems to have been inspired at the University of Wisconsin by Professor Turner."[8]

Beard built a career on plausible provocation. Notoriety threatened but never crippled his reputation among historians—until the last difficult years of his life. His final two books, *American Foreign Policy in the Making* (1946) and *President Roosevelt and the Coming of the War* (1948), struck liberal scholars as irresponsible works that falsely accused the recently deceased Roosevelt of "maneuvering [the] Japanese into firing the first shot." These "maneuvers," Beard argued, including Lend-Lease aid to the Allied powers, the freezing of Japanese assets in the United States, and the secret Atlantic Charter meeting between FDR and Winston Churchill, inevitably brought America into the war. We now know that Beard may have been more right than his critics. Leading up to the 1940 election, Roosevelt did publicly campaign for neutrality while secretly extending the nation's commitments to the British, and he did regard an act of "enemy" aggression (the Japanese raid on Pearl Harbor as things turned out) as crucial to overcoming isolationist sentiment. Beard's conclusions were devastating.

> If the precedents set by President Roosevelt in conducting foreign affairs . . . are to stand unimpeached and be accepted henceforth as valid in law and morals then: The President of the United States in a campaign for re-election may publicly promise the people to keep the country out of war and, after victory at the polls, may set out secretly on a course designed or practically certain to bring war upon the country. He may, to secure legislation in furtherance of his secret designs, misrepresent to

Congress and the people both its purport and the policy he intends to pursue under its terms. . . . He may, after securing such legislation, publicly announce that he will pursue, as previously professed, a policy contrary to war and yet at the same time secretly prepare plans for waging an undeclared "shooting war" that are in flat contradiction to his public professions.[9]

In the aftermath of Vietnam, Watergate, and the second Iraq war, Americans are far more likely than they were in Beard's day to believe that their presidents engage in willful deception. Be that as it may, the interwar Midwest's inability to formulate a plan to pursue a more assertive and constructive role in world affairs undermined much of the moral authority it possessed. The empty response of America Firsters to Nazi fascism and Japanese militarism portended a divided, violent world, almost assuredly more vicious and less secure than even the cold war that followed. Yet as large as this error is, it should not obscure the fact that Beard's pointed warnings against the growth of presidential warmaking powers deserves our careful, respectful attention. After all, his premonition of an imperial presidency has on occasion born bitter fruit.

Beard's leading critics were fellow historians—though what made interventionist-minded scholars including Samuel Eliot Morison, Perry Miller, and Arthur Schlesinger Jr. authorities on American foreign policy is unclear. While Beard published several books on international relations, his chief critics did not. Morison concentrated on New England and maritime history, Miller wrote on Puritanism, and Schlesinger produced several studies on the more influential Democratic presidents. Their fields of scholarship did not converge—but their politics did. They agreed that the isolationism of the 1930s imperiled American security and that attacks on Roosevelt's handling of foreign affairs threatened, by association, the legacy of the New Deal. The future of postwar liberalism seemed to hang in the balance, its reputation not yet secure; its ideology, in a sense, needed to be imposed.

The liberals' rejection of Beard is all the more noteworthy considering his once towering reputation among them. "Within the intellectual community at large in these years," one observer has written, "Beard was *the* American historian. In the 1938 *New Republic* symposium on 'Books That Changed Our Minds,' Beard was ranked second only to Veblen in influence, ahead of Dewey and Freud. A study of college textbooks in 1936 showed that his *Economic Interpretation of the Constitution* had become virtual orthodoxy." In fact, up to his attacks on FDR, Beard's "radical" credentials had been unimpeachable. His first book, *The Industrial Revolution* (1901), featured a blanket rejection of laissez faire intended for a working-class readership. Three years later, he joined Columbia University's political science department and, with the assistance of James Harvey Robinson and James T. Shotwell, helped turn academic history from a stale recitation of military campaigns and legal cases to an exploration of economic motives and social development. As we have seen, Beard's 1913 masterpiece, *An Economic Interpretation of the Constitution of the United States*, respectfully demoted the founders from demigods to self-interested statesmen. Freed of their hero worship, progressives passed through a spate of amendments that chipped away at the deferential republic created by the fathers. "I was more belligerent than was necessary," Beard conceded at the time, "and overemphasized a number of matters in order to get a hearing that might not have been accorded to a milder statement."[10] The same taste for a good quarrel, critics later claimed, pushed Beard's Roosevelt books beyond the pale of responsible scholarship.

If progressives cheered Beard's "belligerent" treatment of the country's power elite, they revered his 1917 resignation from Columbia University. The issue was academic freedom. As America entered World War I, Columbia President Nicholas Murray Butler directed his faculty to cease any and all criticism of the country's foreign policy. Beard, then serving as chairman of the political science department, received an "order" from the trustees "to warn all other men in my department against teachings 'likely to inculcate disrespect for American institutions.'" In the wake of this caution-cum-threat, the trustees dismissed three members of the faculty. The psychologist J. McKeen Cattell and literature professor H. W. L. Dana were sacked for opposing conscription; Beard's friend Leon Fraser, an instructor of politics, was fired for comments critical of the nation's preparedness campaign. In protest, Beard resigned. His letter to Butler— published in the *New York Times*—flayed the trustees as "visionless in politics and narrow and medieval in religion." They had—he slammed the door on his academic career—"no standing in the educational world."[11]

Beard's resignation devastated his students. "I don't need to say I was dumbfounded," wrote one undergraduate, "I don't need to say I was in a swoon like one mightily stricken with grief. . . . He is the big asset of this place. Now he is gone." Another said, "I didn't come here on account of Columbia College being here—it was on account of Beard being here." A similar discontent rippled through the faculty. One professor informed President Butler that Beard's dramatic maneuver had won considerable support among his former colleagues. "If Professor Beard's resignation from Columbia meant merely a personal loss to me, I should not feel called upon to address you at this moment. But it means far more than this. Beard has said in public what many, very many, of his colleagues have been saying in private. The University indeed faces a crisis when a gallant gentleman, an inspiring teacher, and a scholar who has left a deep impress upon American historiography and political science feels that it is no longer consistent with his intellectual independence and self-respect to remain upon its pay-roll."[12]

Evidence that Beard's departure from Columbia enhanced his professional standing can be gleaned from the fact that just days after his resignation, Harvard historian Albert Bushnell Hart advised President Abbott Lawrence Lowell to bring the freshly unaffiliated scholar to Cambridge. "Beard, I know, is a good man," Lowell assured Hart, regretting that budget constraints prevented the appointment. In later years, Columbia moved to repair its relationship with Beard. He returned to Morningside Heights in 1940 as a visiting professor, and in 1944 the Columbia trustees conferred upon him one of the university's highest honors—the degree of doctor of letters, *honoris causa*. These actions by Columbia were taken before Beard published his controversial works on American foreign policy, and it is an open question whether they would have transpired otherwise. "The stage is set for the greatest scrap over the right of academic freedom that this fair land has seen," historian Leyton Carter had written to Beard shortly after his resignation, but he was wrong. The war ended quickly and victoriously for the United States, and despite pressures on professors, flagrant abuses of academic freedom were few. The showdown Carter predicted did not occur until the next great war. On one point, however, he was correct— Charles Beard stood at the center of the storm.[13]

During World War I, Beard flexed an unimpeachable patriotism. He favored American intervention on the Allied side, supported U.S. entry into the League of Nations, and wrote articles for the *War Cyclopedia* (1918), a reference guide critical of Germany. But in the cold morning light that followed the armistice, Beard grew increasingly certain that the old imperial system, not a respectable or enduring peace, had been the true victor. He presumed that the president recognized this arrangement even as he designated the war a democratic crusade. "Either Wilson knew and lied" about the "secret" treaties carving up the Near East between Britain and France, he caviled to a colleague, "or he and the State Department were ignorant of matters known to men in the streets."[14] In the end, a number of factors—disillusionment over the botched Treaty of Versailles, the great economic reversal of the 1930s, the Nye Committee's intimation that "merchants of death" pressured the president and Congress into a declaration of war—influenced Beard's sharp and unforgiving turn away from Anglophile internationalism.

In geopolitical terms, Beard continued to draw insight from the Midwest. The stronghold of prewar progressivism but not—outside of large labor cities like Detroit—a reliable supporter of postwar liberalism, the region consisted of Wasp and ethnic constituencies united in their suspicion of the World Court, the British Empire, and the metropolis's countinghouse connections to Europe. "We need an exposé on the Wilson—F.D.R. mythology," Beard once complained, "but most of the people who deal with foreign affairs are subsidized by the Carnegie peace-slush fund and live by keeping up the mythology."[15] This splintering of the old reform camp into eastern liberal and midwestern progressive wings prefaced America's struggle to respond to the international crisis of the 1930s.

In textbooks written with his wife, Mary, Beard outlined a system of economic and military neutrality that he called "American continentalism." Its main features included domestic reform, immigration quotas, defense of the United States homeland (along with Hawaii and the Panama Canal Zone), and a rejection of the crippling contest for world markets that Beard believed compromised the nation's security. "How lucky that we have the broad oceans between us and the others and can easily defend ourselves," he expressed an opinion embraced by many interwar Americans. "I say let us rather build a strong, democratic society in our island continent by intelligent planning."[16]

The Open Door, a bruising competition with Japan for domination of the China market, blocked Beard's continentalist fantasy. He visited Tokyo twice in the 1920s and demonstrated an acute sensitivity to the economic issues that divided the Showa empire and the United States. In a prophetic 1925 essay, "War with Japan," Beard argued that "trade and profits" constituted "the substance of the controversy" between the Pacific powers. On the surface, he argued, America's actions in Asia seemed inscrutable. The United States, after all, enjoyed both military security and a robust economy. What then explained the steady chatter among the nation's newspapers predicting war in the Far East? Beard laid the blame firmly at the feet of his country's economic, political, and military elite.

> There are war-scare mongers who make profits out of congressional appropriations for munitions and armor plate. There are capitalists, land speculators, and merchants on the Western coast who honestly think that they did not get their fair share of the profits of the last war. . . . There

are labor-politicians in some communities who flourish on anti-Japanese agitation. There are restless navy officers who enjoy fishing in troubled waters and are eager to see the "untoward incident" precipitated—on account of the fun, the glory, the excitement, the honors, the decorations, and the promotions. Some of them are doubtless wondering just how the matter can be started with a show of propriety.[17]

Beard distrusted both Republican and Democratic handling of foreign affairs. He saw little difference among McKinley's Open Door, Taft's Dollar Diplomacy, and Wilson's Liberal Internationalism. As darkening clouds formed on European and Pacific horizons, however, he reserved a special loathing for FDR, the chief proponent of an expansive policy that lavished large appropriation bills on what he jeeringly called the "Big Navy Boys." "The Jefferson party gave the nation the War of 1812, the Mexican War, and its participation in the World War," Beard wrote in 1935; "the Pacific War awaits."[18]

In the late 1940s, Beard maintained a brief but friendly correspondence with Charles Lindbergh and Herbert Hoover—two famous Roosevelt critics. Following the publication of *President Roosevelt and the Coming of the War* (a recipient of Hoover furnished materials, reminiscences, and contacts), Lindbergh congratulated the author: "It's been a great source of satisfaction to watch the success of your latest book. I gather from the place it held on the best seller list that it's had the success it deserves. I've seen it displayed in front windows in book shops all over the United States. I think this is quite extraordinary in view of the recent intolerance toward anything but pro-war and pro-Roosevelt administration publications."[19]

The fates of Beard, Lindbergh, and Hoover are worth noting. They collectively embodied a progressive persuasion that thrived in the interior and flowered in their respective fields of scholarship, aviation, and engineering. As ambassadors of small-town America (Beard's Knightstown, Lindbergh's Little Falls, Minnesota, and Hoover's West Branch, Iowa, have to this day smallish populations ranging from two to eight thousand), they represented an intriguing mix of provincialism and cosmopolitanism, traditional and new. Their opposition to American globalism reflected the last stand of a respectable (though in the case of Lindbergh's anti-Semitism, sometimes not so respectable) nineteenth-century rural midwestern way of life. It succumbed before the combined catastrophes of the market crash, the Great Depression, and the Nazi revolution. The influence of these men plateaued in the 1920s, and they would live out the rest of their lives in the shadow of a precarious cold war liberalism.

Among a great many professional historians, Beard ceased to be taken seriously. Allan Nevins's 1940 review of Beard's *A Foreign Policy for America* discounted that study out of hand. "Of [this] book it is not necessary to say much. The author occupies an important place among American historians. He has won it largely by applying a smart, hard materialism to the interpretation of history, and thus often arriving at clever simulacrum of Truth rather than Truth itself." One critic dismissed his penultimate work on Roosevelt as "an isolationist's treatise. It is in all probability, the last isolationist book that will be written by a progressive."[20]

As the condemnations piled up, the eminent Harvard historian Samuel Eliot Morison emerged as Beard's most determined critic. A Beacon Hill Brahmin, Morison handled the history of New England with loving care, restoring the reputation of the Puritan divines from the acid writings of H. L. Mencken and producing a multivolume tribute to his Cambridge alma mater. There is today a large bronze statue of Morison planted between Exeter and Fairfield Streets on the Commonwealth Avenue Mall in Boston—a favorite son celebrated as historian, genealogist, and defender of the New England way. Naturally, Morison's politics mirrored his region's. As a cosmopolitan, a Wilsonian, and a liberal internationalist, he believed in the power of gunboat diplomacy to protect and export American commodities and values throughout the world.[21]

Morison's August 1948 *Atlantic Monthly* essay, "Did Roosevelt Start the War? History through a Beard," fairly dripped with condescension. Beard is alternately referred to as "Farmer Beard," the "Sage of New Milford," and "Charles the Prophet." Armed, Morison argued, with a simple detestation of war, a cynical view of humanity, and an irrational hope that a "new Jerusalem" of American continentalism, socialism, and isolationism might be built, Beard had grown to hate Roosevelt, the New Deal, and the metropolitan sway of twentieth-century American life.[22]

Morison's review unearthed a few factual errors in *President Roosevelt and the Coming of the War,* and its author persuasively argued that Beard's midwestern origins shaped his "conception of reality." The unasked question, of course, is whether the same could be said of Morison. His own worldview hinged on certain "truths" that were powerfully challenged by Beard: objectivity, the efficacy of a big navy, and the character of a president whom Morison revered. Describing himself as a "sea-going historiographer," Morison had successfully petitioned Roosevelt in 1942 to serve as a lieutenant commander with the "Big Navy Boys" in order that he might write, from the vantage of a participant-observer, the history of the American fleet in World War II. He was perhaps, this country's first "embedded" historian.

Morison's personal and professional investment clouded his objectivity and found a focus in the sarcasm of his review. "May [the Beards] rise above the bitterness that has come from brooding over their lost horizon of a happy, peaceful, collectivist democracy insulated from a bad world. May Dr. Beard recast his frame of reference once again, [and] raise his sights a little higher than the Connecticut hills."[23]

Morison continued his anti-Beard crusade through the offices of the American Historical Association. His 1950 presidential address, "Faith of a Historian," pointedly rebutted Beard's 1933 AHA presidential paper "Written History as an Act of Faith." In the earlier essay, Beard had vigorously defended the idea of historical relativism. "Has it not been said for a century or more that each historian who writes history is a product of his age, and that his work reflects the spirit of the times, of a nation, race, group, class, or section?" The holy pursuit of an elusive objectivity left Beard cold, and he advised his colleagues to bring an end to the "tyranny of physics and biology" in historical thought.[24]

On the surface, Beard's embrace of relativity might appear to cut against his "transparent," "literal" midwestern inheritance. Yet as the progressive persuasion declined, Beard understood that any prevailing conception of normative truth would be both defined and wielded by a rising eastern liberalism. To soften its authority, he advanced subjectivity as a plausible alternative. While other factors no doubt contributed to Beard's rejection of objectivity—including well-publicized breakthroughs in the new quantum mechanics and the emergence of cultural anthropology (and thus cultural pluralism)—his sensitivity to relativism's capacity to bolster regionalism influenced his thinking. At root, he knew that the great captains of industry, the social Darwinists, and the liberal internationalists craved structures of certainty to defend their vast concentrations of wealth, their stiff racial hierarchies, and their quest for overseas possessions. Beard refused in his AHA address to award the privileged yet another advantage—refused, that is, to give power a science of history that pandered to its prejudices.

Beard's remarks were consistent with the intellectual currents of his youth, and he wrote within a rich tradition of social theorists that included Thorstein Veblen, Lester Ward, and William James. But Beard's archetype of the historian as hero—performing an act of faith in a subjective universe—faltered in the 1940s. Faced with the threat of Nazism and the expansion of Soviet power, Americans looked for enduring principles to sustain their civilization. Called upon first to enlist their sons and daughters in a great war against totalitarianism and then to construct an impregnable cold-war state, they needed to believe that their sacrifices furthered the cause of grand, inspiring, and eternal principles. Beard's unsparing dismissal of history as Truth—"History is chaos and every attempt to interpret it otherwise is an illusion"—now struck a false note.[25]

It certainly stuck in Morison's craw. "The faith of a historian," he assured his own AHA audience seventeen years later, countered all chaos, illuminated all illusions: "with honesty of purpose, balance, a respect for tradition, courage, and above all, a philosophy of life, any young person who embraces the historical profession will find it rich in rewards and durable in satisfaction." Morison's insistence that "no person without an inherent loyalty to truth, a high degree of intellectual honesty, and a sense of balance, can be a great or even a good historian" was preached to a congregation of the converted. And these saints needed a sinner against whom they could shine. "I wish that every young historian might read Beard's final book, *President Roosevelt and the Coming of the War*," Morison boomed, "as an example of what happens when a historian consciously writes to shape the future instead of to illuminate the past; of a man becoming the victim or the prisoner of his 'frame of reference.'"[26]

These are shrewd, suggestive remarks, though I suspect Morison said more here than he realized. What happens, after all, when a historian *unconsciously* "writes to shape the future"? Recall that Morison had scolded Beard for making the past partisan, though he too had taken sides, on the war, on presidential leadership, and on Beard himself. Beard's bitter reaction to World War I, Morison wrote, "taught that no war was necessary and no war did any good. . . . It only rendered the generation of youth which came to maturity around 1940 spiritually unprepared for the war they had to fight." Lieutenant Commander Morison appeared, in this remark, to be making the case for (objectivity be damned) a nationalist history, one that might best prepare young minds for the rigors of the unfolding cold war. He discounted in this passage Beard's "pacifist" approach not necessarily because it was wrong but rather because it was not *relevant* to Americans in the atomic age.[27]

Two years later, the interior replied to Morison. In 1952 Merle Curti, a Pulitzer Prize–winning social and intellectual historian at the University of Wisconsin, rose to the presidency of the Mississippi Valley Historical Association. A native of the Middle West, a vigorous champion of public education, and Frederick Jackson Turner's last student, Curti had impeccable progressive credentials. A physically small, bespectacled, and soft-spoken man, he was blessed with a searching mind and seemingly boundless energy—he seemed to know and correspond with every historian in the country. As an unreconstructed Beardian, Curti felt an obligation in his own executive address to challenge Morison's remarks. And yet the prospects of crossing swords with an old friend must have made this an uncomfortable contest. "I became kind of a protégé of Sam," Curti later recounted of his Harvard days. As part of his New England initiation, Morison had dutifully squired the wide-eyed graduate student to Concord, where they took tea at the Ralph Waldo Emerson house and looked over the family library. But that was long ago. "By this time," Curti later recalled of his mid-century break with Morison, "Sam disapproved of me because I had written so much on the peace movement and he didn't really approve of that. Though he had a certain interest in left-wing liberalism when I knew him at Harvard, he'd become very conservative in later years."[28]

In his address, Curti spoke in favor of historical relativism (a "realistic, pragmatic approach") and praised "presentism" as the wellspring of intellectual discovery. The New Deal, he reminded his audience, had inspired the liberal Arthur Schlesinger Jr. to reconceptualize the early republican past and create a provocative new synthesis in his award-winning *The Age of Jackson* (1945); Alice Felt Tyler's popular *Freedom's Ferment* (1944) had similarly discovered in the reforms of the 1930s a template for exploring the reforms of the 1830s. Such well crafted—and not wholly objective—studies, Curti maintained, helped Americans to better understand the complex nature of their evolving democratic institutions.[29]

The following year, Curti's Wisconsin colleague Howard Beale produced his own rejoinder to Morison and the guild that lined up behind him. In a harsh, unforgiving essay, "The Professional Historian: His Theory and His Practice," he let fly with a full disclosure of dirty academic secrets. Dull seminars, esoteric dissertation topics, and racial discrimination topped his long list of failings. Having cut his colleagues down to size, Beale set off to save the profession's favorite great white whale—Charles Beard—from the howling pack of Ahabs. He turned the tables on his fellow historians, accusing *them* of intellectual dishonesty for meekly acquiescing in the government's informal screening of historians (determining whom it would and would not allow into the nation's archival records). Citing "national security" needs, bureaucrats, Beale pointed out, had routinely denied Beard's requests for documents as he researched the tangled path to Pearl Harbor. "Many officials and particularly diplomats, military men, and Department of Justice officials," he complained, "do not comprehend why in a democracy it is important to give the people and their historians full knowledge of what has been done in the past." He further denounced Roosevelt's "court historians"—the men allowed in the archives—for abandonment of critical analysis as the fee charged for nearness to power. "Alas, there are historians among us," he wrote in a rather obvious reference to Morison, "apparently delighted to cooperate in the policy of government censorship by accepting commissions to write history under government blessing or even government assignment from archives open to them but closed to others who are therefore unable to check their work."[30] Censorship, with a deep bow from the academy, Beale concluded, had made a mockery of the high-minded "objective" and "fair play" standards that scholars like Morison posited as a reply to Beardian relativism.

As true as many of Beale's criticisms may be, there is little doubt that they were a product of his progressive politics. He too operated from a frame of reference. A Beardian to the bone, during the late interwar period Beale had anxiously observed Roosevelt's every move in foreign affairs, convinced that the president planned to throw American might on the Allied side with or without congressional consent. During the 1941 debates on the Lend Lease Bill, Beale anticipated in its passage an alarming growth of executive power at the cost of representative democracy. "I do feel strongly," he wrote his friend the perpetual Socialist Party presidential candidate Norman Thomas, "that the present policy of the President . . . is inevitably drawing us into armed conflict that will mean the sending of American boys in enormous numbers to die in foreign lands. I heartily oppose this foreign policy. . . . I believe the power it gives to the President is a threat to democracy itself. I believe it is the second great step following the Conscription Bill last summer in the establishment of a totalitarian government in this country." Beale's robust continentalism, aversion to centralized authority, and pacifist politics were respected in progressive Madison, and there is certainly something both honorable and defensible in his concern over the growth of executive powers. Taken as a whole, however, his argument for isolationism belied the intellectual's quest for breadth. "The older radicalism" celebrated by Beale and his midwestern colleagues, George Mosse points out, "had certainly brought a feeling of élan into a usually staid discipline, but it had proved rigid in its America-centeredness, which may have encouraged a certain social conservatism as well. Their patriotism, though anti-imperialist, through its very isolationism had its price to pay."[31]

In an era of great dictators, Beale detected in Roosevelt's remarkable popularity and command over vast public-works programs unsettling signs of an American Caesar. He counseled a return to a revived progressivism. "I am . . . much less optimistic about democracy than ever before," he wrote Curti in 1936. "I still believe in democracy, but it must be a reformed democracy. New York radicals cannot save us from the dilemma. With all their sincerity they can only throw us into the arms of fascism. But I do believe that there is still in America a group who can by the democratic method, by stirring up the old liberal reform spirit and teaching it economic realism, bring about a better social order in America before we must choose between the dread alternatives of fascism or communism."[32]

Following the war, Beale watched anxiously as the far right reaction to the New Deal predicted by Beard set in. While some historians argued that the old Populist-Progressive tradition gave direction to this brewing anti-liberalism, Beale dissented, believing that McCarthyism arose within the context of World War II, when most Americans—and most academics—acquiesced to the slighting of civil liberties in the name of fighting fascism. Liberals had it backward, he insisted. Red-baiting reflected a thorny case of too little rather than too much democracy in America. "I wonder," Beale wrote to Curti, ". . . . when people will come to see that this is all the logical outcome of our having tried to save democracy by abandoning it for the duration of a war under the delusion that you can strengthen democracy by force and can defend it by negating it for a long period of war to protect it. Many of our college professors who will be themselves destroyed as this thing grows were a few years ago using the same techniques in OSS or even more recently were defending secrecy or censorship of historic documents 'to win a war' in order to save our right to freedom."[33]

Following Beard's 1948 death, loyalists circled the wagons. In the face of an ascendant liberal academy, Curti, Beale, and the young Princeton historian Eric Goldman fought an exhausting uphill battle to produce a Beard festschrift. They faced two great hurdles: the disinclination of several scholars to offer essays and the resistance of publishers to handle the book.[34]

Initially, prospects for the tribute were bright. In 1946 Beale and Goldman approached Alfred Knopf, who agreed, Beale wrote, "to assume all the cost of publishing it if we could get it together." From there the situation unraveled. The 1948 publication of *President Roosevelt and the Coming of the War* polarized the profession. That spring Curti, playing around with the idea of writing a Beard biography, distributed a survey to select colleagues requesting their opinions on the controversial historian's scholarship. The returns were not encouraging. Schlesinger replied that "Beard's views on World War I seems to me most naïve. His opposition to the Lend Lease Act in 1941 seemed to me an act of great irresponsibility. I find his two books on Roosevelt's foreign policy thoroughly vicious." Stanford historian Thomas Bailey condemned the FDR studies as "a disgraceful mishandling of the evidence. One is forced to ask one's self whether the author is a dolt or intellectually dishonest. . . . Beard is guilty of suppressing facts, hand picking others, overstepping others, and misrepresenting still others—for all of which shysterism we would flunk the dissertation of a Ph.D. candidate in history." Yale historian Samuel Flagg Bemis counseled Curti to drop the project entirely. "Leave it mercifully to time. If you overappraise him now, time may not be so merciful."[35]

The following year, Knopf, despite his earlier commitment to distribute the book, dropped the project. The publisher's insistence that the essays were unworthy of publication is curious. Despite some historians' refusal to contribute papers ("I can't do it," Henry Steele Commager said; "I think he did incalculable harm to our people"), a number of notable scholars including Curti, Beale, Goldman, Richard Hofstadter, Max Lerner, and Harold Laski did. Supreme Court Justice Hugo Black wrote the foreword. Knopf's about-face stunned Beale. "If I knew what to do I'd still try to do something," he fumed to Curti. "There have been three festschrifts come out this year for unimportant people of the old-fashioned dull sort, and it seems amazing to me that no one will do this one."[36]

To complicate matters, Mary Beard lost confidence in the project. Following her husband's death she had endured a steady stream of requests to comment on his scholarship, politics, and personal life. These inquiries—many coming from an unsympathetic academy—understandably taxed her patience. A Yale historian's questionnaire was dealt with coldly. Yale: "Did Beard, in your opinion, overstress the personal economic motives—rather than class and group interests—in *An Economic Interpretation of the Constitution*?" Mary Beard: "No, read it again." Yale: "What did Beard mean by 'collectivist democracy?'" Mary Beard: "Can't devote myself to this." Yale: "Perry Miller has suggested that . . . the real tragic flaw in Beard was that he allowed his unmasking impulse to strip away not only the ideals with which men clothed their real interests but all values as well." Mary Beard: "How mad!"[37]

The publication of Goldman's 1952 Bancroft Prize–winning book *Rendezvous with Destiny* opened a deep and ultimately irreparable rift between Mary Beard and the festschrift coterie. In this work Goldman drew an altogether respectful sketch of Charles Beard, but his description of the heretic historian as "a lonely old man, glooming out his last years on his Connecticut hill," angered Mary, who wrote a letter of protest to Alfred Knopf, Goldman's publisher. Knopf's reply—"I don't think I am wrong in saying that Eric feels a great sense of devotion to Charles however he may have represented him"—is parsed in the margin by Mary's handwritten rebuttal: "Eric was more modest then . . . has in fact damned him."

Figure 3. American Pastoral: Charles and Mary Beard.
Photo by Walter Sanders/Time & Life Pictures/Getty Images.

Knopf referred in the letter as well to the difficult task of identifying a capable Beard biographer. Curti—linked with Goldman on the would-be festschrift—now proved unsuitable to Mary Beard. "As for a biography of Charles, I am sure you were right not to take Curti," Knopf wrote. "The problem is a very difficult one. I don't think you could count on any of the older men and you may have to wait for some really promising youngster to develop." Beard scribbled on the side, perhaps with some relief, "I'll be dead by that time."[38]

The odds against the Beard festschrift were now overwhelming. And yet the book slowly moved forward. "We loved him and honored him," Beale assured Goldman. "He has been much maligned. I feel very strongly that we should go ahead with the volume. . . . In the long run, we will be glad we have done so."[39] The University of Kentucky Press published *Charles A. Beard: An Appraisal* in 1954.

The vilification of Charles Beard softened over the years. The passing of Morison's generation and the recovery of evidence lending support to Beard's profile of a corner-cutting FDR forced a respectful reevaluation of his work. Too, the disastrous war in Vietnam alerted American historians to the dangers of unimpeded presidential power. A post-1960s academy no longer asked whether Roosevelt deceived the nation but whether he was justified in doing so. The responses were mixed. Robert Dallek maintained that a "need to mislead the country in its own interest" acquitted the president's actions. Warren Kimball disagreed: "As much as one sympathizes with Roosevelt's dilemma, the national election is the one time every four years when the President should be obligated by his own conscience and the nature of the American political system to be totally honest and candid with the public."[40]

If Beard has in some sense been vindicated, it is an acquittal that comes with rather large qualifications. He celebrated America's natural oceanic defenses as a lasting hedge against invasion or attack, yet rapid technological advances in aviation, submarines, and missiles swiftly shattered the old security. And his opposition to a Lend Lease program that provided critical support to British and Russian forces in their desperate efforts to beat back fascist armies appears in hindsight a disastrous position. No responsible historian today would fail to acknowledge that this was money well spent.

Still, if Beard underestimated the dangers of neutrality, he correctly warned that Roosevelt's policies could very well leave America with unintended and difficult consequences. A crusade to promote democracy in

Europe ended with Stalin's armies occupying half the continent; Japanese power in northern Korea gave way to a native authoritarian regime; the Open Door in China slammed shut with the victory of Mao's Chinese Communist Party. At home, critics argued that Beard's vision of American continentalism encouraged a belligerent nationalism coupled with a garrison-state mentality, yet the cold war had much the same effect on American life. Historians like Morison believed that the United States could have security only by destroying the Axis powers. But the great peace never came—not after Wilson's war to end all wars, not after Dresden and Hiroshima, and not after the collapse of communism. And now, in our newly born century of terror we must again reckon with Beard. His provocative epigram of the American predicament—"perpetual war for perpetual peace"—continues to strike a true and troubling chord.[41]

PART II

The Liberal Age
1945–1970

As we look toward the future—our own future and the future of other nations—we are filled with foreboding. The future doesn't seem to hold anything for us except conflict, disruption, war.

HENRY LUCE, 1941

FOUR

A House Divided

I have a profound distaste for the type of scholarship produced by the Nevins-Commager-Morison-Schlesinger clique in the Harvard-Columbia axis.

WILLIAM HESSELTINE, 1948

The historical profession's founding fathers considered their work a branch of science.[1] Yet much of the history written by that generation clearly reflected the regional backgrounds of its authors. Rather than approach the past as a mixture of multiple imaginations, cultures, and economies, the historian was often subject to a creeping localism that shaped his sympathies and clouded his window to the world. The personal point of view, that is, triumphed over the open archive. Even Frederick Jackson Turner—a towering figure in the early social scientific community—embraced an elusive and exclusive frontier that appealed to the very intellectual narrowness he spoke and wrote against. Illusions of catholicity, after all, were the order of the day. A long view of historiographical trends reminds us that regional schools were, until recently, *the* propelling impulse behind American historical writing. From the old East Coast patricians (1700–1890) to the midwestern progressives (1890–1945) and the postwar Ivy League liberals (1945–70), the telling of our nation's story has chimed in time to peculiar dialects.

Among the Puritan divines, Cotton Mather holds a special place in colonial-era historiography. His pious jeremiad *Magnalia Christi Americana* (1702) chronicled the Calvinist flight from England, its courageous effort to make a new Jerusalem, and the maturing settlements' inevitable spiritual decline. American civilization, Mather pessimistically argued, stood hostage to a sinful heritage. "It must, after all, be confessed, that we have had one enemy more pernicious to us than all the rest, and that is 'our own backsliding heart,' which has plunged the whole country into . . . degeneracy."[2] The *Magnalia* depicted the building of the Bay Colony as something far greater than just another episode in the guns-and-drums annals of English colonization. It reflected, rather, a broader marriage between history and mission among a people destined to carry the Word into a new world's wilderness. Succeeding generations of post-Puritans worked diligently within the framework established by Mather. Be they Congregationalists, Unitarians, or freethinkers, the heirs of the old church hierarchy followed their fathers' faith. New England's past foretold America's future.

For much of the nineteenth century, the Harvard-educated Jared Sparks (class of 1815), George Bancroft ('17), and Richard Hildreth ('26) were among the country's most popular historians. Though politically divided—Bancroft was an enthusiastic Democrat, Hildreth a dyed-in-the-wool Whig—they agreed that New England's patriot departed had tamed the land, founded the nation, and carved out the political and religious freedoms enjoyed by all Americans. The Boston-led American Revolution, they pointed out, advanced representative government over monarchy, while the sectional crisis culminated with Yankee saints thrashing southern sinners. Often referred to as "national historians" because their work celebrated the rise of American power and influence, these Harvard men in fact hewed closely to the curious "universal provincialism" first evident in Mather's *Magnalia*.

By the 1890s, Bancroft's generation had given way to a fresh cluster of New England historians known collectively as the Imperial School. This group, including the notables Herbert Levi Osgood and George Louis Beer, rose to prominence in the wake of the Spanish-American War, by which the United States—depending on one's viewpoint—either backed into an empire or eagerly joined the "Great Game" of gobbling up overseas possessions. By scrutinizing Britain's uneven relations with its North American colonies, their work sought to inform the nation how—and how not—to administer its own newly won dominions. Contemporaries of Turner, the Imperial scholars cut against the Turnerian focus on the western frontier, interpreting the American past through the prism of a European-centered Atlantic world. Mather's belief in the Puritan mission of moral redemption reverberated powerfully through Osgood and Beer's implied call to project American mastery over the far reaches of the globe. And like Mather's, their America was at heart a New England nation—patriarchal, Protestant, and capitalist. The hum and reach of Lowell mills and Boston finance, the intellectual influence of Cambridge and New Haven, and the cultural residue of Calvinism (in the face of an increasingly post-1890 Catholic and Jewish immigration) were examples, they insisted, of a dynamic and robust civilization. New England's scholarly defenders legitimized local aspirations, idiosyncrasies, and moral judgments, characterizing them as coast-to-coast characteristics rather than merely the patched and imperfect views of a particular people.

The old Northeast's hold on historical writing failed to survive the nineteenth century. In the age of Turner, Beard, and Parrington, interior writers internalized the public's passion for nostalgia and its growing concern over the urban-ethnic influence in the United States. In this respect, the Progressive historians mimicked their eastern cousins—local histories and cultural references were mistaken for a general perspective. In Madison, Wisconsin, the academic center of a thriving midwestern historical persuasion, a number of demographic trends worked in favor of a sentimental nationalism. "Wisconsin lent itself to this vision of an American arcadia," writes Paul Buhle. "With no metropolitan centers outside Milwaukee, with relatively little mass production and few of the 'new' southern and eastern European immigrants, the state could cling to an earlier vision of politics and life."[3] And from this vision emerged new themes and new heroes. The *old* American Revolution—the patriot campaign against a wicked empire—may have garlanded the proud brow of New England, but the *new* American Revolution—the Populist contest against a corrupt business state—gave fresh meaning to ideas of independence, morality, and democracy in a nation struggling to reconcile industrialism with republicanism.

As long as midwestern historians held the high ground, the Populists received solid reviews. Wisconsin's John Hicks produced the profession's most sympathetic appraisal of agrarian radicalism—*The Populist Revolt* (1931)—while his talented Madison protégés Theodore Saloutos and George Mowry completed dissertations strongly supportive of the Populist-Progressive tradition. Their dominance did not last. By 1950, the maturation of ethnic scholars in America countered the Wasp consensus in historical writing, producing studies sensitive to the largely literary and sentimental anti-Semitism of Populism. These scholars stressed midwestern support for William Jennings Bryan's multiple presidential runs and for the third-party bids of Theodore Roosevelt in 1912 (Bull Moose), and Robert La Follette in 1924 (Progressive Party). Too quick to view coalitions outside the Republican/Democratic mainstream as products of the same warped mass politics that gave rise to Hitler and Stalin, some cold war intellectuals denounced expressions of democratic activism that operated beyond or challenged from within the two-party consensus. A glance across the Ohio Valley seemed to confirm their worst fears. In 1948, the Iowa agricultural scientist and former vice president Henry Wallace ran a left-leaning (pro-

Soviet, some critics claimed) presidential campaign; shortly thereafter, the Wisconsin senator Joseph McCarthy became the poster child for the era's arch anticommunism. Though neither Wallace nor McCarthy received significant support in the Midwest, their personal ties to the region encouraged an important and influential concentration of scholars to regard the "Heartland" as the center of the nation's problematic politics.[4]

Below the surface of this political struggle lay a deeper cultural clash that split American reformers between an older progressivism and a budding postwar liberalism. Representatives of the former taught mainly in ethnically homogeneous universities, resisted conflating Populism with McCarthyism, and equated the containment theories of foreign policy "realists" with the kind of troubling internationalism that drew America into the Pacific War. Cold war liberals, by contrast, constituted an ethnically mixed group, drew from McCarthyism a deep suspicion of mass behavior, and favored the expansion of U.S. commitments around the globe. In the spirit of the new liberalism, Columbia University's Richard Hofstadter accentuated in his Pulitzer Prize–winning book *The Age of Reform* (1955) the crank side of the Populist movement—its "irrational" fear of an efficient industrial state—and courted controversy by charging the farming class with Jew-baiting. In the wake of the Holocaust this was just about the most damning accusation that one could make.

Just about. The quickest route to professional oblivion in the postwar academy ran straight through the Communist Party. After combing through dozens of manuscript collections, I have yet to recover evidence that a single member of the iconic Wisconsin history faculty belonged to the CP or any of its appendages. No doubt some of their students did. What we do know is that a few members of the department supported Norman Thomas's Socialist Party but leaned no further left. These men were in the main tied to an older Jeffersonian vision embracing egalitarian democracy and rejecting global interventionism. In a 1941 letter to Thomas, Howard Beale outlined his recent contributions to the party: "I have been speaking against Aid to Britain and against other measures that will lead us into war as frequently as my time and strength will permit."[5] One would be hard pressed to distinguish Beale's "radical" objection to American internationalism from its more conservative Robert Taft Republican form, which also developed in the Midwest. It is a telling indication of just how far postwar liberalism moved to the center that old-line progressives like Beale and Merle Curti were accused of harboring Marxist sympathies.

But accused they were. Paul Schrecker, a European philosopher touring American universities in 1944, made in the pages of *Harper's Magazine* a suggestive observation about the historians he encountered in Madison: "I noticed with surprise how much their approach is influenced by Marxian theories, even without themselves being conscious of this influence." Curti, at that time seeking a seventy-five-thousand-dollar grant from the Rockefeller Foundation for a study of American civilization, moved quickly to refute Schrecker's claim. "None of us," he promised one Rockefeller official, "could in any sense be said to be Marxists, or to have been influenced as much by Marx as, say, by Dewey and Veblen." Yet Curti and his colleagues could do little to dispel the belief—even among certain of its alumni—that Wisconsin had gone red. One indignant southerner complained to the Madison historian William Hesseltine of an antisegregation piece that he had recently published: "If you are 'shocked' at the resistance of Tennesseans to integration, it is nothing to the feeling of outrage which moves intelligent people in our state when they see educators attempting to 'Brain-Wash' college students with socialistic and communistic ideas, under the guise of Christian Democracy. As a graduate of the University of Wisconsin, it distresses me to learn of the manner in which subversives operate there."[6]

Many liberal historians in the northeast no doubt shared this southerner's suspicion of the "subversive" political culture nursed in the more radical midwestern enclaves. In 1953, Madison doctoral candidate Warren Susman reported to Curti that his recent job interview at Princeton failed on political grounds.

> Although there is some regret on my part, I can't say I was really disappointed since I never felt I had a chance for the job after the interview— the hostility toward Wisconsin and its products was too evident. . . . I have been in contact recently with people at Harvard, Yale, Columbia, and Princeton, and you would really be amazed at the mass of misconception held about the Wisconsin department by grad students and the staff alike, really incredible. It is a wonder you place anyone east of the Mississippi—the hostility seems too great. Of course, a great part of this hostility is ideological (I've heard it said that you were all socialists!). . . . And you do represent a certain approach to history which seems at the present terribly on the defensive, especially in the east.[7]

The historical approach favored by Susman's mentors celebrated the old reform heritage: Veblen's critique of American capitalism, Beard's insights on relativism, and Dewey's faith in democratic public education. More than any of his contemporaries, Curti pushed these ideas into the postwar era. Living up to Susman's high acclaim—"I think that you are the heir to Becker and Beard"—he cast off the notion of eternal and unchanging social systems, arguing that conservative regimes routinely justified their privileged positions on such self-serving falsehoods.[8]

In his youth, Curti had witnessed the heeling of an American industrial aristocracy before the principled coupling of public power and university expertise. Among their tactics, the reformers had broken the old guard's monopoly on ideas. Prior to Progressivism, the academy shilled energetically for the status quo. Economists agreed that the "natural," unregulated flow of commodities explained—and thus excused—the country's undemocratic allocation of resources; sociologists appealed to Darwin's theory of natural selection as proof that the few were fit to rule over the many; and political scientists privileged individual rights over community rights, declaring that government existed to protect the claims of property above all else. Curti's intellectual exemplar, John Dewey, took the lead in dismantling this classical artifice. He argued for social arrangements that encouraged human intervention as a preface to cultivating a more equitable society. A robust public democracy made the new system work. Dewey, Curti wrote, with obvious admiration, "argued that all concepts of human nature are, as it were, politically determined. The theory that human nature does not and cannot change was, he insisted, a view functional to and prevalent in aristocracies. The democratic scheme of human nature emphasized thinking as problem solving and living as a cooperative social enterprise in which experience was reconstructed on ever more satisfying levels, individual and social."[9]

Dewey's ideas offered Curti the promising insight that a fluid and evolving *American* form of human nature undergirded the nation's democratic institutions. And he responded by embracing a progressive ideology that resisted the worship of "permanent" truths, conditions, and classes. As we have seen, the popularization of historical relativism by Beard offended eastern scholars certain that a soft, "subjective" practice of the past would compromise the nation's ability to fight hot and cold wars. In their own way, these historians believed in absolutes as dogmatically as did the old industrial class. Curti sensed in this line of thought a concentrated if unrecognized effort by postwar intellectuals to pick up where the robber barons had left off—imposing elite control over the masses. During World War I, psychological testing on soldiers, including the first extensive use of IQ assessment, indicated a shockingly low average intelligence. These flawed and prejudicial exams raised serious questions about the cognitive ability of Americans to carry out the most basic functions of republican citizenship, including informed voting and holding public office.

Support for a cerebral gentry received additional support over the years from a wide spectrum of scientific and philosophical circles. Eugenicists emphasized the virtues of replicating the human race's most prized heritable traits while proposing contraception and more radical measures, including forced sterilization, to shrink the pool of perceived mental incompetents. "Those least fit to carry on the race are increasing rapidly," argued Margaret Sanger, the controversial birth-control advocate; "funds that should be used to raise the standard of our civilization are diverted to maintenance of those who should never have been born." On the cultural right, Harvard's New Humanism thinkers, Irving Babbitt and Paul Elmer More, rebelled against the Progressive era's democratic drift. They advocated an "ethical aristocracy" imbued with a "moral imagination" that favored moderation over modernity and classical education over utilitarian learning. More warned against the dangers of creating a vast "intellectual proletariat" in the state schools, while Babbitt's student Norman Foerster wondered about the wisdom of mixing gifted and middling minds. "The very atmosphere of the university seems oppressive with the weight of concern for helpless mediocrity," he wrote, "as if it were an intellectual sick chamber." [10]

The attack on democracy found a popular prewar voice in the serious satire of H. L. Mencken. His blistering *American Mercury* send-ups of the "boobocracy" mocked the tastes, lifestyles, and politics of the parvenus, who, he thundered, possessed too much influence and too few brains. Sinclair Lewis, the first American writer to win the Nobel Prize, exposed a "progressive" Midwest wallowing in shysterism and hypocrisy. In the interwar dystopias of Gopher Prairie, Minnesota, and Zenith, Indiana, men like George F. Babbitt talked endlessly and emptily about escaping their suburban prisons, yet retreated into a stultifying conversational black hole of sports, weather, and the wonders of Ford automobiles. In his classic 1935 book, *It Can't Happen Here,* Lewis portrayed an anxious and angry Middle America running over liberals and leftists alike to make a president out of the *petit* folk fascist Berzelius "Buzz" Windrip. If the novel missed the prophet's mark (the "masses" rejected the Far Right and kept voting Roosevelt), it more perceptively anticipated the messy divorce between cold war intellectuals and the working class.

Looking back on events now, it is striking how strong the attack on democracy became in certain quarters of the American academy. Despite the fact that the nation's economic and political elites created the investment and Federal Reserve systems that failed in 1929, and despite the fact that large democratic armies volunteered to fight Nazism in Europe and Japanese aggression in Asia, intellectuals often dismissed the "people" as ignorant biblical literalists, rednecks, and crypto anti-Semites. While the United States worked feverishly during these early cold war days to export democracy abroad, important corners of the academy ironically assailed popular politics at home.

Scholarly prejudice against the masses peaked with the 1955 publication of *The New American Right,* a collection of essays edited by the sociologist Daniel Bell. Of the nine contributors, seven were either currently or formerly affiliated with Columbia University. None of the authors hailed from the Midwest, the South, or the West. Briefly, this Columbia School identified in McCarthyism a shadow movement against intellectuals, liberals, and perhaps even American Jews. Adopting experimental categories—"status anxiety," "anti-intellectualism"—it took up where the antidemocratic Nietzschean elitist Mencken had left off, but with the imposing apparatus of a new scientific nomenclature to prop up its claims. Peter Viereck described McCarthyism as an "outburst of direct democracy" and argued that "the McCarthyites threaten liberty precisely because they are so egalitarian, ruling foreign policy by mass telegrams to the Executive Branch and by radio speeches and Gallup Poll." David Riesman and Nathan Glazer suggested a curious linkage between the American far right and an alleged Teutonic authoritarian personality—"a good deal of McCarthy's support represents the comeback of the German Americans after two world wars." In total, the essays make seven references to Nazism, five to Hitler, and one each to Goebbels, Goering, and Speer. In a book that purported to dissect ultraconservatism in the United States, the authors' glancing but revealing references to the Third Reich raised altogether different questions.[11]

Four years after *The New American Right* appeared, Curti responded to the Columbia intellectuals in his ambitious case study of frontier democracy, *The Making of an American Community.* This work—a lively defense of progressive historicism in a liberal age—rejected Bell and company's negative assessment of folk politics in America. A portrait of the cultural and ideological development of Trempealeau County, Wisconsin, it set out to prove that the people of Trempealeau (and by inference Wisconsin, and by a still larger inference the Midwest) were, as Turner had insisted, liberal and democratic.

The Columbia School's use of social psychological categories gave its work a gloss of intellectual rigor that made Turner's studies on the frontier look underresearched and amateurish by comparison. In reply, Curti (with the aid of a small army of research assistants) adopted quantitative analysis to press his case. Specifically, he compared the socioeconomic development of Trempealeau with a control group—an area of Vermont—for the period 1850–80. The results vindicated Turner on every important question. "All the immigrant groups did well.... Decade by decade the foreign-born, including those from non-English-speaking countries, were increasingly represented in political and cultural activities, and . . . intermarriage increased." A pleased Curti confided to one colleague that "the results are more positive and affirmative than I had earlier supposed, and, all in all, it seems to me perhaps the best work I have done, certainly from the point of view of using methods seldom used by historians to point the way to an operational attack on a highly controversial issue—the Turner thesis as it must now be considered." On the critical issue of whether the backcountry promoted or prohibited popular government, Curti (since 1947 the Frederick Jackson Turner Professor of History at Wisconsin) happily concluded that his study "lends support to . . . the main implications of Turner's thesis about the frontier and democracy."[12] Of course the Columbia School never denied that rural America advanced democracy; its fundamental quarrel was with democracy itself.

It may be helpful at this point to note the convergence of ethnicity and ideology in midcentury American academic life. Bell and Hofstadter were the sons of Russian and Eastern European Jewish fathers. The former attended the City College of New York because Columbia University's Jewish quota was full; Hofstadter took his undergraduate degree at the ethnically mixed University of Buffalo. Early in life, in other words, they could both make claims to a kind of intellectual or social marginality amidst the broad contours of Wasp America.

Curti also bore the impress of an immigrant experience, though a very different one from that of either Bell or Hofstadter. Raised in rural Papillon, Nebraska, he knew something about the frontier and its European peopling. His father, a pharmacologist turned insurance salesman, arrived in America in 1865 from Rapperschwyl, Switzerland. His mother migrated from Vermont and watched her parents fail in the unpredictable Omaha cattle shipping industry—she remained, but her family returned home. As a child, Curti crossed half the country every summer to be with his New England grandparents. In this way, from the dreamy three-day journey of a Pullman car, he saw America. Negotiating a cultural landscape that connected Czech and German neighbors on the prairie plains with Yankee relatives in the Green Mountains made an indelible impact on the young boy. "I had two sides," he later observed. "I think I learned to appreciate America as much from my father as I did my mother and her family. They were quite conscious of being Vermonters. I think my father [on the other hand] had a very deep appreciation of the American West."[13]

This regard led John Eugene Curti to adopt an American identity rooted in the nation's interior. And far from developing a sense of limitations or cultural otherness imposed by ethnic differences, he sent his son to Harvard, where he fell under Turner's spell. Unlike the metropolitan-based Columbia social scientists, Curti could note with pride that "both the frontier *and* the immigrant contributions to America helped develop my early interest in the national history."[14] As a product of two traditions, he linked his second-generation progress to the progress of frontier mobility—the linchpin of democracy. In contrast to either Bell or Hofstadter, in some vital sense both outsiders to the older Protestant progressivism, Curti felt very much an insider.

As such, he watched with dismay the steady erosion of progressive politics in the 1950s. The Mencken-era attacks on the masses by psychologists, eugenicists, and the New Humanists had picked up steam in the postwar period. Specialists, technocrats, intellectuals, and social scientists moved rather openly against the idea of broad civic engagement formally advanced in the Wisconsin Idea. Curti detested the elitist strain of the new liberalism, its suspicion of the people it purported to represent, and its problematic faith in absolutes. The moral necessity of fighting the cold war seemed to most liberals beyond dispute, and scholars who raised serious questions about the effects of U.S. foreign policy on American civil liberties risked their disfavor. This had a chilling impact on the academy. While the Columbia School warned against a culture of "anti-intellectualism" that threatened higher learning, it was the academic gentry who produced a state-friendly consensus history, acquiesced to loyalty oaths on their campuses, and opened their universities to military recruiters and Department of Defense contractors. The fall of this liberal/intellectual leadership in the Vietnam tragedy—driven home by Nixon's "silent majority" rise to the presidency—powerfully questioned the aristocratic vision of "the best and the brightest."

The Columbia-Curti quarrel, emblematic of the wider ideological argument within reform politics, made a strong impression on interior professors and graduate students alike. William Hesseltine spoke for the old guard when he insisted that "the New Deal failed because it departed from the fundamental concepts of the American progressive tradition. Its liberal supporters were led, first gradually and then precipitately, down a path which went diametrically opposite from the direction in which Jefferson, Bryan, La Follette, and a host of other progressives had pointed. For long decades before the New Deal, the progressive forces of America had been waging a ceaseless struggle against big-business monopoly and the aggressions of government." Unreconciled to the *über*-centralized state hammered in place by the Roosevelt administration, Hesseltine warned that swollen government bureaucracies, a burgeoning military establishment, and the ominous growth of presidential power grievously endangered the republic. In comparison to a liberal meritocracy that embraced Keynesian capitalism, technology, and the rule of experts, "American progressives preferred the slower but more productive process of democracy and freedom."[15]

It may be tempting to dismiss Hesseltine's remarks as the lamentations of a passing political generation. Yet many of the interior's brightest graduate students were then adopting progressive points of view. The radical historian Herbert Gutman is a case in point. He began studying the American working class at Columbia under Hofstadter and Richard Morris, but nothing really clicked until he arrived in the Midwest for his PhD. "The Madison years made me understand that all my left politics had not prepared me to understand America west (or even east) of the Hudson River. Not in the slightest. None of my preconceptions held up. The Progressive historians, my fellow graduate students, and the undergraduates helped me unload my dogmatic blinders." Gutman discovered in Wisconsin's commitment to civil liberties, receptivity to questioning the status quo, and democratic sensibilities "in a time of liberal surrender and communist duplicity" a wonderfully instructive and vital model for students.[16]

But Madison proved to be an aberration. In the emerging postwar political realignment, much of the Old Left had made its peace with cold war liberalism. In the process of surrendering certain "dogmatic blinders," some of the more radical among Gutman's academic generation abandoned the metropolis in search of an interior oasis that might provide intellectual and ideological space to create a new leftist tradition.

What they were leaving behind might be glimpsed in Hofstadter's provocative 1953 essay "Democracy and Anti-intellectualism in America." In this indictment of egalitarianism, Hofstadter warned of a "great crisis" imperiling American universities. McCarthyism no doubt informed the diagnosis, as did its author's involvement in the first Adlai Stevenson presidential campaign. In a political struggle between the slow and the smart, the former, Hofstadter believed, had exercised a smoldering contempt for intellect by making the plain-minded Eisenhower president.[17]

The 1952 election convinced Hofstadter that popular power threatened the American mind. Democracies, his essay observed, typically failed to cultivate, respect, or reward gifted thinkers; they tended, rather, to resent their presence and prerogatives. In the United States, he continued, evangelical Protestants, Jacksonian Democrats, and Bryan antimodernists formed a solid phalanx historically hostile to intellect. By comparison, the Gilded Age industrialists (the bane of the reformers) showed a striking sympathy for mental talent. The old money barons may have abused their workers, bribed congressmen, and made a mockery of social mobility, but they were damned respectful of professional learning, creating some of the nation's best temples of instruction. As a stark statement of academic protocol, "Democracy and Anti-intellectualism in America" put forth what its author considered an unpopular if inescapable truth—high minds and classes went hand in hand.

One might fairly accuse Hofstadter of scholarly snobbery, and many did. His casual dismissal of a democratic university system compromised by open enrollments, the cult of varsity sports, and preprofessional curriculums both undercut and underestimated the missions of these institutions. Stereotyped as football and dairy colleges, the state schools represented outposts of intellect in secondary cities like Bloomington, Indiana; Ames, Iowa; and East Lansing, Michigan. Middle-class Americans were proud of their local campuses, worked hard to send their children to them, and believed they connected their communities to a broader world of ideas. Hofstadter—despite having taken his own undergraduate degree at the University of Buffalo—seemed unimpressed. His allegiance had now shifted to the urban style of intellectual activity familiar to him at Columbia. And he sought during this period to separate gifted minds from the pressures of mass culture—"the primary fact is that this elite must maintain a certain spiritual autonomy in defining its own standards."[18]

Three months after his essay appeared, Hofstadter received a cold letter from Curti suggesting that in the future he try to "point up a bit more the positive accomplishments of . . . academic freedom." To another correspondent Curti flatly rejected the "essentially anti-democratic and elitish tone of the analysis" advanced by Hofstadter. These communications brought him no joy. Before coming to Wisconsin in 1942, Curti had taught for a number of years at Columbia's Teachers College. There, he had mentored Hofstadter and served as the major adviser on his dissertation—an attack on social Darwinism written within the progressive tradition. The two men now found themselves uncomfortably divided on the crucial issues of postwar politics and culture.[19]

Curti's opportunity for a public response to Hofstadter soon arrived. In his combative 1954 American Historical Association presidential address, "Intellectuals and Other People," Curti argued that the position staked out by his former student badly misrepresented the public's relationship to talented minds. Intellectuals under duress? They enjoyed incomes and social prestige far beyond what most Americans could ever hope to attain. And rather than serving as useful social critics, the thinking class too often reinforced a host of intellectually bankrupt stereotypes and superstitions. The Ivy-trained triumvirate of Madison Grant (*The Passing of the Great Race*, Yale '87), Lothrop Stoddard (*The Rising Tide of Color against White World Supremacy*, Harvard '05), and Fairfield Osborn (an influential promoter of eugenics, Princeton '77) had pioneered the field of scientific racism in America. What did these brilliant men discover? Curti slyly queried. "That colored people were hopelessly inferior in native ability to think—though they were fine at singing!"[20]

Curti had no doubt that the intellectual's fever for reason blunted his sensitivity to productive "nonrational" factors in social life including instinct, faith, and intuition. He persuasively noted that such wise and original thinkers as William James, Reinhold Niebuhr, and Thomas Merton were profoundly guided by their spiritual convictions, while D. H. Lawrence, Henry Miller, and Sigmund Freud enlarged the Western world's understanding of the inner life by emphasizing the often inexplicable and irrational side of humanity. To summarily dismiss these essential if less visited byways of intellectual life was, well, anti-intellectual.

As a disciple of Dewey, Curti was quick to contradict Hofstadter's dim assessment of progressive education. While some cold war liberals emphasized a great divide between intellect and activity, Dewey, Curti reminded his colleagues, had long ago shattered this sham dualism by demonstrating that thinking *is* activity, and more, that thinking is most noble, generous, and useful when it enriches the nation as a whole rather than a few universities, literary magazines, and professional organizations. In postwar America, he tersely noted, "the ivory tower can become a pretty dull place, and rather unproductive, too."[21]

While intellectuals resented the public's suspicion of their work, Curti believed that such honest doubts were entirely justified. Americans were expected to support the country's universities through tuition, state revenues, and gifts but not inquire about the kind or caliber of their work. In a decade of big science, impenetrable specialization, and the rise of multiversity campuses, such oversight might have been healthy on a number of levels, including building a bridge between the thinking class and the middle class. As things currently stood, Curti complained, academic snobbery cut against the nation's democratic traditions and justifiably put the public on edge. "Some intellectuals . . . have continued to invite resentment by the way in which they hold their learning. Somehow the impression is conveyed that they feel a moral superiority to the hillbillies, the masses of common people, because they know that El Greco is better than Gains-borough, Emily Dickinson than James Whitcomb Riley." Drawing his audience back to the democratic theme, Curti observed that intellect had long flourished outside the academy. "Sometimes we forget that it was a boy born in a crude log cabin who grew up to write the Gettysburg address, that a humble Massachusetts fish peddler wrote letters that will be long remembered, that the great religious leader of the Western world was a carpenter."[22]

Coming to the crux of his argument, Curti pointed out that Hofstadter's hope for a kind of intellectual segregation cut against the country's deeply entrenched ideological principles. Aside from the peculiar examples of the Puritan clergy and southern planter gentry, American history provided little evidence of elite rule. There simply were no philosopher-kings. "For any group consciously to set itself up, because of its abilities and training, as superior to other groups in society," Curti protested, "is inconsistent with democracy." Rather, the nation's past revealed a prolific melding of the mental and the active. Benjamin Franklin united theory and practice in his useful inventions, while the founding fathers popularized political philosophy in the name of a people's revolution. In more recent times, Curti continued on a personal note, "one might also consider the successful experiences of experts in economics, political science, and law at the University of Wisconsin in serving the progressive movement by blueprinting social legislation and by staffing the state commissions." Turning Hofstadter's argument on its head, he maintained that intellectual freedom in America enjoyed its greatest periods of security and public esteem when sustaining the nation's democratic mission (the 1930s and 1940s, for example, when FDR's "Brain Trust" combated the Depression and Manhattan Project scientists gave their country a brief nuclear monopoly). Pleas for intellectual autonomy sounded to his ear like a dangerous call for intellectual secession. Such a perilous choice, he concluded, would place his colleagues on the sure path to oblivion. "March without the people," he quoted Emerson, "and you march into the night."[23]

The ideological tensions that set apart interior progressives and eastern liberals constituted but one sectional skirmish in the postwar historical profession. A second involved a fight for civil rights. For years, tensions had been building between reform-minded midwesterners and southern traditionalists over control of the Mississippi Valley Historical Association. In the early 1950s a small clique led by Curti and Cornell historian Paul Gates

Figure 4. Postwar Progressive: Merle Curti.
Courtesy University of Wisconsin–Madison Archives.

brought the battle into the open. Their goal was simple: modernize the MVHA by redirecting its culture from a parochial, racially segregated body toward one in tune with shifting demographic, educational, and racial realities. They faced a deeply entrenched opposition, the nature of which might be best explored in a brief overview of the association.[24]

In 1907 Clarence Summer Paine, secretary of the Nebraska Historical Society, summoned his Ohio and Mississippi Valley counterparts to Madison with the aim of creating an organization committed to providing greater treatment of the Middle West's history and archival treasures. His proposal caught fire. The following year historians representing eighteen states gathered in the Tonka Bay Hotel in Minnetonka, Minnesota, to participate in the inaugural meeting of the MVHA. There the association's first vice president, Clarence W. Alvord from the University of Illinois, called for a rewriting of American history to reflect parity among the sections. "The planting of Boonesboro in Kentucky or of Marietta in Ohio," he maintained (perhaps reaching a bit), "is of equal importance to the landing of the Pilgrim fathers at Plymouth."[25]

In 1914, the MVHA expanded its reach by commencing publication of a quarterly journal. "The development of interest in American history has been very rapid during the last thirty years," the inaugural edition of the *Mississippi Valley Historical Review* declared, "and this is true in the West, where there has grown up a very active school whose members are reaching out into all fields of research offered in this part of the region." In particular, the new periodical requested of its readership original essays on Native Americans, the exploration and colonization of the West, and the "amalgamation of the various nationalities" mixing beyond the Appalachians.[26] Clarence Paine died in 1916, but the association and *Review* were by then on solid footing.

Paine's wife, Clara, served as the association's perennial secretary-treasurer from 1916 until her resignation in 1952. These were years of substantial growth for the MVHA; what began as a small, regional historical society quickly mushroomed into the nation's largest organization for American history. But expansion beyond the valley brought controversy. The incestuous, undemocratic appointments of Paine loyalists to leadership positions discouraged younger and more liberal members, as did the holding of MVHA conferences in segregated cities. Even the association's title came under attack—the appellation was symbolic, critics insisted, of a constricting regionalism that no longer reflected the organization's true character and composition. Something had to give. "Our geographical limitations gave us a sense of unity and excuse for organizing," one observer to this brewing family feud wrote in 1953, "but our programs and functions have fitted a whole nation's need, and our fellow historians outside the Valley have been understanding and ready to participate in an expanded cooperation without respect to geography."[27]

The great demographic changes in postwar higher education had a profound impact on the MVHA. Student enrollments increased dramatically, faculty slots trebled, and a building boom literally reshaped the old universities. These trends challenged the tight circle of Mississippi Valley scholars long attached to Clara Paine. Operating the MVHA from her home in Lincoln, Nebraska, Paine held no elective office within the organization but ruled rather by suggestion, persuasion, and the courtly deference of her male colleagues. No doubt she loved the "old" association, felt a proprietary claim on its offices, and worked diligently to maintain control of its agenda by limiting the eligibility of leadership positions to her supporters. In 1924 she informed the association's executive committee that in her opinion "officers and editors should not be elected who reside outside the confines of the Valley."[28] And for several years this "suggestion" carried the credibility of a papal bull. Not until 1931 did the first easterner—Arthur P. Whitaker of Cornell—win a seat on the executive committee; Harvard's first representative on the committee, Oscar Handlin, arrived in 1953. As the size of the MVHA grew, however—from eighty in 1907 to about fifteen hundred in 1950—the old guard's grip weakened.

Many among the new membership hoped to bar the MVHA from holding its annual meetings in segregated cities. Its elder sister organization, the American Historical Association, had once convened regularly in the South—to be precise, on seven occasions between 1903 and 1935. But from 1936 to 1972 it never met below the Mason-Dixon Line—except in desegregated Washington, DC. During this same period (1936–72), the MVHA and its successor, the Organization of American Historians, met twelve times in southern cities. Two observations are worth noting: the AHA, a larger and more eclectic body, liberalized between the world wars and consciously avoided holding its conferences in Jim Crow venues. Second, if one looks closely at where the MVHA met in the South before 1950 (including New Orleans, Columbia, and Austin) and after 1950 (including Lexington, Louisville, and St. Louis), it is obvious that the association abandoned the Deep South (one generation after the AHA) for those cities on the southern periphery that guaranteed equal rights to all of its members. How this happened is part of our story.

The struggle to desegregate the MVHA must be understood within the broader context of regional politics. Paine's midwestern loyalists may have cringed at the blunt racial practices of their Dixie colleagues, yet they found themselves allied with southern members who were equally disturbed by the growing power of easterners in their ranks. Not surprisingly, the pressure to reform the association came most aggressively from scholars at Wisconsin and Cornell. These men resided in areas—upstate New York, the upper Midwest—historically known for accommodating, even encouraging, a more liberal line on race than perhaps anywhere outside the old New England abolitionist stronghold. They would be successful only if they could convince enough of their colleagues to abandon politics as usual—and that, considering the conservative, deliberate leanings of the MVHA, would mean an ultimatum.

In 1946, Merle Curti began the revolution. "I am disgusted," he wrote Howard Beale shortly after that year's annual meeting, "at the absolutely undemocratic and drinking sort of politics that govern the Association." He pointed out that a three-member nominating committee selected the

MVHA president—who then circularly appointed future members to the nominating committee! "There are no elections at all," he complained, and he noted that the historians typically elevated to the presidency—Ralph Bieber, Herbert Kellar, William C. Binkley—were known less for their scholarship and leadership than for their devotion to Clara Paine. "I think," Curti advised Beale, "we had better make a concerted move to choose someone and get him elected and above all to use him as the focus of democratizing the machinery of the Association."[29]

Politicking or not, Curti became that "someone" in 1951, the year he ascended to the presidency of the association. MVHA executives served for a single year, and if the young Turks hoped to instill a new organizational culture, they would have to move quickly. Emboldened by Curti's success, Beale sent a brief, cryptic note to Paine that prefaced the reformers' clash with the Nebraska clique: "Could you send me, in time for me to study them before the Cincinnati meeting, a copy of the constitution and by-laws of the Mississippi Valley Historical Association?" With the opportunity to use the popular Curti to bring about open elections in the society's offices, momentum swung against Paine. The incoming president's independence made this change possible. "My own judgment," Gates wrote Curti,

> is that the Mississippi Valley Historical Association needs to get out from under the influence of Mrs. Paine, who has been a retarding factor in every substantial development over the course of years. Her dead hand and the respect that the older members have for her have made difficult numerous things which we have suggested in the past. I see no reason why we should continue to defer to her at this late time. You will be, I believe, the first president who has not come up through that western matriarchy, as you call it, and that should assure us independence if we do not achieve it before you assume office.

University of Chicago historian Bessie Louise Pierce shared Gates's view of the situation and counseled Curti to handle Paine less delicately than his predecessors had: "Unless some of you men lose your sense of so-called chivalry and treat her on the basis of merit as you would treat a man, you will continually be confronted with the situation you now have." As things turned out, Pierce had nothing to fear. With the foothold gained by Curti and his supporters, there would be no retreat. The wheels of change turned slowly, but turn they did, and in 1955, the MVHA adopted a resolution that created a nominating committee of five members elected by the total membership. It selected candidates for openings on the executive nominating committee—again, to be elected by the entire membership.[30]

Before that happened, the MVHA, again under Curti's prodding, began the process of cutting its once firm ties with southern cities that discriminated against its black members. In February 1951, two months before the annual meeting assembled in Cincinnati, the association's executive committee voted to hold the 1952 conference in New Orleans. Everyone knew what this meant. Black historians would be barred from staying in the same hotels, eating in the same restaurants, and perhaps even attending the same sessions as their white colleagues. As the incoming president, Curti strongly considered resigning in protest. Fred Shannon, a University of Illinois historian, counseled otherwise. "My advice is that you do not resign. Instead fight it out at the Cincinnati meeting. Make it clear that the choice of New Orleans for the 1952 meeting was made before a rump session of the executive committee; that so serious a matter as this should not have been settled until the facts had been taken; that the matter be reconsidered and that if the committee will not reconsider the matter, at least you will not attend any meeting and will not give your presidential address at any meeting that is held under Jim Crow auspices."[31]

Men like Shannon hoped to push the association into the future—yet it was by no means certain that the reformers constituted a majority. Gates reminded Curti that "the southern contingent in our membership is undoubtedly substantial and probably larger in numbers than the liberal element that would fight to keep away from segregated communities." And some of the "liberal element" mentioned by Gates may have opposed segregation in principle but felt a stronger impulse not to embarrass or "insult" their white southern colleagues. Curti nevertheless forced the issue by indicating his refusal (as Shannon had suggested) to read his presidential address in the Crescent City. When the executive committee agreed to revisit the question of where to hold the 1952 conference, association conservatives (certain of their numerical advantage) proposed in lieu of discussion a simple up-or-down vote on New Orleans or its alternative, Chicago—and this by mail ballot. Presumably such a glancing maneuver would save time and reputations and reduce the likelihood of a protracted and potentially divisive debate about the racial ethics of the MVHA. But a debate was precisely what Beale wanted. At the association's business meeting, he moved "that the referendum ballot on the choice of cities for the 1952 meeting of the Association be accompanied by a full statement of the issue involved in the choice in terms of the reception that would be accorded Negro members of the Association at a meeting in the two cities."[32] This led ultimately—without the showdown Beale anticipated—to New Orleans's being dropped. But the controversy did not end there. A battle over where to hold the 1953 meeting (liberal Lexington won out over segregated Memphis) ensued the following year, and Topeka was dropped in 1954 after its delegates could not guarantee hotel accommodations for black MVHA members. At that point, a reform-dominated executive committee quietly took care of future controversies by refusing invitations to hold conferences in segregated cities.

Curti's actions in 1951 put the Mississippi Valley Historical Association's race problem plainly in the open. His refusal to preside as president in New Orleans set in motion a series of actions and arguments that ultimately scuttled Jim Crowism within the association's offices. What he and other reformers hoped to accomplish that year—the desegregation of the association, the enlargement of its mission to encompass a national historical perspective, and the adoption of democratic measures to run its offices—made him the most important and constructive president in its history. The clubby and cordially racist culture of the MVHA broke before the combined weight of the civil rights movement, the rising power of postwar liberalism, and the growing influence of northern and West Coast historians. In 1952, the year Curti delivered the association's presidential address, an outmaneuvered Clara Paine retired as secretary-treasurer. One year later her son and successor, Clarence, completed the family's swift reversal of fortune—the association fired him for embezzling nearly three thousand dollars from its coffers. The days of the Nebraska matriarchy had come to an inglorious end.[33]

The progressive racial politics practiced by the MVHA's midwestern reform wing had clear limitations. If it championed the inclusion of black historians at its conferences, it almost never hired them as departmental colleagues. Its record in regards to Jewish scholars is also problematic. Unlike black scholars, who were segregated in black colleges and universities, Jewish scholars had the proper pigmentation (if not always the right names) to teach anywhere. But getting hired was another matter. Before the war, Jewish academics encountered severe obstacles to career advancement in the Midwest as well as in other regions. They had to contend with a horribly tight Depression-era job market and competed with European Jews escaping Hitler for the few positions actually awarded to non-Gentiles. Too, they were often stereotyped as ideologically radical. The following 1935 letter to Cornell's Carl Becker from C. H. Oldfather, dean of arts and sciences at the University of Nebraska, illustrates the uphill battle Jewish scholars faced at this time. "Thanks very much for your letter of the 26th regarding men for our position here. I may be quite frank and say that

[Leo] Gershoy and Rosenberg . . . are out of the picture for the very simple reason that they are Jews. It just so happens that over the past five years, during which I have been dean and for a couple of years acting chairman of the Classics Department, I have brought in three Jews and am now trying to get back a man who is probably at least half Jew if not one hundred per cent. It would be unwise for me to consider another one."[34]

Eight years later, Becker's young colleague, Paul Gates, requested from Curti a list of prospective candidates for a new post at Cornell. Curti's response reveals the distasteful business of assessing a Jewish candidate's "Jewishness," typically defined in terms of physical appearance and "temperament"—that is, intellectual aggressiveness:

[Bert] Lowenberg is a fine scholar, but as you say, is, alas, Jewish! Less obviously "Jewish" in the popularly accepted sense is Eric Goldman, who is very charming, and to whom Greenfield and others at the Hopkins are devoted, as I know full well. He had a very raw deal there, and has made a good place for himself at Princeton. . . . I think he will go further, in research and writing in social-intellectual history, than any of his age group I know anything at all about—much further than Lowenberg, for example. But he is Jewish; and maybe that excludes him. . . . I like [Oscar] Handlin's book very much, but have heard the same "reports" you got about his personality; I don't know him personally at all. Is he, too Jewish? How dreadful this question has to be raised at all.[35]

Curti's belief that his friend Goldman had made "a good place for himself at Princeton" may have been true at the time, yet within a few years Goldman himself contradicted this encouraging assessment. He informed Curti in a searching, self-pitying 1949 communication of the difficulties that he and all Jewish scholars faced in the American historical profession.

I had to smile ruefully when you brought up the question of whether Illinois or Texas would be congenial for me. I'm afraid I'm no longer in a position to be choosey about anything. . . . The academic profession does not readily make offers to men named Goldman. I have been teaching 11 years, and except for the instructorship at Princeton, I have received exactly two offers. One was an Assistant Professorship at Brooklyn, at a time when I was an Assistant Professor at Princeton and at less salary. The other was from Chicago, an Assistant Professorship at a time when I was already an Associate Professor at Princeton and at about the same salary. Both offers were during the war-created shortage of manpower, as, of course, so were my promotions at Princeton. The academic profession praises men named Goldman, it continually asks them to read papers at meetings and contribute to various books. It does not readily offer them jobs.... I write this way partly because I want to raise with you again the question I raised once before—whether it is wise to encourage in any way Jews to enter the academic profession.[36]

Considering the reluctance of interior schools to hire Jewish historians and Curti's studied understanding of how the game was played ("is he, too Jewish?"), Goldman's complaints to his patron are particularly poignant. Wisconsin may have been a politically progressive university and a leader in popularizing a critical style of historical thinking, but its relations with ethnic scholars and students were neither particularly welcoming nor enlightened. Hesseltine wrote in 1938 that "the administration is alarmed over the spread of communism, and the faculty sees a Red under every hooked nose and feels that Stalin is stalking behind every Yiddish accent." Within a few years, circumstances abroad made this attitude (at least in its most ugly, overt forms) untenable. Decolonization movements in Asia, Africa, and India anticipated a U.S.-Soviet struggle for the "third world" that brought into sharp relief the shortcomings of the old Euro- and America-centric history favored in Madison. In response, Wisconsin began offering coursework in fresh geographic areas—and it had to hire more historians to do so. In September 1945, enrollment stood at 7,779, but just one year later, with the GI Bill in full swing, that figure spiked to an astounding 18,598.[37] Adapting to both cold war and enrollment realities, sections in Russian, Latin American, and East Asian history began to appear in the curriculum catalogs. Robert Wolff, a Russian specialist hired in 1946, was Wisconsin's first Jewish historian.

In a department that harbored quiet forms of racial stereotyping, Howard Beale's anti-Semitism constituted yet another thick layer of the man's complex, idiosyncratic personality. An insufferable moralist given to bouts of erratic, even explosive behavior, Beale arrived in Madison in 1948 following several years at Chapel Hill, where he advised the dissertation of C. Vann Woodward. "He was a great fighter," Curti remembers, "really loved a good fight, and though he certainly was not liked in many circles—the administration and no doubt elsewhere—he contributed a great deal to the Department of History." Beale met Curti in the East while the two were graduate students at Harvard. They shared the same Norman Thomas politics, and both men read the past through the progressive prism of conflict and relativism rather than through the liberal lens of consensus and objectivity. Here the similarities ended. Curti's midwestern origins were modest, while Beale was to the manor born; his family speculated in farm-land and owned stock in several companies, including Borden Milk. "Beale was the only radical Beardian we knew who owned half of Iowa," Walter LaFeber wryly notes. "I think he admired Charles Beard almost as much for operating a successful dairy business in Connecticut as for being a great historian."[38]

Beale tended to "abuse" all graduate students, but his sense of Wasp decorum made him particularly sensitive to the differences—real and perceived—in Gentile and Jewish students. In 1956, George Rawick, a doctoral candidate descended, as he once put it, "of radical rabbis and failed businessmen," privately requested that Beale be barred from serving on his dissertation committee. "I can never forget," he wrote Curti, "his childish, and in my opinion idiotic, petulance at my master's exam—he almost drove me out of history altogether—or his comment to me 'out of the blue' two years later, 'Rawick, I must tell you that I will never sign any Ph.D. warrant for a neurotic student, no matter how brilliant.' In addition, his virulent anti-Semitism also it seems to me disqualifies him. I realize that you consider this last accusation irresponsible and paranoid—but I consider the kind of 'I am a liberal and love Jews' attitude of Beale coupled with his parroting of every vicious slander of the American Council of Judaism basically and essentially anti-Semitic."[39]

Curti shepherded Rawick's dissertation through the program—though at times tension overtook even their genial relations. Rawick's topic—the history of communist front organizations in the United States—caused his sponsor no little worry. Could a radical historian, Curti wondered, write an unbiased account of this topic, and could a radical historian writing on this topic get a job? Rawick hotly contested the assumption that a leftist scholar might exhibit less objectivity than a liberal scholar. "I fear," he wrote Curti, "that there is a problem in the fact that you and I have a different frame of reference in particular toward the nineteen-thirties and the New Deal. I am both a socialist and a Marxist and an anti-Communist. And this provides me with a frame of reference. And I can write as honest history as Republicans and Idealists and anti-Communists of the Right, or as Liberals, Instrumentalists, and non-Communists. I hope that you will judge my work on . . . whether within my frame of reference I do an honest and scholarly job."[40]

While Rawick's plea emphasized abstractions like "objectivity" and "frames of reference," Curti was probably more worried about the concrete—a New York Jewish Marxist writing a dissertation in the Mc-

Carthy 1950s on communism in America. He knew what kind of polished scholars the academy preferred ("is he, too Jewish?"), and he may have had differences with Rawick's dissertation out of a well-intended (if intellectually patronizing) paternalism. Perhaps he wanted to be able to write for Rawick the kind of innocuously positive letters he was then drafting for his student Herbert Margulies: "Personally, Margulies is an attractive man. He is neat in appearance, reliable, and mature. He gets along nicely with others and would in no sense create any problems for you or your colleagues. He is a rather quiet fellow, and in no sense aggressive." An oppositionist by nature, Rawick could not conform to this depressingly narrow conception of what a historian ought to be. Considering his struggles at Wisconsin, it comes as little surprise that he wrote of his time there, "I, for one, never found the Holy Land to be located in the Department of History of the University of Wisconsin-Madison. . . . The faculty was made up of a bunch of what appeared to me to be weird old men, at least in American history, mostly Beardians. Most of these folks with their small-town midwestern and southern roots and their Populism prepared me to believe that Populism in America was more reactionary than radical."[41]

The distinguished Madison economist Selig Perlman shared Rawick's concern about the "reactionary" side of the Wisconsin historians. In 1950, he informed the department that because of its reluctance to hire Jewish scholars, he would no longer serve on dissertation committees for PhD candidates in history. He blamed a recent illness on a psychosomatic reaction to years of tolerating low level anti-Semitism among his colleagues. "I have tried to analyze [what] . . . produced this change after a considerable stretch of well being," he wrote Curti.

> [I] am now convinced that it is the seething indignation at your department's behavior on this issue of appointing Jews to professional posts. For a quarter of a century, graduate students in your department have been "minoring" with me for the Ph.D., and have presumably benefited from the blending of my historical sense, with its awareness over three millennia, with what I got from the Anglo-American culture. . . . Your department has been willing to receive the fruits of the above development *without* contributing its share. For you can never convince me that a large department, covering the whole world and all times, has never been able to find one man stemming from a great historical people fit to be a professional colleague![42]

Curti responded to Perlman sympathetically ("your letter distressed me very much because it is plain you wrote with a deep sadness"), but he cannily defended his department's hiring decisions. "I have always opposed everywhere, any expressions of anti-Jewish feeling," he insisted,

and I have done a good many positive things to redress here and there in the few situations I could influence, what rankles in me as a great injustice. I cannot recall that in discussing new appointments in our department this question has arisen; if it had, I know I should have spoken in the same vigorous way I did on one occasion when I thought I detected a note of anti-Semitism in the remarks of one of my colleagues. Such feelings some of my colleagues may have, but in justice to them, they have never raised any such point in speaking of new appointments. Not long ago after we had made every effort to keep [Robert] Wolff someone asked if he were not Jewish, and the chairman said he had never thought of asking or even considering the question.

Curti closed by reminding Perlman that another personnel "issue" haunted the department—the lack of a woman historian. "I have regretted this," he wrote, "but when we have made new appointments in the American field I was unable to suggest any woman scholar that seemed as good as the men that were being considered. I hope we may yet have one." As things turned out, six years passed before the department replaced Wolff—departed to Harvard—with another Jewish scholar (George Mosse), and nearly two decades more before it hired a woman historian (Diane Lindstrom, in 1971). Apparently the idea of a black colleague was so far beyond Curti's (or Perlman's) comprehension in 1950 that he did not think of it in terms comparable to his department's failure to hire Jewish or female historians. [43]

As Perlman's letter indicates, the Wisconsin School's Wasp consensus led to certain cross-departmental tensions between colleagues. It also divided—if generally only in light and largely unspoken ways—the department's graduate students. After a string of one-year appointments, Warren Susman despaired of ever finding a permanent situation. Frustrated, he complained to Curti that the historical profession prized a certain type of candidate—a type he could never be. "Of course a person like Dave Cronon is easy to place. He has published and what is more is sufficient of a type which must have special appeal. I mean this without any bitterness or antagonism of Dave who is a friend of mine. But he remains a kind of perfect young Anglo-Saxon of a being—liberal without being in the slightest way unrespectable—religious and sincere." [44] Despite his youthful apprehensions and insecurities, Susman went on to teach for many years at Rutgers University. He also correctly predicted his classmate's professional success. After teaching at Yale and the University of Nebraska, Cronon returned to

Madison, where, over a long and fruitful career, he served as department chair, dean of the College of Letters and Science, and coauthored volumes three and four of *The University of Wisconsin: A History*.

In the early postwar decades, an era customarily recognized for its commitment to a consensual view of the American past, conflict absorbed the attention and energies of professional historians. Interior scholars were in the vanguard of resistance. The more radical among them dissented from the new politics in the East and the old politics in the South—the Columbia School's attack on popular democracy and the sharp racial practices of the Mississippi Valley Historical Association. These clashes emphasized the persistence of regionalism in an expanding university system and, more, the impact of ideology on a supposedly neutral and objective academy. In abeyance, the middle-western professoriate was forced to recognize that it no longer represented the dominant tone or trend of reform politics in America. That had been ceded to the New Dealers. In stark terms, the insiders had become outsiders—political and intellectual refugees in their own country.

Like any proud pack of contrarians, they wore their opposition to contemporary historiographical trends openly and honorably. To be sure, their incomplete vision of America suffered from the provincialism implicit in their native outlook. Yet the perspective they gained by circulating on the margins of postwar liberalism gave the Midwestern School room to challenge the new consensus on the cold war and the rapid growth of an antidemocratic technological and intellectual elite. As a consequence, its historical vision remained fresh, critical, and appealing to students.

Recently, Columbia historian Alan Brinkley reflected on the art of textbook writing for undergraduates, and more specifically his role in taking over the popular survey *American History* (first published in 1959) from its three original authors, Frank Freidel, T. Harry Williams, and Richard Current—all trained at the University of Wisconsin. "It may seem strange," Brinkley wrote,

> that a textbook that made its appearance in the late 1950s could survive through the extraordinary changes in scholarship we have seen since then. I think this book survived in part because it was written by people who were outside the northeastern, consensus school type of scholarship that dominated the 1950s. The three authors had all been graduate students together at the University of Wisconsin, and had, one way or another, all worked with William Best Hesseltine, to whom they dedicated the

book. They were part of the old Wisconsin school Progressive tradition. The book was built around conflict, around battles over power. It wasn't polemical—it wasn't like reading Charles Beard—but it was different from the other textbooks of its time. And this made the book more compatible with the world of the 1960s and 1970s.[45]

Brinkley's judicious observation illuminates the attractive interpretive approach that drew young minds back to Beard's generation. In eclipse, the old progressives were discovered by the New Left. Together, they anticipated the culture's coming break with consensus.

★ FIVE ★

Remaking American Radicalism

The Radical Tradition runs deep at the University of Wisconsin. . . .
Yet if a radical tradition still remains, the students are now its custodians.

ANDREW HACKER, 1960

In 1959, a small group of graduate students at the University of Wisconsin began publishing the radical journal *Studies on the Left* (*SOL*). Depending upon one's perspective, *Studies'* appearance signified either an act of supreme courage or supreme foolishness. In the days of the great postwar boom, after all, the American leftist tradition looked lost, anachronistic, and hopelessly irrelevant. The Depression had not returned, universities reported record enrollments, and the new Keynesian economics promised a cornucopia of full employment, home ownership, and as much Tupperware as one could negotiate into a Frigidaire. The older socialism, by comparison—a product of economic deprivation and indifferent distribution—limped gingerly into the 1950s. Cast in the midcentury imagination as a curious relic from the bygone days of the handlebar-mustachioed robber baron and the Lower East Side sweatshop girl, it preached a sad sermon of want before a swelling congregation of satisfied consumers. In the dawning days of the cold war, the anguish of American radicalism seemed complete.

Because of their marginal status as critics of a celebratory postwar consensus, *Studies'* founders (including David Eakins, Lloyd Gardner, Saul Landau, Martin Sklar, and James Weinstein) were ideologically free to explore and record liberalism's recent failures to break fresh ground in the areas of reform, intellect, and the arts. The new politics struck the *SOL*ers as a dismal departure from the earlier Populist/Progressive/socialist tradition made romantic in the Bryan and Debs crusades for social and economic justice. The academy too, they claimed, had shifted from a conflict-centered curriculum to an acquiescent and quiet conservatism. "A few of the many [topics] we feel need radical surveillance," insisted one *Studies* editor, his eye firmly fixed on the universities, include "current myths in American scholarship." Certainly the fat biographies of the old business tycoons produced by Columbia University's Allan Nevins fell into this category. The subtitle of his multivolume *John D. Rockefeller: The Heroic Age of American Enterprise* left little doubt regarding its author's sympathies. And Hofstadter's student Stanley Elkins published in 1959 the controversial *Slavery: A Problem in American Institutional and Cultural Life,* a work that compared southern plantations to Nazi concentration camps. The psychological burden of servitude, Elkins argued, produced a lazy, regressive "Sambo" personality type among slaves. The study trafficked, its critics claimed, in racial stereotypes, and they pointed to contemporary black agency in the emerging civil rights movement as proof of its inadequacy. Finally, the influential diplomatic historian Thomas Bailey had declared in his book *America Faces Russia* that U.S.-Soviet relations need not result in World War III—as long as the Soviets accepted American global hegemony. His assertion that "we can hardly hope to achieve an enduring peace unless the present techniques and ultimate aims of Russian communism are substantially modified" seemed more appropriate to a State Department policy paper than to a historical treatise.[1]

While the "myths" of American scholarship elicited a critical response from *Studies,* the journal strove to be much more than a political publication as politics is typically and narrowly defined. It appealed, rather, to the intellectual curiosity of left-leaning students in the social sciences and explored contemporary trends in literature, history, art, and public policy through the lens of politics. More akin to the communal coffee-shop culture of Europe than to the rigidly specialized structure of the modern American university, *Studies* proved to be an immensely valuable intellectual experience for its creators. Perhaps even more important, it nurtured a midwestern-centered dissent of the consensus fifties into the protest sixties.

A generation before *Studies* appeared in print, Philip Rahv and William Phillips had founded *Partisan Review,* the most important American radical journal of the twentieth century. Its eclectic mélange of political and intellectual topics captured the imagination of an emerging second-generation immigrant class newly educated in Manhattan's second-tier universities. Among the most gifted of these "New York Intellectuals" was Irving Howe. "The Stalinists," he once wrote of his *PR* education, "were middlebrow, the Trotskyists were highbrow, because they thought in the kind of terms that you had when *Partisan Review* started coming out, the union of two avant gardes, a political avant garde and a cultural avant garde. We prided ourselves on reading Joyce and Thomas Mann and Proust, maybe not completely, but at least dipping in, whereas they were reading palookas like Howard Fast." Diana Trilling, a *Partisan Review* contributor, remembered with obvious pleasure her relation to the *PR* milieu. "It was very extraordinary to find a magazine and a group of people who shared one's left-wing anti-Communism, one's, if I may put it that way, one's advanced notions about books and the arts and also one's anti-Communism. This was a very, very extraordinary thing."[2] Something like this sense of intellectual excitement accompanied the creation of *Studies*. If it lacked the polished sophistication of *PR* (and how, as a journal produced by graduate students, could it not?), *SOL* nevertheless reinvigorated leftist politics for a generation of young Americans who had moved beyond the older Marxism—which made so few concessions to the literary arts—and sought a relationship with a culturally respectable radicalism.

Partisan Review made its peace with liberalism in a 1952 symposium, "Our Country and Our Culture." Composed largely of prewar radicals, the *PR* circle had changed its mind about the postwar United States. "We have obviously come a long way from the earlier rejection of America as spiritually barren, from the attacks of Mencken on the 'booboisie' and the Marxist picture of America in the thirties as a land of capitalist reaction," read the symposium's editorial statement. The old *PR* protested American provincialism and resistance to European culture and politics; it looked to socialism and communism as viable alternatives to the progressive capitalism that collapsed in the Great Depression. The new *PR* praised the New Deal for providing government assistance to artists, poets, actors, and intellectuals; it acknowledged the American military's role in destroying fascism, critiqued European thinkers like Sartre for sidling up to Stalin (their own leftist leanings permanently leveled by the Moscow Trials and the Nazi-Soviet Pact), and saw the United States as the center of a revived Western civilization. To be sure, they acknowledged, America wrestled with the perils of a sprawling and often erratic culture, but to a remarkable degree, they believed, discerning minds were coming in from the cold—and on their own terms. "For the first time in the history of the modern American intellectual," symposium contributor Lionel Trilling winked, "America is not to be conceived of as *a priori* the vulgarest and stupidest nation of the world."[3]

The abrupt change in attitude (and politics) of the American thinking class discouraged a rising generation of radicals. The liberal position ap-

peared to posit a false choice: criticism of the Soviet system meant uncritically accommodating the American system. This either-or argument had a
resourceful champion in Arthur Schlesinger Jr., who wrote for the *PR* symposium that, yes, the 1920s may have represented in all its fundamentalist,
prohibitionist, Harding-Coolidge-Hoover splendor a depressing decade
for American thinkers, but "next to Himmler, even Babbitt began to look
good."[4] So naturally any non-Stalinist society required the patient understanding of social critics. But younger radicals—with no apologies to make
for joining Stalin's party in the 1930s—rejected this approach. They advanced a critical (and typically anti-Stalinist) politics that made few com-
promises with either communism or capitalism. Generational differences,
in other words, contextualized the ideological differences that separated
PR and *SOL*. The former experienced firsthand the great dictatorial horror
shows of the twentieth century—watched the rise and fall of Nazism and
observed with great hope and finally greater disappointment the devolution of the Soviet experiment into a gulag state. *Studies* came of age amidst
a different set of suppositions: American power did more than contain the
Russians, it actively served as an agent of empire, and further, it seemed
perfectly plausible to reject Stalinism without embracing liberalism.

Studies began as a response to the long cold-war fifties (1947–64), yet its
opposition to a ruling liberalism prefaced the protest sixties. At heart, it
rejected the cliquish Democratic-Republican arrangement that had rolled
back a once healthy and recent tradition of multiparty participation in
America. In the century's early decades, vigorous debate had informed
ideological discussions. Populists, Progressives, Bull Moosers, Socialists,
Single Taxers, and others won the attention of a wide spectrum of voters critical of the industrial process and disillusioned by the failure of the
major parties to do anything about it. This electoral openness narrowed
in postwar America, and we should note the irony of its demise. Repelled
by the single-party systems that distinguished fascism and Soviet communism, Americans touted their "plural" politics as a viable alternative to the
twin authoritarian regimes on the ultraright and Far Left. Yet following the
destruction of Nazism, political pluralism in America all but disappeared.
It was against the backdrop of this diminishing democracy that *Studies*
rebelled.

The ghost that haunted the radical mind answered to "consensus." More
than a tidy label to define the era's dominant historiographical direction,
the consensus idea reflected a broad range of ideological, economic, and
cultural concepts that shaped midcentury American thought. Synonymous with liberalism, the two-party system, and Keynesian capitalism,

consensus contained within its quest for uniformity certain psychological triggers that responded to clear political and spiritual needs. Commentators have often remarked on the quasi-Christian underpinnings of Soviet Marxism—faith in a holy trinity (Marx, Lenin, and Stalin) to bring about a heaven on earth (apotheosis of the working class). The American liberal consensus also discovered—in its dream of a free-enterprise techtopia— meaningful ways to redirect religious energies in a secular age. God, after all, had given to America big universities, big science, big weapons, and a big economy. These graced components pulled in divine harmony to contain its enemies while ending poverty, eliminating racism, and ratcheting ever upward the country's standard of living. The post-Depression worker had already experienced a political conversion to a risen Democratic Party; the pearly gates of a suburban paradise with a two-car garage and a nuclear deterrent beckoned.

As a symbol of the liberal consensus, the New Economy stood supreme. Philosophically, it promised an end to recessions, depressions, and the periodical troughs and hiccups fitfully endured by an earlier unregulated money supply. Through prudent management of the nation's finances, a chorus of economists claimed, government could circumvent the uncertainty of the nation's business cycle. John Maynard Keynes pioneered this argument in the Depression 1930s, explaining in a private meeting with President Franklin Roosevelt that the failure of individual savings to be used for investment typically exacerbated unemployment. His solution? What the individual failed to do, the government should do in his place. Through a judicious manipulation of the country's currency—"priming the pump"—the Federal Reserve might stimulate a sluggish economy by lowering interest rates and slow a speeding economy by raising them.

The Harvard economist John Kenneth Galbraith proved to be postwar America's most imaginative and articulate promoter of the New Economy. In his influential study, *The Affluent Society* (1958), Galbraith gazed with wonder (and not a little disgust) at the vast array of kitchen appliances, comic books, and mouthwash that flooded the consumer landscape and, raising his vision above the Appalachian and urban poor, declared in a moment of raw optimism that "Western man has escaped for the moment the poverty which was for so long his all-embracing fate."[5]

It should come as no surprise that *The Affluent Society* received a sour reception in Madison, Wisconsin. The historian William Appleman Williams, a mentor to several *Studies* editors and a *SOL* contributor, pulled no punches (and spared little sarcasm) in his claim that "Galbraith's imaginative report on his meanderings in a mythical land called *The Affluent Society*, is a complacent, inaccurate, misleading, and dangerously stultifying exercise in self-congratulation." In his own work *The Great Evasion* (1964), Williams insisted that severe poverty prevailed among tens of millions of cold war Americans, good jobs were in decline, and a competitive (rather than humane) use of technology promised the systematic replacement and thus penury of unskilled labor. "American capitalism," he lectured the Keynesian converts, "has never since 1861 functioned effectively enough to decrease economic misery over any significant period of time, save as it has been stimulated by war or cold war."[6] The great goods-and-services machine ran, he concluded, in fits and starts, and a welfare-warfare philosophy kept it knocking along at an unpredictable pace, producing an uneven bounty.

Interpretive differences aside, no one denied that the affluent society had introduced deep changes in American life. The New Economy advanced a popular culture of suburban sameness that anchored politics in the shallow stream of a conservative and monochromatic two-party system. This compressed ideological climate made it possible for Americans to believe that they had always enjoyed common political goals. Richard Hofstadter had argued as much in his classic statement of consensus historiography *The American Political Tradition* (1948), declaring that the nation lacked a radical past. In an influential chapter in that book, "Andrew Jackson and the Rise of Liberal Capitalism," Hofstadter criticized progressive studies that purported to find in Jacksonian Democracy vibrant artisan and trade movement associations that challenged factory owners for control of the nation's economy. Rather, he wrote, "the typical American was an expectant capitalist, a hardworking, ambitious person for whom enterprise was a kind of religion, and everywhere he found conditions that encouraged him to extend himself." The familiar ideological dichotomy "liberal versus conservative" had little meaning in Hofstadter's book, for in a nation dominated by entrepreneurs and small-scale capitalists, all politicians—Jacksonians or Whigs, Democrats or Republicans—responded alertly to their constituents' demands for widening economic opportunities. Hofstadter's narrative ended with the New Deal, but Galbraith extended its findings into the 1950s, writing in *The Affluent Society* that "on a great many modern social issues . . . the consensus is exceedingly broad. Nothing much divides those who are liberals by common political designation from those who are conservatives. The test of what is acceptable is much the same for both."[7]

Galbraith's musings on the consensus theme fit the mood of the times and harmonized nicely with the prevailing attitude of the postwar academy. Accustomed to fending off "anti-intellectual" critics who regarded higher education as a latent threat to the nation's egalitarian principles, the universities were delighted to be embraced by important segments of the culture. Far from residing in the ivory tower, they pointed proudly to their recent contributions advancing the New Deal (making vast public works programs run efficiently), World War II (atomic scientists), and civil rights reform (legal counsel). The future promised even greater glory. Both the social and the natural sciences benefited from the explosive growth of the 1950s economy, winning lucrative defense contracts for their laboratories, advising presidential administrations, and basking in their close relationships with key sources of political and corporate power. There was, of course, a price to pay. The postwar "multiversity," a system of research and instruction that educated millions of undergraduates on sprawling campuses across the nation, alienated its youthful clientele. Before the free-speech protests at Berkeley, before the unrest at Columbia, and before the killings at Kent State, *Studies on the Left* anticipated the coming day of the student movement. Its sensitive and searching commentary on domestic and international issues lent intellectual seriousness to the demonstrations that followed in its wake.

According to James Weinstein, a founding member of *Studies,* "the main purpose of the journal was to re-legitimize a left presence in academia that took the Marxian tradition seriously."[8] Rather than recite a thick catechism of economic theory or defend a dense dialectical materialism, *Studies* accentuated the humanistic side of Marxism—and this led it to more contemporary expressions of radicalism. Among young intellectuals interested in applying the existentialist philosophy of Sartre and particularly Camus to the American scene, the concept of alienation enjoyed a certain vogue. Kitsch culture, organization men, gray flannel suits, and the reflexive worship of technology imparted, its discontents insisted, a sterile vision of national life among the great American middle class.

Too, the booming postwar economy ensured that any serious discussion of Marxism or alienation would have to concentrate on the perils of prosperity rather than poverty. The existentialist response to the twentieth century—emphasizing the isolation of the individual in a world indifferent to human aspiration—appealed to critics of conformity, many of whom blamed the efficacy of the industrial system for creating a soulless state. And yet the *SOL* circle never came near nihilism. Unlike the drifting, confused characters in Jack Kerouac's Beat ode *On the Road* (1955), *Studies* seemed certain of its mission. As the basic patterns of America's industrial development, its mixed race record, and its aggressive cold war maneuvers were read through the eyes of alienation, a coherent picture began to emerge. Abundance not only failed to solve the country's most urgent problems but created a few of its own. While a small number of academics made this case—most notably the Wisconsin-trained sociologist C. Wright Mills—the historical profession remained largely wedded to an unapologetic vision of national cohesion.

Against this campus inertia, *Studies* hoped to revive American radicalism, not begin a fresh radical folklore. To understand the immensity of its task, we might remember that according to a number of notable midcentury thinkers there was no legacy on the Left to revive. In his influential book *The Liberal Tradition in America* (1955), the Harvard political scientist Louis Hartz had claimed that absent both a feudal past and a state church, Americans lacked a conservative, hierarchical heritage. Rather, as products of a civic culture that privileged individualism, the rights of property, and the rule of law, they proved themselves once, again, and always to be Lockean liberals. With a creed so common, they had seen no need to name it. "There has never been a 'liberal movement' or a real 'liberal party' in America," Hartz wrote; "we have only the American way of life, a nationalist articulation of Locke which usually does not know that Locke himself is involved."[9]

But in making liberalism the ideological alpha and omega of American political culture, Hartz had to deny not only a conservative heritage in the United States but a radical one as well (dismissed in a brief section, "The Failure of Marxism"). And here he took curiously little account of either "native" radical movements—the antimarket evangelicalism that swept through parts of Jacksonian America, the Farmers' Alliance, and the Industrial Workers of the World—or the great and historically recent migration of southern and eastern European Italians, Slavs, Russians, and Jews into the United States. Some among these peoples brought with them a patrimony of anarcho-syndicalist-Jacobin thought that merged with their minority status in a nation of Wasps to infuse American politics with an unusually strong passion for labor organization, civil rights, and municipal reform. *The Liberal Tradition in America* threatened to erase the nation's radical past from the textbooks, and thus it struck young scholars on the left as an example of the gaping intellectual limitations—and curiously ahistorical perspective—of the Consensus School.

The militant tradition celebrated by *Studies* had played an important role in the rise of modern America. The great capital-versus-labor feuds of the 1890s combined with the Populist revolt to underline unmistakable signs of discontent with the new industrial order. By 1912, the Socialist Party in the United States counted a membership of nearly 120,000, it published over three hundred newspapers with a circulation of two million, and its presidential candidate, Eugene Debs, won 6 percent of the popular vote in that year's election. The intense if fleeting prosperity of the 1920s weakened radicalism, but the Depression 1930s reinvigorated the Left. In 1932, a number of distinguished writers including Ernest Hemingway, John Dos Passos, Katherine Anne Porter, Langston Hughes, Richard Wright, and Edmund Wilson endorsed Communist Party presidential candidate William Zebulon Foster.[10] And then circumstances changed dramatically. The cold war, McCarthyism, and Truman's 1947 National Security Act promoted a climate of fear that checked ideological pluralism in the United States. Predictably, criticism of the American system declined sharply. Henry Wallace's Progressive Party defeat in 1948 concluded half a century of respectable left-wing political opposition at the national level. While presidential aspirants Debs, Thomas, Foster, and Wallace never came close to capturing the Oval Office, their ability to consistently draw respectable minority support—combined with the ebb and flow popularity of socialism in America—demonstrated undeniably that a native radical heritage did exist.

Studies tapped into this tradition and retooled it to meet contemporary needs. Consensus emphasized affluence—*Studies* noted the unequal distribution of income; consensus pointed to the amazing abundance of consumer items available to the working class—*Studies* drew attention to the sterility of suburban life; consensus praised the United States for exporting democracy abroad—*Studies* highlighted the problematic imperial structure that informed U.S. foreign policy. By questioning the shaky assumptions that underpinned the consensus artifice, *Studies* helped lay the intellectual foundations for the New Left. While much ink has justifiably been spilt on East and West coast contributions to the 1960s protest culture, it is interesting to note that the earliest expressions of student opposition came from Madison, Wisconsin (*Studies,* 1959) and Ann Arbor, Michigan (Students for a Democratic Society, 1962). Here, in the Midwest, converged two rich traditions of radicalism, the older Gentile Populism/ Progressivism and the more recent Red Diaper Babies—the children or grandchildren of New York Jewish communists.

The University of Wisconsin's reputation as America's premier progressive institution made it a magnet for left-leaning students dissatisfied with the "provincial" educations they received elsewhere. As Jeffery Kaplow, an undergraduate in the 1950s, remembers, "Given my origins . . . I was a New Yorker, Jewish (of the atheist, Yiddishist, and radical persuasion), a first- or second-generation immigrant . . . living in Madison was like discovering America." The relationship was far from one-sided. Recalling his Madison days, film critic Richard Schickel noted the steep learning curve encountered by all parties:

> About half of [Madison's] population was drawn from a Midwest previously unknown to me, the small-town Midwest, and they were thus truer products than I was of the now-dwindling Populist tradition of the region. . . . The midwestern WASPs had a certain phlegmatic quality about them, a sense that most crises were not terminal, that the seasons, the world, would roll on in their accustomed ways, McCarthyism or no, Cold War or no. The "New Yorker," on the other hand, bristled with the nervous energy that was the heritage of their city and, yes, their Jewish leftist backgrounds. What they had learned at their mothers' knees was that you really could not count on anything, that cataclysms—indeed holocausts—could and did happen. If the WASPs had a healthy sense of security about history's reliable course, the Jews had an equally healthy sense of its unreliability.[11]

More hopefully, Selig Perlman trusted that Wisconsin's rich reform tradition reflected a fruitful blending of American and European customs in a slowly emerging post Wasp community. "I don't believe," he observed of his first years in Madison,

> that you could find anything like it in America, perhaps anywhere in the world, because of the spirit of optimism the whole thing radiated. You felt that here was a people who had escaped—because the mark of Europe was still upon a good many of them—who had escaped the European social system, with its class consciousness, with the upper-classes looking down on the lower-classes. Well, they had escaped that and they showed in every one of their movements the feeling that this is a new land, this is a new deal, so to say, for them and that they were intent on making the best of it, for themselves and for their children and for anybody that wished to come in.

Ultimately, Perlman concluded, Madison rejected the harsher strains of American individualism and capitalism to embrace those parts of the European socialist tradition that spliced evenly into the region's peculiar political culture. At the University of Wisconsin, he remembered, "a good many people felt that here at last, you're getting something in America which will bring it closer to modern Europe."[12]

The proliferation of the postwar academy broke the tight grip that Ivy Coast universities customarily held on East Coast students. "New York's centrality as political, cultural, and publishing locus of the intelligentsia diminished considerably after the 1950s," writes historian Paul Buhle. "The geographic dispersion of intellectual energies during the expansion of vast college systems pretty well obliterated the possibility of one 'center' and posed the prospect of a multiple succession to intellectual leadership. Madison's burst of energy in the 1950s, like the very different one in San Francisco, arguably foreshadowed events." Among some talented young Jewish leftists, the University of Wisconsin stood poised to take "intellectual leadership" primarily because it offered what no other university could—an indigenous radical tradition. In the 1950s, Berkeley remained a historically conservative institution that bowed before McCarthyism by hastily imposing a loyalty oath on its faculty. The University of Michigan, the University of Chicago, and Stanford also lacked reformist campus cultures and consciously aspired to a more exclusive status. As *the* distinguished midwestern public university, Wisconsin legitimized dissent as a respectable, even obligatory exercise of intellectual activity. And those who sat at its seminar tables might expect to find a sanctuary of sorts. For that reason, Madison proved an inviting location for Jewish students eager to join in a kind of heartland radicalism. This intellectual conversion process proved terribly consequential on two accounts—it gave direction and legitimacy to the metropolitans while helping to break down the provincialism of the midwesterners. "This movement," *Studies* associate James Gilbert remembers of the dynamic ethnic mix that descended upon Madison, "created a hybrid, an enormously creative view of American politics, culture, and history."[13]

Without the cooperation of the Wisconsin historians these connections might never have bloomed. Curti, Beale, Hesseltine, and Merrill Jensen shared with their students an informed and selective disenchantment with contemporary American society, and their status as respected scholars raised a protective veil over those who studied under their wings. None of these men were connected to the founding of *Studies*—but their new colleague William Appleman Williams was. Hired in 1957, Williams quickly surfaced as the central figure in the history department, a radical pied piper and bona fide sixties academic superstar whose ability to meld American progressivism and European Marxism fascinated a broad constituency of graduate students. "Williams," *Studies* editor Saul Landau remembers, "was the great germinator. He put Beard and Marx together, and this attracted both radical Jewish students and uptight Midwest kids." Other hires complemented Williams's presence. George Mosse, a German Jewish refugee who became one of the nation's leading scholars of European nationalism, culture, and sexuality, joined the faculty in 1956; the historian of French radicalism Harvey Goldberg arrived in 1963. Gilbert emphasizes that "Mosse and Goldberg were as important as the Americanists in the department. The graduate students were very Marxist in their thinking and while the professors were not, they were tolerant of it."[14] As the campus radicalized in the 1960s, the department's old guard Americanists died off (Beale in 1959, Hesseltine in 1963), retired (Curti in 1968), or moved into administration (Williams's mentor Fred Harvey Harrington became president of the university in 1962). In their wake, the trio of Williams, Mosse, and Goldberg emerged as the Wisconsin School's new stratum of stars.

On the Americanist side, Williams proved to be the seminal figure. A complex and not altogether consistent thinker, he held social and cultural values of a latent conservatism that informed his writings and relations with colleagues and students alike. Mosse recorded in his perceptive memoir that

> Bill Williams stood apart from the student unrest at the time of the Vietnam War because of what he saw as the students' aggressiveness, which ran counter to his ideal of well-thought-out and intellectually prepared change. But the fact that he disliked the student leadership, which was largely eastern and Jewish, played its part. He was not an anti-Semite in the usual meaning of the term, and certainly his teachers would have denied such an imputation. But still, as I used to say, Bill Williams was always looking for the blond and blue-eyed Iowa Socialist, one who shared his own roots, which lay deep in the Iowa prairie.

Interestingly, the two major intellectual programs in 1960s Madison—*Studies on the Left* and the Wisconsin School of Diplomatic History (to be discussed in the following chapter)—revealed certain ethnic distinctions. "*Studies* was pretty much Jewish," recalls Gilbert; "in fact people used to tease me about being the only person on it who wasn't Jewish. During the period of my involvement I was perhaps the only Gentile editor." By contrast, the foreign policy school led by Harrington and Williams attracted both Jewish and non-Jewish students, yet its most notable graduates were the midwesterners Walter LaFeber (Walkerton, Indiana), Lloyd Gardner (Delaware, Ohio), and Thomas McCormick (Cincinnati, Ohio). Their Christian roots and interest in a Beardian historical framework helped to illuminate their paths to the past.[15]

LaFeber recalls that a shared opposition to liberalism brought the two groups together. "The thing that united us with the people involved with *Studies* was a mutual questioning of the New Deal. People like Marty Sklar and Saul Landau grew up looking at the New Deal from the Left. A lot of us grew up in the Midwest criticizing the New Deal from the Right. My father was a small grocery store owner in Indiana, and he hated the New Deal because of all the bureaucratic requirements they imposed and the taxes and his belief—much like Beard's—that Roosevelt lied us into the war."[16]

If a common antiliberalism distinguished the Wisconsin historians and the *Studies* set, certain ethnic and regional distinctions stood out. Gilbert, a Chicago native, remembers that "some of my fellow students from New York used to call the people in Madison 'Americans.' It was a joke, but not entirely a joke. Someone once said to me, 'You know, Jim, for a long time no one trusted you because of where you came from.' It was a joke, they were laughing at themselves, really, because they were thinking they were so foreign, and felt it, and celebrated it, and at the same time felt guilty about it." Further, this dual identity meant "that the East Coast students could find a community in Madison. Here were all these New Yorkers in the Middle West; if they had been on their own they would have been miserable. These were basically children of the Communist Party, children of the Socialist Party. They were kids who grew up comfortable with a radical tradition particular to their ethnic group. Then they arrived in Madison and saw in someone like Williams an American style of radicalism."[17]

This cultural exchange flowed both ways. The political attitudes and modes of expression favored by the easterners suggested new avenues of intellectual activity to the midwestern Gilbert, a graduate of Carleton College in suburban Northfield, Minnesota. "The New York tradition is the coffee house tradition—a lot of open debate and arguing—and this just stunned me when I arrived at Wisconsin. At Carleton, no one ever objected to anything; we were all good little Protestants. Madison was wild. Students really engaged their professors, and I think professors really liked it. It was such a vibrant life, and I've never seen anything like it since. I don't think anyone in my generation thought about getting a job in academia—and that's the way the New York world worked. Public intellectuals were writers, they were editors, they were a variety of things. The problem with history today is that it is peopled exclusively by historians."[18]

Studies was published in Madison from 1959 to 1963, when the departure of several editors resulted in its removal to New York. It was conceived as a quarterly, but early issues of *SOL* appeared irregularly and usually later than scheduled—hardly a surprise considering that the editorial staff consisted of fewer than a dozen harried graduate students. During its Madison years, revenue from over-the-counter sales and subscriptions were insufficient to cover costs, and readers' contributions, small grants, and most importantly the considerable assistance of Weinstein—scion to a Manhattan real-estate fortune—kept the magazine afloat. By 1962, *SOL* had discovered a slight if steady source of income in New York, where nearly 450 copies were regularly distributed to twenty-nine bookstores and newsstands. A much smaller number was shipped to San Francisco, Berkeley, and Palo Alto. Operations were necessarily informal—bank records were kept in longhand, with the vast majority of entries showing at "$2.50," the price of a year's subscription. The New York outlets earned informal imbursement codes that ranged from the easy ("pay well") to the near easy ("give a nudge, he will pay") to the downright difficult ("we had to threaten to sue to collect").[19]

Of course the success of a venture like *Studies* is typically measured in variables other than circulation (which peaked at ten thousand in 1966). Influence is the ultimate end, and here the record is interesting. In an age of ideological conformity, *Studies* initiated a fresh challenge to cold war liberalism, one that was distinctly centered on higher education. Combined with the civil rights and antiwar movements, *SOL* modeled a spirit of campus activism that helped transform the postwar universities from passive bodies into critical institutions. The establishment soon took notice. In his 1960 *Commentary* essay "The Rebelling Young Scholars," the conservative Cornell political scientist Andrew Hacker prophetically argued that the academy stood on the cusp of an uncertain new era. "The intellectual awakening symbolized by *Studies on the Left* at Wisconsin," he wrote, led the way. "These young men and women will be the college and university professors of the next generation. Their revolt against the professors has only just begun: what they do when they come to power in our universities—and their coming to power is only a matter of time—will have an important bearing on the intellectual life of our country."[20]

Hacker's observation offers valuable insight into the fragmentation of the post-1960s academy. In our quarrelsome age of "identity politics" and "culture wars," synthesis has proven elusive. And in recent years a new genus of criticism—backlash books—has made good coin for some conservative commentators who long for a return to the imaginary days of a depoliticized academy. Among the most popular include Hoover Institute Fellow Dinesh D'Souza's *Illiberal Education: The Politics of Race and Sex on Campus* (1991), University of Pennsylvania historian Alan Charles Kors's *The Shadow University: The Betrayal of American Campuses* (1998), and any number of studies by social activist and occasional Fox News analyst David Horowitz (see particularly *The Professors: The 101 Most Dangerous Academics in America,* a sort of twenty-first-century blacklist of the liberal university intelligentsia).

Studies had hoped to avoid the kind of fragmentation that now divides the academy. Sensitive to the possibilities of an alliance between minorities and radical whites, *SOL* aimed to unite its readership behind a call for racial and ideological inclusiveness. In a 1960 letter to *Studies'* other editors, Martin Sklar laid out his vision for how the new journal might promote bona fide change within American communities. He adamantly rejected politics as usual: "Student and negro radicalism disregards and bursts through the bonds and standards that define political programs in terms of: a) the two party system, b) the corporate economy, c) the trade union movement, d) congressional maneuvering for bit-by-bit legislation, e) court litigation, f) American 'world leadership' in the fight against communism." He argued instead for a hard realism among the Left that would replace "the 'universal' or 'utopian'" aspects of liberalism (that is, vacuous calls for "democracy" and "freedom") with "practical and audacious forms of struggle [including] simple issues like the right to sit and eat or ride the bus in dignity." *Studies'* commitment to the "practical radicalism" of a reinvigorated left, he insisted, represented the future of antiliberal thought and action in America. "What we are witnessing in the student and Negro movements, then, is a process that contains the seeds of a new American left capable of becoming a politically viable movement nationally, a process in which the new left is learning those forms of struggle that will make a radical movement relevant to the American body politic."[21]

In essence, Sklar called for a new "consensus"—the unification of a badly balkanized left. To be sure, radical politics in America had taken a beating in the 1950s. McCarthyism, the Soviet invasion of Hungary, Khrushchev's de-Stalinization speech, and the bourgeoning New Economy forced political dissidents to question their ideological commitments. Before the first issue of *Studies* appeared, Weinstein, smartly recognizing the impossibility of uniting every stripe of Stalinism, anti-Stalinism, Marxism, neo-Marxism, etc., offered the following advice to his fellow editors: "We must be much broader than the total of the organized left, and, in any case, we will not get favorable responses from all segments of it, and run the danger of becoming identified with one part before we get off the ground. That would be fatal. We must be able to present *all* points of view in our magazine, but we will only be able to get away with it if we are identified with none, and if as broad a group as possible are in on the founding of the magazine and on the adoption of this principle." Put another way, as Eleanor Hakim did to one *Studies* critic: "God-damn it, we're American left-wingers and don't have to justify ourselves either one way or another in terms of the Soviet Union."[22]

In the interest of maintaining a kind of left "neutrality," a proposal by *Science and Society* editor Eugene Genovese to share subscription lists with *Studies* was gently rebuffed. "Our reason for this decision at this time is politic rather than political," Madison responded. "We are still trying to extend our readership base among the various groupings on the left. Although we seem to be appealing to the 'new left,' we are still held in suspicion by certain factions of the left who tend to read a 'Stalinist line' into every comma and hyphen no matter how much we affirm and assert our policy of publishing material of all shades."[23]

These "factions of the left" included their own. Curti's student George Rawick accused *SOL*'s editorial board of Stalinist sympathies and declined several invitations to write for the journal. "If you all are so clean, then tell me why no clear statement on the Soviet Union? As I consider the Soviet Union to be a more reactionary social phenomenon than Nazism I find it difficult to write for a publication whose editors are friendly to the Soviet Union." Responding on behalf of the editors, Hakim informed Rawick that *Studies* was an inclusive radical publication and had to be in order to survive. "For, political bickering would split the journal and ruin something that is bigger than any of our individual outlooks. We all realize this and are quite scrupulous about it." She then concluded by giving Rawick a quick tutorial on the nuts and bolts of making *Studies,* a thoroughly apolitical process, she assured him: "You'd be amazed were you to sit in on a Board meeting. Do we discuss Marxist theory? No. De we rehash the latest viewpoint of what *really* happened in Hungary? No. Do we even plan for the new left movement? No. What we do is haggle over whether we should get a ½ or a ¼ page ad in *Commentary.*"[24]

The first edition of *Studies* appeared in the autumn of 1959. In what amounted to a declaration of intellectual independence, it flatly rejected (à la Beard and Curti) the traditional "objective" commitment to scholarship demanded by the academy. This "noble dream" blood oath, the *SOL* editorial board argued, favored consensus while giving the illusion of fairness through an open-minded search for truth. It noted that in the American university system, book contracts at prestigious publishing houses and coveted jobs at distinguished institutions were typically awarded to professors who wrote within the main currents of the liberal establishment. Were there any tenured communists in the Ivy Leagues? Did the Big Ten schools hire scholars holding far right positions? Historians, *Studies* argued, went to the archives under the pretense of objectivity, but the questions

they asked and the way they consciously or unconsciously chose to interpret evidence often demonstrated an unmistakable personal interest in the
outcome of their work. Far from holding objectivity as the grand ideal to
which every academician should aspire, *Studies* proposed a fruitful blending of archival research and social commitment. The notion of frankly disinterested recoveries of the past mortified the editors, for this struck them
as a fast track to intellectual inertia. "Scholarly dispassion," they warned,
"is the true medium of the scholar satisfied with (or browbeaten by) things
as they are."[25] A stale academy, they continued, cut off promising areas of
historical exploration by defining "appropriate" topics as those which supposedly had no distinct connection to the author's personal interests, politics, or values. In this way, radical critics of American liberalism writing on
American liberalism could be summarily dismissed without their work's
needing to be taken seriously.

Of course, every historian should scrupulously utilize source materials
and, more, change his or her mind if the evidence dictates. Yet the subjective struggle for historical truth emphasized in *Studies* may prove as compelling in the search for answers as the objective struggle for historical
truth. As in our legal system's adversarial philosophy, scholars should enjoy
the conversational space to argue their cases with vigor. In the Darwinian
marketplace of ideas, the bad history should (one hopes) fall before the
good.

As matters stood in 1959, however, a very limited marketplace of historical ideas existed. Neither the Old Left nor the new conservatism (soon
to jell in the Sunbelt's support for Barry Goldwater) had yet to present a
cogent challenge to liberalism. Worse, liberals solidified their base in the
academy by declaring that with "the end of ideology"—a phrase coined by
Daniel Bell to explain a post-Hitler/Stalinist world—neither the Far Right
nor the Far Left had legitimate complaints against the current politics. This
defensive and self-serving attitude damaged the nation's prospects, *Studies*
argued, for it justified the expansion of presidential powers, soft-pedaled
racial segregation, and turned a blind eye to the disturbing growth of American militarism. Its editors knew that a liberal academy struck neither an
"objective" nor a "dispassionate" posture; rather, it contributed its libraries,
its laboratories, and its intellectual capital to advancing the status quo.

In the case of historians, a number of the profession's finest wore their
politics quite openly. Daniel Boorstin testified before the House Committee on Un-American Activities in 1953 that his books *The Lost World of
Thomas Jefferson* and *The Genius of American Politics* highlighted certain values in the nation's past that students might productively use to reject com-

munism. Arthur Schlesinger Jr. took part in the Congress for Cultural Freedom, a liberal front organization whose bills were paid by the CIA; years later, his services to the Kennedy Administration included a less visible contribution—participating in the lead-up to the Bay of Pigs. Days before the invasion, Special Assistant to the President Schlesinger drafted an anti-Castro address that was then delivered by the president before the Organization of American States. Schlesinger's years of researching and writing the definitive account of the New Deal (the three-volume *Age of Roosevelt*) were put to good use: in the midst of revising the speech Kennedy asked the Harvard historian "whether I could not find an appropriate quotation from Franklin Roosevelt. I dug one up in the next few minutes."[26]

To adulate objectivity imperiled historical scholarship on two fronts, *Studies'* editors protested. First, it weakened the academy by committing its energies to the maintenance of a mythical grand narrative. Second, it compromised the historian's ability to conduct research of a controversial nature. To merely imitate a style or a school proved depressingly contrary to the pursuit of knowledge—it was anti-intellectual. Better to explore fresh terrain by asking new questions than to write harmless books based on perceived wisdom. But how were new voices to be heard in liberal America? in a liberal academy? "It was largely in response to a growing feeling of frustration, to a feeling of irrelevance as intellectuals who desired to help change society," the editors explained, "that we conceived and organized *Studies on the Left*."[27]

Sklar no doubt experienced such "frustration" when he received a letter from an old friend, Duke sociologist James Vander Zanden, detailing why he would not—*could* not—subscribe to *Studies*. "As time has passed," Vander Zanden wrote, "I've lost my interest in politics, *per se*. I perceive myself as a sociologist—this is my profession—and as such you probably consider me an ideologist—an ideologist who for the most part produces in the spirit of contemporary American sociology—i.e., its mainstream—I have no interest in reform—again perhaps you consider this bankrupt—the world is the world as it is, and if I'm going to find personal happiness, I'll make my peace with it." Vander Zanden touted his survival of the publish-or-perish whip that commodified scholarly output—"I have now had some nine articles either published or accepted for publication, so in this regard the pressure is considerably relaxed"—and questioned whether radicals sought to create "alternative" journals because their own research rested "on poor scholarship . . . [that] just wouldn't make it regardless of the ideological content." With a good job ("I love teaching and my students are very responsive to my materials"), a good personal situation ("I've developed a love life—a very sweet splendid gal—a nurse here at Duke Hospital"), and a wary, knowing eye on his surroundings ("I feel [*Studies*] is a little 'hot' to touch when residing in the South"), there really was only one possible reply for a careful young academic to make to Sklar's entreaty—"I'm going to pass up on your suggestion that I subscribe."[28]

Rejections aside, *Studies* moved forward with early editions assessing the progress of the civil rights movement, the Cuban Revolution, and President Kennedy's "New Frontier" at home and abroad. The editors condemned JFK's "dirty war" against Castro and cheered on the possibilities of socialism in South America. Ernesto "Che" Guevara and C. Wright Mills (both international symbols of radicalism destined to die young) received space in *Studies*—their essays brought a star rebel cachet to the publication (as did Jean-Paul Sartre's "Ideology and Revolution"). In 1963, Sklar and Weinstein returned to New York and took the journal with them, maintaining a small number of editors and associates in Madison. In Manhattan, *Studies* moved in a different direction, one far more influenced by literary criticism, philosophy, and above all, community action. Too, it discovered "the sixties" and gave increasing attention to Vietnam, the peace movement, and the rise of student power.

The critical issue that preoccupied liberals at this time—ultraconservatism—held little interest for the journal's editors. They chafed under the liberal assertion that fear of the Left mobilized the Right; the "failed" policies of the New Deal order, they countered, empowered the Sunbelt "extremists." Goldwater and his followers, in other words, were not the problem, the consensus commitment to economic dominance through global conflict was. "For the left to view the irrational right as the major threat to freedom or progress and to look for the development of an opposition from some vague tradition of Jeffersonian liberalism," the editors insisted, "is to follow a comfortable but ultimately fated path."[29]

In its New York permutation, *Studies* became deeply committed to community coordination projects. While this form of "print" activism appealed to the movement politics of the day, some long-time readers were disappointed in the journal's evolution from an ideas-centered publication to one increasingly dedicated to grassroots organizing. The change in both zip code and philosophy prompted one *SOL* editor to raise the following concerns: "I don't know what the new *Studies* is going to look like but I have an idea it's going to look like all the other journals of the left, which is more than a damn shame. . . . There was more to moving from Madison than just losing our corn-fed cachet. . . . Radicalism sounds so much more encouraging when it comes from Madison rather than NY."[30]

As *Studies* moved further away from its middle-western roots, articles on history, sociology, and theory were replaced by items on "the SDS March on Washington . . . the Cleveland Conference of the Poor . . . [and the] New Brunswick Community Action Projects." Evan Stark, a Madison graduate student and fan of the old *Studies,* was deeply disturbed by what he considered the morally pretentious, intellectually soft, and ahistorical direction of *Studies* East. "There is nothing intrinsically wrong," he caustically wrote, "with pen-pushers playing as leaders of the proletariat. But when they continually renounce the ideas of the past and pretend to get notions about 'what is needed' from the 'people themselves,' they merely serve to legitimize the strangulation of historical sense and creative thought which the government, the media, and the professional journals have been engaged in for years."[31] Stark's comments underlined a growing tension within *Studies* between those who pressed for its return to its scholarly roots and others who wanted to see *SOL* "on the streets" and in the vanguard of radical action. By 1967 these ever-sharpening ideological differences among editorial factions—compounded by the kinds of personal grievances that invariably crop up among a group of young people conducting work in a critical environment—proved irreconcilable, and the journal ceased publication.

During its Madison years, the *Studies* circle advanced a new and controversial historical idea: corporate liberalism. A bold reassessment of the early twentieth-century reform movements, it rejected the consensus school's portrayal of this period as a golden age of government activism in which the states worked hand in hand with the first Roosevelt and Wilson administrations to check the power of the great industrialists. The older generation's peace with progressivism is easy enough to understand. Its formative political and intellectual experiences occurred in the 1930s as the New Deal expanded a regulatory state that traced its origins to TR's Square Deal. Their younger critics, by contrast, grew up in an era that celebrated big business and passively permitted a "military industrial complex" to marry the fortunes of the corporations and the cold war. Wisconsin students Sklar, Weinstein, and Gabriel Kolko argued in a number of books and essays that the great Progressive reforms—workers' compensation, railroad regulation, the Federal Reserve System—were initiated by a self-interested business class looking to manipulate markets, destroy competition, and undermine the labor movement. Fearing socialism, worker autonomy, and loss of economic control to the federal government or the states, industrialists squeezed out just enough concessions to stave off the kind of violent revolution that, in the eventful years 1911–17, destroyed the Porfiriato in Mexico, the Manchu Dynasty in China, and the Russian czarist aristocracy.

But as Madison's radical young scholars made clear, the forced, truncated, and conservative nature of the American reform movement prevented not merely "anarchy" but widespread democracy among laboring men and women as well. The European working class enjoyed more freedom than its counterpart in the United States because it played an important role in regulating factory conditions, bargaining over pensions, and negotiating state welfare programs. By contrast, American workers—once the most powerful and potentially revolutionary voting bloc in the nation ("the bone and sinew of the country," Andrew Jackson had vowed)—lost power over the liberal decades, and the twentieth century belonged to a modern corporate elite. Progressivism, in other words, did not constitute an age of reform; in Sklar's words, "corporate liberalism" ruled the day.

In its broadest meaning, the corporate liberal thesis argued that progressivism, the New Deal, and the Great Society were the handiwork of capitalist apparatchiks using the state as a cover to carry out programs beneficial to corporate power. The industrial titans preferred to rule by shrewd centralization of the economy rather than through fierce competition or naked force. Top-down control ensured efficient production, which led to an expanding array of affordable commodities and provided services— social security, federal deposit insurance, farmer subsidies—that an unregulated laissez-faire system might never get around to supplying. During the Great Depression, organized labor stood its best chance of gaining power and influence in the national government. Yet by offering (in the context of a national crisis) relatively mild reforms, corporations siphoned off dissent and solidified liberalism's hold.[32]

In important respects, the corporate liberalism thesis revived Charles Beard's penchant for portraying American history as a struggle between the haves and the have-nots. Propertied interests, he had argued, drafted a constitution sympathetic to property holders, later crushed the anticapitalist agrarian South, and still later pulled the United States into twentieth-century imperialist wars in Europe and Asia. Beard's Wisconsin descendants were less overtly conspiracy minded, arguing that the expansion of corporate hegemony in the United States was a mindset, a way of looking at the world shared by most Americans, rather than a wicked plot conceived by a small band of power brokers. The public, after all, had enthusiastically allied with the government and the progressive presidents to create a welfare state amidst a more powerful business state. The reformers had failed to realize that in the end they could not control industrial power—it would control them. As Weinstein put it in his 1968 book *The Corporate Idea in the Liberal State* (assuming a greater sophistication on the part of office-park policy makers than perhaps existed), "Businessmen were able to harness to their own ends the desire of intellectuals and middle-class reformers to bring together 'thoughtful men of all classes' in 'a vanguard for the building of the good community.'"[33]

In return for what amounted to near monopolistic economic powers, the great business barons promised abundance and expansion. Faced with a growing backlash to the bruising methods employed by the old Gilded Age titans, modern capitalists eagerly sought partnerships with municipal leaders that would produce (enough) reform to fend off the much-feared revolution. The demands of Populists, the Knights of Labor, socialists, and share-the-wealthers could not be summarily dismissed, and the new industrialists shrewdly positioned themselves in the vanguard of change. They eventually embraced the principles of collective bargaining, workers' compensation, and social security, realizing that these issues were not going away.

Attentive to historiographical trends, the Corporate Liberalism School accused consensus scholars of ignoring this antireform side of the reform impulse. Schlesinger had written in his popular *The Age of Jackson* (1945) that "liberalism in America has been ordinarily the movement on the part of the other sections of society to restrain the power of the business community."[34] In subsequent books, Schlesinger carried this argument through the New Deal (the aforementioned *Age of Roosevelt*) and into the 1960s (an insider history of the Kennedy presidency, *A Thousand Days*). The question, of course, begged to be asked: if liberalism was successful, why was it so easily—and repeatedly—overcome by "conservative" interests? If Jacksonian Democracy had triumphed, in other words, how do we explain the Gilded Age? If progressives had reformed the industrial state, why did the industrial state dominate the Babbitt 1920s? And if the New Deal reduced the power of corporate America, why did corporate America ("what's good for General Motors is good for America") hold so much power in the postwar decades? Schlesinger countered that "cycles" of reform and reaction dominated American history and that public interest characterized liberal eras while private interest distinguished conservative periods. But this dichotomy struck the corporate liberalism scholars as false, or rather as "false consciousness." Weinstein put his finger on the problem when he wrote that

the confusion over what liberalism means and who liberals are is deep-seated in American society. In large part this is because of the change in the nature of liberalism from the individualism of laissez faire in the nineteenth century to the social control of corporate liberalism in the twentieth. Because the new liberalism of the Progressive Era put its emphasis on cooperation and social responsibility, as opposed to unrestrained "ruthless" competition, so long associated with businessmen in the age of the Robber Baron, many believed, then, and more believe now, that liberalism was in its essence anti–big business. Corporation leaders have encouraged this belief. False consciousness of the nature of American liberalism has been one of the most powerful ideological weapons that American capitalism has had in maintaining its hegemony.[35]

An example of the confusion generated by the labels "liberal" and "conservative" is evident in the economic posturing of the two-party system. While Democrats and Republicans made much noise about their supposedly separate and distinct identities, the Corporate Liberalism scholars replied that their "differences" were superficial and unremarkable. One side championed a free market, the other a mildly regulated free market. From Milton Friedman to John Kenneth Galbraith, conservatives and liberals alike agreed that the American economy was the best game in town. This consensus naturally encouraged agreement in other areas of social policy including racial, labor, and military. The participants of the "one-party" arrangement may not have marched in perfect lockstep, but, according to *Studies'* editors, they found enough common ground to live with Jim Crow, Taft-Hartley, nation building, and nuclear brinksmanship. Under the rule of corporate liberalism, its Wisconsin critics concluded, the nation celebrated a legacy of progressive reform that in reality laid the foundation for undemocratic governance and destroyed the best hope for authentic popular change—socialism.

The students affiliated with both *Studies* and the Corporate Liberalism School were part of a broader generational rebellion against the cultural conformity that had swamped postwar America. The historian John Higham captured the uneasy mood in his recollection of a public lecture given by William Whyte at Rutgers University in the late 1950s. Whyte's *The Organization Man* (1956), a compilation of essays on corporate life and the suburban middle class, explored the alienation of white-collar workers as they ascended the company ladder. A slyly dystopian account, the book chucked conventional wisdom out the door. American mythology argued for a nation of go-getters advancing by dint of talent, intellect, and initiative; but in the business world, Whyte countered, conformism was key. The too productive or too smart antagonized their colleagues—better to get along and go along with the lions of mediocrity and groupthink than to blaze an independent path. The students listening to the lecture, wrote Higham, were "unsettled" by Whyte's pessimistic description of "how modern business was turning college graduates into 'organization men.' His hearers wanted some prospect of escaping that fate; he had little to offer. By the early 1960s, a hunger *for* deviance, for some posture of radical dissent that could create new identities, was tugging strongly at the kinds of people attracted to the study of history and society. The intense urge of a new generation of students to build oppositional subcultures supplied the manpower and womanpower essential to the development of schools of historical writing that would rally around their own sustaining orthodoxies."[36]

Among these schools, *Studies on the Left* took the lead in seeking new roads to a postliberal historiography. A quick glance at its roster of writers, associates, and affiliates, including Genovese, Gardner, Staughton Lynd, Tom Hayden, and Carl Weiner, reads like a who's who of early sixties student radicalism. They, and many others like them, discovered in *SOL* a response to the consensus state that spoke to their generational experiences and articulated their alienation. In its pages the intellectual wing of the New Left cut its teeth. Before the 1960s really hit, before Vietnam, political assassinations, black power, the women's movement, and the student revolt, *Studies* had already pushed American radicalism into a conservative age.

SIX

Liberal Nemesis
William Appleman Williams

I was born and reared in our American womb of empire, but my experience and my study of history have enabled me to understand that we must leave that imperial incubator if we are to become citizens of the real world. Our future is here and now, a community to be created among ourselves so that we can be citizens—not imperial overlords—of the world.

WILLIAM APPLEMAN WILLIAMS, 1980

Only in its infancy, with Turner's ascendant frontier thesis, had midwestern historiography launched an original idea that captured the intellectual high ground. The scholarship that came after struck a decidedly defensive pose. Beard, Curti, and their followers had written against the prevailing American Century principles that sustained their country's rise to global dominance. None among them managed to control the field quite as Turner had. His work suggested a crucial connection between expansion and democracy—and in a dawning age of empire this insight met the culture halfway. As long as public confidence in liberal internationalism held, nostalgia for the old progressive continentalism remained in check. And for a generation it did. But the problematic containment of Soviet power, accompanied by a host of interventions, invasions, and occupations, sapped the republic's vigor. The Vietnam War closed the era and took with it any lingering claims to innocence.

Beginning in the 1940s, a Wisconsin School of Diplomatic History challenged long-standing assumptions about America's relations with the world. In the seminars of Fred Harvey Harrington and the scholarship of William Appleman Williams came a floodtide of provocative opinions that rejected conventional thinking on foreign affairs. While liberal scholars emphasized the *ideological* origins of the U.S.-Soviet split (a struggle, they agreed, between communism and democracy), the Wisconsin School stressed its *economic* roots. The constitutional monarchies of Georgian Britain and Wilhelmian Germany in 1812 and 1917 and the Mexican republic in 1846, after all, were no more successful in avoiding war with the United

States than were the Japanese imperial government and the Nazi Third Reich. And in more recent times, the United States had moved against the democratic Mossadegh and Arbenz governments in Iran (1953) and Guatemala (1954).

In place of ideology, the Wisconsin School substituted the open door. In 1899, U.S. Secretary of State John Hay circulated letters to Japan and the major European powers requesting their respect of Chinese territorial and administrative integrity—essentially a call to promote competition and free trade in the colonized coastal Manchu territories. Recent events prompted the plea. In 1896, the Russian government had concluded the one-sided Li-Lobanov Treaty creating the Chinese Eastern Railway. In 1898, Germany received a free hand in Shangtung along with a ninety-nine-year lease of Kiaochow Bay; the British shortly thereafter won similar control of Kowloon (near Hong Kong), while the French and Japanese too gained valuable concessions. These bold maneuvers threatened to corner the China market at the precise moment that the United States was emerging from the Spanish-American War with imperial designs of its own. Though never formally agreed upon by the great powers, Hay's call for an open door became the guiding principle of America's Pacific strategy through the 1930s. It led—depending on one's point of view—either directly or indirectly to the Japanese attack on Pearl Harbor before collapsing completely with the victory of Mao's communist forces in 1949.

Historians had long understood Hay's notes in the context of a particular time (1899) and place (eastern China). But the Wisconsin School broke with this tradition by enlarging the idea of the open door to encompass the whole of American history. More than a mere policy paper to promote overseas trade, the notes struck Williams as a clear continuation of Jefferson's call for the United States to transform itself into an "empire of liberty." Jefferson spoke, of course, to the needs of an agricultural nation moving rapidly across the continent, while Hay addressed a rising industrial power looking to drum up business abroad. They harmonized, however, on the only point that really mattered: America's well-being hinged on expansion. And much more seemed to be at stake here than the price of wheat. A keen sensitivity to the place of open space on the democratic imagination had anchored Turner's observation that the American mind craved physical expansion—the closing of the frontier threatened that impulse but could not quell it.

A half-century after Turner's Wisconsin heyday, Madison became the center of a scholarly revolt against the open door. Harrington trained the first generation, including Wayne Cole (a specialist on American isolationism), Robert Freeman Smith (who moved from the Left to the Reagan right), and Williams. When a talent for administrative work took Harrington out of the classroom, he searched for a suitable replacement. Only one of his "boys" would do. Williams returned in 1957 to become the history department's major figure in foreign affairs; his influence soon exceeded that of his mentor, attracting talented young scholars such as Walter LaFeber, Lloyd Gardner, and Thomas McCormick. "When I moved into administration," Harrington acknowledged, Williams "had much more time for them then I and [was] much stronger on rapping with graduate students—that is [he was] quite willing to spend the whole night." Though the historical profession tended to regard Williams as an intellectual rebel, Harrington believed that his protégé adopted rather than introduced the radical ideas that secured his fame. "Bill made his reputation advocating an economic interpretation of foreign policy. But when he arrived, he was in no sense economic. We fed him Charles Beard, which is the core of his work."[1]

The Beardian approach fine-tuned at Madison appealed to both a neo-isolationist right and an anti-imperialist left. Many years after the fact, Wayne Cole recalled with real enthusiasm his introduction to the progressive argument against internationalism.

> [Harrington's] informal two-hour lecture and interpretive overview of the history of American expansion that he delivered in [a] proseminar on October 6, 1948 was the most intellectually exciting and mind-shaping lecture I ever heard at any time. . . . Of course I knew then and came to realize more fully later that Harrington's interpretive themes reflected, in part, the approach that Charles A. Beard advanced in his 1934 book on *The Idea of National Interest* and in other books and essays. But Harrington gave those interpretive ideas a clarity, consistency, and precision that Beard never provided me so effectively.[2]

Beard's provocative book *The Idea of National Interest* offered readers a clever conspiratorial gloss of American diplomacy. Surveying the first decades of the twentieth century, its author lamented the damage done to the nation's security by an industrial class that placed profits (self-interest) above patriotism (national interest). This powerful constituency demanded low tariffs, foreign loans, and greater involvement in China. Their successful efforts, Beard argued, compressed an already reeling Depression-era job market while simultaneously enlisting America in an expensive and reckless rivalry for global markets.

Beard's book rejected the idea of a Pax Americana, declaring that the philosophic underpinnings of U.S. foreign relations were shot through with false premises: "The conception of national interest revealed in the state papers is an aggregation of particularities assembled like eggs in a basket. Markets for agricultural produce were in the national interest; markets for industrial commodities were in the national interest; naval bases, territorial acquisitions for commercial support, an enlarged consular and diplomatic service, an increased navy and merchant marine, and occasional wars were all in the national interest. These contentions were not proved; they were asserted as axioms, apparently regarded as so obvious as to call for no demonstration."[3] Beard countered that a long-term expansionist policy on the part of the United States would arouse resentment among the global community while turning the American Athens into an American Sparta.[4] By the late 1940s, Beard's worst fears appeared to be coming true. In a mood of exultation underwritten by atomic victory, the nation implemented the mutually reinforcing policies of liberal internationalism and containment. Designed to enlarge the dimensions of American capitalism while curtailing Soviet expansion, these programs entered the public consciousness as critical pillars of postwar prosperity.

Historians roundly rejected Beard's diplomacy studies, and the ruling ideas of American foreign policy fell firmly into the hands of two dominant coastal scholars—Samuel Flagg Bemis of Yale and Stanford's Thomas Bailey. In his classic textbook *A Diplomatic History of the United States,* Bemis ("Wave the Flagg" Bemis, some students teased) taught the liberal international manifesto to generations of undergraduates. Its main assumptions: the United States is by nature an anti-imperial power; it stabilizes Western civilization as a moral force against an autocratic East; and it promotes freedom and democracy around the globe through the example of its superior economic, political, and cultural institutions. Even with most scholars ready, willing, and eager to enforce this view, two inconvenient historical episodes threatened its monopoly—America's naked imperialism of the 1890s and its complicity in the cold war. The hurried annexation of Hawaii and the Spanish War windfall that included U.S. control of the Philippines, Puerto Rico, and Guam seemed, after all, to support Beard's view. Bemis simply brushed it all aside, tidying up that fateful decade as "a great national aberration."[5] On the cold war, the Yale scholar failed to analyze the specific repercussions of America's nuclear monopoly, its historic hatred of communism, and its rapid economic and military encirclement of the Soviet state. His assessment of the East-versus-West showdown lacked multidimensionality, portraying the cold war as a Manichaean struggle for freedom's future. "There was," he wrote,

One World of general Western preference and renewed American fancy. It rested on the political thought of Burke and Bagehot and Woodrow Wilson. It was what Franklin D. Roosevelt thought of as a world family of Democratic Nations. It envisaged collective security for individual liberty and political democracy, functioning nationally and constitutionally under a new league of nations, backed this time by an international force of righteousness. On the other hand there was the Revolutionary world of Marx and Lenin and Joseph Stalin. It was based on a totalitarian power, to be seized and wielded in the name of the proletariat. It sacrificed the freedom of the individual to the omnipotence of the state. The Marxian World, under its mighty Russian dictatorship, avowed an irreconcilable conflict between capitalism and communism.[6]

One did not have to be an apologist for Soviet actions to sense that Bemis's work failed to wrestle with the full range of issues that underlay the cold war.

At Stanford, Bailey produced a spate of books warmly receptive to America's foreign policy decisions. His 1950 study *America Faces Russia* praised the United States for engaging in a principled moral crusade against Soviet oppression. Bailey's unintended thesis statement could be found opposite the title page—an illustration showing a long row of luckless Russians forcibly marched through a violent snow squall on their way to a deadening Siberian exile. This wincing image of communist aggression is reinforced by the author's leading prose—"Russian menace," "Soviet darkness," "the Soviets put the screws on their neighbors"—and blanket defense of the recent and dramatic growth of American military power and commitments. Liberals had assailed the progressive interpretation of American diplomacy as reductive and laced with an agenda—yet the same criticism could be fairly made of Bailey's work. His books took little account of the cultures or histories of nations forced to "choose" between East and West; they boiled painful and complex decisions down to a simplistic axiom: "prosperous nations that have known freedom do not willingly choose Marxist-Stalinist chains." And while Beard endured a hard hazing for questioning the objective nature of historical writing, Bailey too strayed from the prim path of archival evidence to offer personal opinion and advice to his readers. "We must 'sell' democracy vigorously," he wrote in *America Faces Russia,* "even militantly." Considering the ideological climate of postwar America, the Wisconsin School's rejection of Bemis and Bailey ranged far beyond revision; it constituted an open act of intellectual secession.[7]

This defiance, it must be acknowledged, took several years to mature.

Before Williams hit it big, consensus scholars held a virtual monopoly in the field of foreign affairs. Because of their radical leanings, Wisconsin historians working in this area were careful to tiptoe around their liberal brethren. In 1953, Cole's important work *America First: The Battle against Intervention* appeared. Developed out of a dissertation directed by Harrington, the book made great use of the Hoover Institute's archival holdings located on the grounds of Stanford University. While there, Cole received a letter from Harrington advising him to be careful with whom he discussed his work; Harrington was obviously concerned that Palo Alto's liberal historians would show little sympathy for a midwestern progressive. "I am sorry, really, that you saw Bailey, but suppose it was inevitable. . . . Guard your findings; don't tell Bailey or his students the best of what you find. . . . And in talking with Bailey make sure he realizes you are not an isolationist. He's not, of course, but your choice of subject and the Wisconsin tie may make him suspicious. Remember too that Bailey is anti-Beard."[8]

A native of Watertown, New York, Harrington had made his first Madison connection at Cornell, working under a Turner PhD, the distinguished progressive historian Carl Becker ("he was not close to his students, but was a great man whose courses . . . had a way of developing one's ability to look into the past"). Anticipating a State Department career, Harrington went to Washington in 1933 to take the Foreign Service examination—which was unexpectedly canceled, not to be offered again for three years. "I was left high and dry," he later recounted; "I had nothing to do." As a backup he studied history at New York University, becoming Henry Steele Commager's first PhD student. In 1937, at the age of twenty-five, Harrington took a nontenurable position at the University of Wisconsin teaching American foreign relations and Latin American history. After three years, he accepted a more substantial post at the University of Arkansas. An ambitious man, Harrington seemed to have it all: imposing height (6' 4"), a razor-sharp intelligence, and charisma uncompromised by a large ego. Introduced to the young president of the University of Arkansas, William (later Senator) Fulbright, Harrington did what came naturally—he impressed the hell out of a potential patron. At twenty-eight he chaired the department. "It was a second-level school," he later acknowledged, but a good place to prove himself. When Wisconsin offered a permanent post in 1944, he happily accepted.[9]

In a department filled with lively and competitive personalities, Harrington emerged as a dominating force, his success bolstered by a natural air of authority and an uncanny ability to read people and situations.

While Curti published major works that drew students to him, Harrington never did. His single book on international relations, *God, Mammon, and the Japanese: Dr. Horace N. Allen and Korean-American Relations* (1944), failed to spark wide professional interest. Consequently, his reputation as a historian stands largely on the shoulders of his students. His 1984 letter to Walter LaFeber reveals the context of his accomplishment:

> I handled doctoral students in diplomatic history less than a dozen years, perhaps a third as long as Bailey and Bemis. But our people certainly stand out. Why the high quality? Not being a towering figure as an historian when I started the diplomatic seminars, I did not attract students nationwide, as Bemis and Bailey doubtless did, & as Hicks & Curti did at Wisconsin. Well, why then? Because Wisconsin attracts good graduate students because of its enduring reputation in U.S. history, its progressive/activist traditions, the loyalty of its graduates (many, like you, steered here by undergraduate teachers). Also, probably, because of our public university character, low tuition, teaching-assistant system—slave labor, doubtless, but providing support for lower income types, & maybe even a little training.[10]

Harrington's ambitions were bigger than the classroom, and he steadily moved up the administrative ladder, becoming president of the university in 1962. His support for Williams as his replacement proved an inspired choice that helped—along with the unpopular Vietnam War—to revive a once respectable middle-western isolationism. Yet it also caused Harrington to wonder in years to come if he had made the right choice. Eclipsed by Williams's rising star and troubled that *his* Wisconsin School fell prey to a New Left radicalism that wrecked his presidency, Harrington came to regard Williams as something of a popularity seeker, his scholarship insufficiently critical of Soviet actions. "These New left historians," he observed in the early 1980s, ". . . leave the thought that the Russians aren't all that bad, or that the Russians are better, more right, than we. . . . It's a view that I don't like . . . . That is, I think, a key to my difference with some of my own students with reference to their interpretation, and it means that the Wisconsin School of diplomatic history ought not to be just associated with the New Left." Harrington clearly recognized differences between the old Beardianism and the new radicalism—and he resented Williams's tug toward the left as a deviation from the progressive training he had absorbed at Madison. "Somehow," he remarked shortly after Williams's death, "Bill and I never quite agreed on anything."[11]

Given these differences, what inspired Harrington to bring Williams back? According to David Cronon, "Fred was a correct middle-class man. He was not an iconoclast like Bill, but he felt the department needed them, and he hired Williams for that reason." Lloyd Gardner adds that "when Williams came to the University of Wisconsin . . . the graduate program in American history was languishing. The era of the giants at Wisconsin had not yet passed, but there was a feeling that many were tired giants, and if not tired, no longer much interested in graduate teaching. Within a few months of his arrival, Williams had significantly changed the atmosphere." Walter LaFeber believed that the hiring of Williams benefited both the institution and the individual. "Wisconsin and Bill were a perfect match. He needed room and encouragement for what he wanted to do, and Wisconsin was probably the only place in the United States that could provide both." Certainly the University of Oregon, his former employer, could—or would—not. Wisconsin's salary proposal of $7,600 exceeded Williams's Oregon earnings by a mere $400—yet his colleagues in Eugene refused to match the higher offer.[12]

To this day, some wonder whether Williams played a role in Harrington's 1970 resignation from the Wisconsin presidency. The student demonstrations that engulfed the university in the late 1960s found especially supportive allies in both Williams and his colleague Harvey Goldberg. Their lectures drew hundreds and frequently played to the revolutionary themes that rattled the cage of Madison's radical student culture. Professors, some have argued, incited students to acts of campus violence which in turn forced an increasingly conservative board of regents to apply pressure on Harrington to shut the protests down. While this interpretation unduly minimizes the independent politics and aspirations of Wisconsin's students, it does accurately stress their eagerness to find intellectual models among their professors. In a 1982 interview, Harrington recalled Williams's theatrics during those fragile years. Interviewer Laura Smail (wife of John Smail, a Madison historian) pursued the matter cautiously: "I didn't mean to imply that Bill Williams was inciting students. I merely meant that his lectures had enlightened students too . . . " But Harrington cut in, "Well, I think it's proper to say he did incite students." Again, Smail seemed to be on the verge of pursuing a softer line—"Maybe he wasn't . . . "—when Harrington firmly reiterated his point: "He did incite students."[13]

Williams's radicalism emerged from the Plains-states populism that had once moved the Midwest. Born in rural Atlantic, Iowa, in 1921, he grew up in an agricultural community that had a generation or two earlier lodged chapters of the National Grange and the Northern Farmers' Alliance. "One learned early and at firsthand how the farm was tied to the world market-place," Williams wrote of his youthful political awakening. "As in the case of my grandfather, who exported his beloved and prize-winning hunting dogs to England and France, and Germany and even Russia, until the Great Depression destroyed his market—nearly destroyed him." A "blue-eyed Iowa Socialist," Williams felt a certain calling to make sure the historical community treated the Populist Party fairly. He rejected both the liberal (Hofstadter's scolding of the farmers as far-right proto-McCarthyites) and radical (Yale scholar Norman Pollack's overpraising of the farmers as proto-socialists) interpretations of the farming revolt. He emphasized, rather, its conservative nature. "I have spent about 5 weeks working the Populists and other agrarians, 1885–1895," he wrote James Weinstein, "and have come to the conclusion that Hofstadter and Pollack are *terribly* wide of the mark. These farmers such as Allen and Simpson are extremely intelligent and rational. . . . The idea that they had a 'new' vision of America is ridiculous; they are trying, like everyone else, to prevent a real social upheaval and tie themselves very intelligently and thoroughly to the Jeffersonian-Jacksonian set of ideas, policies, and tradition."[14]

Interestingly, Williams's *bete noir* Arthur Schlesinger Jr. (a case of the ultra-"radical" and the ultra–"court historian") also spent part of his childhood in Iowa. The similarities end there. Unlike Williams, Schlesinger bore the distinct markings of an academic brat brought to Iowa City after his father, the noted social historian Arthur Schlesinger Sr., received a teaching post at the University of Iowa. Following four years in the corn and hog belt, the older Schlesinger accepted an appointment at Harvard, an environment in which young Arthur—an avid attendee of his father's Sunday afternoon teas—thrived. Williams, by contrast, never lost his suspicion of the metropolis. Acute physical discomfort accompanied his infrequent travels to "enemy" territory, alcohol medicated his mounting anxiety, an affected midwestern twang underlined his defiance.[15]

In a 1980 interview for *Radical History Review*, Williams credited Atlantic's conservative small-town sensibilities with shaping his worldview. It all sounded more like Norman Rockwell than Norman Thomas (as Williams pointedly put it, "I'm just a little boy from Iowa"). He ruminated on the love and support of his relatives ("people who had community values at the center of their lives") and fondly remembered summers working on the family farm and the pride of scholastic and athletic spoils ("good grades and good basketball got me into college"—a prized appointment to the United States Naval Academy). Midwestern village life, Williams emphasized, had granted him the perspective, work ethic, and encouragement to succeed as

Figure 5. Empire's Agonists: Fred Harrington (left) and William Appleman Williams (right). Courtesy University of Wisconsin–Madison Archives.

a "radical" historian. He sought now to use that radicalism—informed by a Populist past and contemporized by an American empire that threatened the weak and the small—for purposes of preservation.[16]

In the crosshairs of a widening capitalist market, tiny Atlantic lay at the mercy of powerful commercial forces beyond its control. "Those who turned the soil and harvest the crops," Williams wrote of his Iowa kin, "met

others who sold and fixed the tools of the farm, and still others who handled livestock, poultry, and gingham and ice cream. And there was always
the railroad. Nobody went home until the night express had stopped for
water and then huffed-and-puffed its way down the line west to Omaha
and Denver and San Francisco. Atlantic was part of the empire."[17] Williams
fought in the name of this vast apparatus, receiving the Purple Heart during World War II, but it repelled him—both intellectually and emotionally. As a professional historian he produced scholarship challenging the
imperial tectonics of cold war liberalism, and as a citizen he made his home
on the empire's periphery. After eleven combative years at Madison, Williams retreated even deeper into the pastoral, taking a position at Oregon
State University and living in tiny Waldport, a spare seaside town of about
two thousand.

From Atlantic to Madison to Waldport, Williams cultivated a curious
mixture of dialectical materialism and midwestern militancy. "Obviously
I consider myself a Marxist," he once wrote, "no apologies and no deny-
ing the problems inherent in all that. But, to start with, one does have to
separate the tradition into the intellectual and activist traditions. I think,
on balance, that intellectual Marxism offers the most insightful mode of . . .
making sense of the world."[18] As a highbrow materialist, Williams stressed
social alienation as the inevitable outcome of capitalist individualism. The
market uprooted communities, mocked moral convention, and tempted
the republic with endless wars, interventions, and occupations. As an interpretive tool, Marxism offered the "little boy from Iowa" a buoyant future.
Released from the pressures of overproduction and overconsumption,
America might elude the crucible of foreign entanglements. It might, on
its better days, even look a bit like Atlantic.

The idea of empire had won the attention of the Wisconsin School
long before Williams arrived in Madison. In an 1896 *Atlantic Monthly* essay,
Turner had written that "for nearly three centuries the dominant fact in
American life has been expansion. With the settlement of the Pacific coast
and occupation of the free lands, this movement has come to a check. That
these energies of expansion will no longer operate would be a rash predic-
tion; and the demands for a vigorous foreign policy, for the interoceanic
canal, for a revival of our power upon the seas, and for the extension of
American influence to outlying islands and adjoining countries, are indica-
tions that the movement will continue." Two years later, the United States
beat up Spain and took its empire. Turner's description of a limitless frontier proved to be the point of departure for Williams—and he unhesitat-
ingly aligned himself with Turner on this score. "It is time," he wrote in

1962, "to stop treating Frederick Jackson Turner as a historian (let alone as a social scientist!). He was a poet. A poet botched by his education, to be sure, but nevertheless a poet. He saw the central role of the American frontier and in a moment of profound insight called it 'a gate of escape.'"[19] The illusion of a limitless, unsettled area allowed America to regard itself as an anti-imperial nation while paradoxically pushing its power across a continent. Jefferson christened his country's collection of western lands an "empire of liberty," implying that the greedy exploits implicit in European expansionism repulsed his countrymen. This construal struck Williams as delusional, and in his own moment of profound insight, he recast Turner's "gate of escape" as the "great evasion."

If Turner provided Williams with the analytic framework to understand the American empire, Charles Beard offered a more concrete criticism. "Beard was asking the crucial question," Williams maintained: "Could liberal internationalism be sustained without imperialism and without subverting private property? His answer was 'Yes'—if the nation abandoned the frontier-expansionist theory of history and allocated its human and material resources in a more rational and equitable fashion."[20] But was such an outcome likely, or even possible? In their hearts, both historians feared the worst. Beard's cryptic observation of the United States' predicament as "perpetual war for perpetual peace" was echoed in Williams's regret that America waged "empire as a way of life."

Beard shared the progressive presumption that America came late to the table of empire. Only with the industrial expansion of the Gilded Age, he argued, did the nation first stray from the glory road of true republican virtue. Williams disagreed, arguing that the American empire and the American republic were early joined in a fateful embrace. Following the revolution, the country's elite hoped never again to see a popular rebellion. It quickly realized that the standard of living among the lower classes could be increased without a substantial redistribution of income only if the economy expanded. Imperialism in the new nation thus served, Williams believed, as a conservative response to the kinds of revolutionary activities that overturned the French aristocracy in the 1790s. In effect, the American master class smoothed the hard edges of class dissent by creating a broad consumer constituency built on foreign markets.

The country's addiction to abundance, Williams continued, prefaced a long-term commitment to territorial expansion, as consumer cravings would only become more sophisticated and more demanding over time. In the "Age of Mercantilism," Williams argued, the agricultural market served as America's primary unit of wealth. Accordingly, the nation's foreign policy focused on the frontier and removed all obstacles to the emerging free farming and plantation slave complexes in the Ohio and Mississippi valleys. As a result, Indian, French, and Spanish empires alike were uprooted by the end of Andrew Jackson's presidency. Under Old Hickory's Tennessee protégé James Polk, one-third of Mexico fell to American arms, and with the acquisition of California the United States began to envision itself as a Pacific power.

Following the Civil War, Williams argued, America entered an "Age of Corporate Capitalism," touched off by the industrial renaissance that quickly swallowed the old farming gentry. The economic downturn of the 1890s—combined with Turner's popularized fear of a vanishing frontier—inspired the United States to look abroad. This reflex, Williams insisted, was no "aberration," as Bemis had blandly declared. Rather, the expansionist impulse that had earlier pushed Americans into the War of 1812, the Seminole and Black Hawk struggles of the 1830s, and Mexican war in the 1840s prefigured the Spanish adventure.

In Williams's reading of the past, the United States had entered in recent decades a new phase of imperialism. Rather than maintain costly overseas possessions with occupation armies and huge administrative bureaucracies, America pursued a policy of free trade—markets replaced colonies. It was a brilliant move. Under the old system, the European powers had neatly divided up the choicest cuts among themselves. To turn-of-the-century progressives, France, Germany, and Great Britain were as guilty as Rockefeller, Carnegie, and Morgan of monopolistic heresies. In the name of smashing international cartels and protecting the interests of the American consumer, the old Jeffersonian continental empire would have to be overhauled to compete in every corner of the globe.

Taken as a whole, the revisionist argument audaciously challenged the way Americans saw themselves and their country. Followers of the consensus model understood the United States to be an anti-imperialist nation with an open door policy that encouraged global stability by allowing nations to compete peacefully for markets. Revisionists, on the other hand, believed that the United States had long-standing imperial ambitions and that the open door encouraged global insecurity by promoting a cutthroat scramble for markets. The Wisconsin School's critique of American diplomacy made no concessions to the country's self-image—and that explains both its power among left- and right-wing mavericks and the intensity with which the liberal establishment criticized it. *Who* were Americans? *What* did they value? If Williams and his students were correct, the open door philosophy destabilized the modern industrial world and played a major role in igniting the twentieth century's hot and cold wars. "'Isolationism' for America," Williams wrote near the end of his life, "is a denial of its entire cultural tradition of expansion and imperialism. Hence, and rightly so, 'isolationism' is perceived by The Establishment as a fundamental assault—intellectually, morally, economically—upon empire as a way of life."[21]

Williams advanced his ideas most effectively in two books that have become classics of revisionist historiography, *The Tragedy of American Diplomacy* (1957) and *The Contours of American History* (1961). It may help us to place the importance of these studies to note that historians typically write two kinds of books—"research" books and "thinking" books. The former (and most common) tend to be monographic, that is, narrowly focused and heavily reliant on archival sources—a small topic cresting on a mountain of footnotes. Thinking books, on the other hand, tend to be broader in scope and are products less of primary source materials than of the author's imaginative reconstruction of the past. They also tend to be more provocative and suppositional since the composer has greater freedom to selectively shape and argue his thesis. He is not strictly confined, in other words, by the limitations of available documentation.

Thinking books attract an academic clientele, it is true, but their real readership is the general public, and their real intention is not to win tenure, promotion, or a better campus parking spot; their goal, rather, is to influence society. Liberal scholars had produced several thinking books in the postwar decades, including Schlesinger Jr.'s *The Age of Jackson*, Hofstadter's *The Age of Reform*, and Bell's *The End of Ideology*. Williams cracked this consensus monopoly and pioneered a style of revisionist thinking book that continues to influence and shape the work of professional historians. As Patricia Nelson Limerick, the distinguished scholar of the American West, wrote in 2001, "I now acknowledge [Williams] as my predecessor. . . . One of the big changes in my field, maybe *the* big change, has been a reckoning with the fact that what we called, for so long, 'westward expansion,' could also fit in the categories of colonialism and imperialism. A recognition of the centrality of Empire, with a capital e, now drives and energizes my field."[22]

Beyond the academy, Williams's thinking books hit the market at an opportune time—confidence in the American empire plummeted in the 1960s, and the old triumphalism now struck a false note. A sweeping indictment of U.S. diplomacy from the open door to the cold war, *Tragedy* broke sharply from liberal orthodoxy by praising conservative contributions to the nation's foreign affairs. Williams applauded Herbert Hoover's Good Neighbor policy for encouraging the kind of hemispheric self-sufficiency outlined in

Beard's continentalist vision. The internationalism practiced by Wilson and FDR, he countered, threatened to stretch the empire to the point of implosion. In Hoover (himself an Iowa farm boy) Williams discovered a figure who embodied a valuable tradition of voluntary restraints and limitations that, if revived, might unhinge postwar America from the cross of containment. "Maybe Hoover was right, maybe we can make it with the hemisphere," he argued. "We've never tried. It might be worth a go." A resourceful contrarian and a skilled intellectual street fighter, Williams used whatever ideas were available to strike out at the consensus monolith. In this way he found favor with both radical and conservative arguments against empire. "Since there isn't any candid, responsible liberal center or right," he stated, "that means that the left must in truth honor if not in deed rehabilitate the best of our conservative tradition in order to have a serious dialogue."[23]

Williams's continentalist sympathies connected him to a heritage of midwestern self-sufficiency—"a certain retreat into 'fortress America,'" one colleague complained—déclassé among liberals.[24] That the lessons of Atlantic loomed large in Williams's mind is no surprise. That so many others fell under its spell is. Timing tells us why. Liberal internationalism undermined itself in the Bay of Pigs, the Dominican invasion, and Southeast Asia. *Tragedy*'s break from a triumphalist frame of reference gave radical students a conservative alternative.

To be sure, the book's publication did have certain drawbacks. "*Tragedy* obviously upset a lot of people," Williams later remembered, "and in 1960–61 the House Un-American Activities Committee subpoenaed me. . . . They sent my name over to the IRS. And the IRS worked me over for the better part of fifteen years." Among his peers in the academy, Williams's controversial appraisal of the cold war caught most of the criticism. He denounced the containment policy and argued that U.S. pressure rather than the expansion of Soviet power in Eastern Europe had caused the rift with Russia. America, Williams noted, held all the high cards in the late 1940s—a booming economy, security at home, and the world's most sophisticated weapons. "It was," he claimed, "the decision of the United States to employ its new and awesome power in keeping with the traditional Open Door Policy which crystallized the cold war."[25]

At that point Williams simply and unsatisfyingly let the matter of complicity drop. But the neoimperialism plainly evident in *both* the communist East's and democratic West's remorseless pursuit of coalitions and satellite states cast the cold war as a revival of the old "scramble for Africa" and "China market" days. Williams tended to ignore Soviet colonial ambitions by crying poverty—"the United States had from 1944 to at least 1962 a vast preponderance of actual as well as potential power vis-à-vis the Soviet Union." Yet the historical record clearly demonstrates that from the time of the czars, Russia wielded its own version of the open door in the Caucuses, the Baltic Peninsula, Central Asia, Trans-Siberia, and finally Eastern Europe.[26]

Williams was on surer footing when he argued that the containment policy actually preceded the cold war. He pointed out that as president, Jefferson promised the destruction of French power in the New World if it refused to sell the United States the port of New Orleans; Jackson illegally captured Pensacola in 1818, convincing the Bourbon king Ferdinand VII to grant Spanish Florida to the United States; and in 1844, James Polk won the presidency on an expansionist plank that promised to drive American interests into the Pacific Northwest by claiming parts of British Canada. Viewed historically, the penetration of Soviet power into Eastern Europe, its assistance to the Arab states, and its anticolonial appeal to third world countries impressed Williams as simply the most recent challenge to the open door. Americans, as was their custom, resisted the "imperial" designs of a European competitor with overwhelming economic and military power—and this, Williams argued, forced the Soviets to "meet strength with strength." Years of terror and domestic deprivation were endured as the Stalinist state built an army and an atomic arsenal to protect Russia from the encircling American leviathan. NATO in the west, SEATO in the east, and the Baghdad Pact in the south effectively legitimized Stalin's talk of external enemies. The early days of containment may have constituted a life-and-death struggle for a Soviet nation that had barely survived the Nazi invasion, but in the United States, Williams wrote, it was (booming) business as usual—"the Cold War has insured the expansion and success of America's mid-century industrial capitalism."[27]

Williams produced in *Contours,* his most ambitious book, a sweeping and pessimistic history of the cultural and intellectual currents—the worldview—that informed American imperialism. He stood conventional historiography on its head by criticizing the liberal leadership that advanced the ideology of the open door—Jefferson ("moved quickly to initiate a western advance"), Jackson (his presidency "the unfettered triumph of laissez nous faire"), Wilson (a "representative of the intellectual and Christian Capitalist wings of the Progressive Movement"), and FDR ("Roosevelt . . . supported the expansionist approach" to pulling the United States out of the Depression). Conversely, he commended southerners and conservatives whom, he argued, bravely opposed a cancerous capitalist culture. Few liberal historians in the 1960s were interested in praising John

Quincy Adams ("willing to devalue property rights in favor of the general welfare"), Henry Clay ("came to doubt . . . the beneficent results of expansion"), or Herbert Hoover ("had more intellectual courage and imagination" than the architects of containment), but Williams did just that. These men, he challenged his colleagues, embodied the precious hope "that it was possible to build a community—a commonwealth—based on private property without imperial expansion."[28]

Liberals denounced *Contours,* with the Harvard historian Oscar Handlin taking the lead. In a scathing appraisal published in the *Mississippi Valley Historical Review,* he dismissed the work as a bad joke: "In evaluating this book one cannot exclude the possibility that it was intended as an elaborate hoax, that its author has been enjoying himself by ingeniously pulling the legs of his colleagues." From there, the review really got nasty. "Large sections" of the study, Handlin fumed "are altogether farcical"; a "pervasive wrong headedness . . . distorts every page"; the writing resembled "the literary strivings of unskilled freshmen." The book amounted, he claimed in his parting shot, to a "total disaster." In a subsequent edition of the *Review,* John Higham, a student of Curti and classmate of Williams, defended *Contours* and its author. He opened his letter in the *MVHR*'s "Communications" section by noting Handlin's history of attacking progressive scholarship. "Professor Handlin recently reviewed Lee Benson's book, *Turner and Beard* in another journal and made, in the course of his olympian comments, the egregious statement that Beard had no students and slight influence on subsequent scholarship. . . . Handlin has now encountered . . . . a self-confessed disciple of Beard . . . and has given that luckless surrogate a thorough trouncing." Rather than trying to understand *Contours,* Higham complained, Handlin had dismissed it out of hand and, worse, resorted to "tasteless," "disgraceful," and "irresponsible" tactics to do so. "The working of a complex, untidy, independent mind," he appealed to the profession, "can easily elude an unfriendly reviewer. But there is no excuse for bullying."[29]

During America's painful war in Vietnam, liberal stewardship of the state naturally underwent intense scrutiny, and Williams's work began to enter the mainstream. In response, antirevisionists conducted a spirited defense of containment dogma designed, in Schlesinger Jr.'s words, to readvance the idea "that the Cold War was the brave and essential response of free men to communist aggression."[30] Specifically, they confronted Williams and his proxies with a number of compelling counterpoints: the business community is not a monolith, nor does it advance a single economic agenda; political leaders exert more influence on global affairs than do business leaders; the Wisconsin School underestimated the power of irrational politics (jingoism, the yellow press) or altruism (missionaries, economic aid) to shape foreign policy; Stalin was a murderous tyrant coddled by revisionists (as Beard had supposedly ignored Hitler's sins).

The most thorough critique of revisionist scholarship, Robert James Maddox's *The New Left and the Origins of the Cold War* (1973), accused Williams of doctoring source material to make his case. "One of the techniques Williams used most often in *Tragedy*," Maddox pointed out, "was to construct imaginary speeches and dialogues by splicing together phrases uttered at different times on diverse subjects." Williams acknowledged using this tactic, rationalizing it (creatively or weakly depending on one's position) as a form of "seriation quotation," that is, linking separate citations together to make a critical point or draw out more clearly ideas buried deep within the existing written record. Ironically, Maddox had begun his graduate studies at Wisconsin working under Williams. After he failed his preliminary examinations in 1960, the department magnanimously blamed itself and supported Maddox's successful effort to transfer to Rutgers. "Unfortunately," William Hesseltine explained at the time, Maddox "took his [exams] before he was fully prepared for them, and we think he has been a victim of our own system and the defects in it. At any rate, under our rules, he may not continue here; but we are quite unprepared to give up on him and in fact have urged him very strongly to go to another institution and show us up."[31] And try he did.

But Maddox's critical appraisal of the revisionist school ("these books *without exception* are based upon pervasive misusages of the source materials") aroused little interest. The academy—moving in time with the culture—was changing rapidly; Vietnam in particular pressed the radical interpretation of the cold war to the forefront and gave to Williams's work a legitimacy the century's other great foreign-policy revisionist, Charles Beard, had never attained. Handlin responded to what he regarded as the inexplicable indifference of his colleagues with an angry manifesto whose title, "The Failure of the Historians" (1975), indicted an entire profession. "Having read the systematic distortions of the revisionist historians for almost twenty years," he wrote, "I continued to hope that scholarship would ultimately correct the story. . . . The hope was vain. Maddox made the case. But it did not sink in." Handlin went on to describe the revisionists' approach as "inherently absurd" and the liberal scholars now crossing over to their side or simply retreating from the fray as guilty of "betray[ing] their professional obligations."[32] Williams's growing influence, Handlin tartly insisted, reflected a broader cultural illness. A decade of war, racial violence, and student uprisings had caused many scholars to lose confidence in objectivity and, at a deeper level, faith in their country as a force for good in the world. Easier to attack America from the ivory tower (and curry the favor of students) than to cut against the contemporary radical chic.

This line of inquest, when applied to Williams, is particularly ironic. During teaching stints in the 1950s at Washington & Jefferson College, the Ohio State University, and the University of Oregon, Williams had refined the revisionist thesis in a conservative age. There is no doubt that the radical incline of American life in the 1960s popularized his views—but these views were not the product of the 1960s. They emerged, rather, from Williams's prewar midwestern roots, graduate training at Wisconsin in the 1940s, and intensive study of American history in the 1950s. An intellectually serious scholar, Williams did not ride the counterculture to prominence; rather, the culture caught up with him.

And then it quickly passed him by. Personal and professional circumstances conspired to end Williams's prolific Madison run. He was in the midst of a difficult second marital breakdown, years of intense work had left him exhausted, and he needed to reclaim himself from a student movement weaned on his books. "Williams was very bothered by the protests in his final years at Madison," LaFeber remembers. "He didn't know that this is what he was creating intellectually, and he was very uncomfortable by it. I think he felt that some of these people had been in his classes and that they looked to him as a kind of guru. But he felt strongly that any type of protest that threatened violence, especially in a university setting, was unacceptable." In love with the Pacific Northwest, he spent the 1966–67 academic year on leave in Newport, Oregon, angling for a job. He hoped to return to the University of Oregon, but it showed no interest. He next approached Oregon State University in sleepy Corvallis and this time received an offer. While other Madison stars—including Turner, Hicks, and Curti—received positions or feelers for positions from the likes of Harvard, Cornell, Berkeley, and Columbia, Williams practically had to beg his way out of Wisconsin. He went to Corvallis on the cheap, earning a mere $16,700—a 16.5 percent pay cut. Clearly, he had moved on for neither financial nor professional reasons. He felt a deep connection with the Oregon coast, knew that he wanted to retire there, and had the good grace to realize that his moment at Madison had passed. "I am inclined to feel that, all things considered, I gave to myself and to Wisconsin the right things at the right time," he wrote to George Mosse. "And now it is both appropriate and more productive to do something different."[33]

Williams died of cancer in 1990—a year shy of seventy. Months later, the Organization of American Historians honored him by holding a panel celebrating his work and influence. The event gave Harrington, who was nearly eighty at the time, an opportunity to reflect upon Williams's impact. In a letter to Wayne Cole, a scholar he passed over to hire Williams, Harrington summarized his late protégé and the Wisconsin School in deft and bittersweet strokes. The tensions in this once and forever master-apprentice relationship are obvious.

> Odd about Bill; some of his work was good, some poor. He is now a great hero of radical historians, though he broke with them over the violence issue in the '60s, and left Madison for Oregon State, a strange move. His *Tragedy of American Diplomacy* apparently has a [great] deal of influence; but when Bill began graduate work, he was not influenced by economic interpretations.... Bill did influence my students who had not finished their Ph.D.s when I went into administration—Gardner, LaFeber, McCormick, Parini—but LaFeber pretty much outgrew that influence, you...and others were never influenced by Williams, and he had remarkably few good Ph.D.s of his own but turned out over 30. Perhaps he insisted too much on conformity to a party line, which had a paralytic influence on some.... There is a sort of Bill Williams cult now, no doubt soon to fade. But he did arouse interest in many, and that was his contribution.[34]

Soon to fade? Williams is more popular now than when Harrington made his remarks. Of course the world was much different in 1990. The Malta Summit had just passed, marking the "official" end of the cold war. Elsewhere the Berlin Wall had recently come down, apartheid in South Africa was in a state of dismantlement, and the prodemocracy movement in China looked to Tiananmen Square as a template for future change. Who needed a killjoy like Williams? Here was incontrovertible proof that the American Century principles of liberalism, pluralism, and internationalism had worked wonders around the globe.

And then it all quickly unraveled. In January 1991 came Operation Desert Storm, followed by a decade of Yugoslav wars, the 9/11 terrorist attacks, and the invasion/occupation of Iraq. In these bloody times Williams's way of looking at the world remains compelling. He produced in *Tragedy* and *Contours* disquieting books that carried the voice of Atlantic and of a thousand other interior hamlets bereft of a champion since Beard. They raised the ominous prospect that America had become a prisoner of ambition, fatally tied to a flawed and violent international system much of its own making. And perhaps there was no way out. "Is *the idea and reality of America possible without empire?*" Williams asked in his last book. "Is America *even imaginable* only on a global scale?"[35]

PART III

The Conservative Age
1970–

It's hard to avoid the conclusion that this election represents a repudiation of liberalism. The question is, is it a temporary fit of madness, like 1946, of which voters will soon repent when they get further acquainted with Reaganism? Or is it a real turning point, like 1930, signaling perhaps decades of conservative government? What a prospect!

CHRISTOPHER LASCH, 1980

SEVEN

Populist of the Heart

Christopher Lasch

The political scene could hardly be more dreary. Surveying the wreckage of the sixties, one is amazed at how little has been accomplished. . . . It's hard to believe that only two years ago Paris, Columbia, McCarthy's candidacy, Johnson's withdrawal, and the emergence of Kennedy all seemed to give hope that the monolith was really beginning to break up and that all the intense political activity of the sixties, however chaotic and discordant, was going to produce changes. . . . In fact nothing has thawed and nothing has changed.

CHRISTOPHER LASCH, 1970

As the 1960s came to an end, so did the long run of liberal historiography. Dependent on the consensus of American Century principles, it succumbed to the cultural upheaval that overtook the era. A metaphorical frontier had closed, again—and with it the boom years that had distinguished the nation's incredible postwar growth. In this season of decline, nostalgia threatened a once resonant interior vision. Trapped in a confidence-shaking Rustbelt, a tired midwestern progressivism looked lost. Its lecture-hall heroes were now just names on the seminar rooms and scholarships that make the institutional memory so intensely vivid in places like Madison, Wisconsin. Among their number, the old Beardian Merrill Jensen sighed in 1971, "I sometimes despair about history."[1] He soon retired from the profession. His pessimism, no doubt encumbered by generational baggage, seems to us now misplaced. New scholars and fresh fields emerged to enlarge the scope of historical activity. The time was ripe for a postprogressive, postliberal reckoning with the past.

Enter Christopher Lasch, heir to a downsized American dream. Vietnam, Watergate, and a host of crises—oil, energy, and hostage—startled the nation and raised serious questions about its prospects. As a critic of both liberalism and capitalism, Lasch's political commitments were complex. Radicals delighted in his pointed denunciations of the cold war consensus while the right embraced his cultural conservatism. Neither could properly claim him. Nor did he warm up to the old progressive idealism, the long time hobbyhorse of midwestern historical writing. The reform impulse had no doubt helped bust trusts, he acknowledged, but under

its aegis, a rising professional class of marriage counselors, social workers, and psychologists pathologized a once dominant bourgeois culture.
As the unwitting ally of market individualism, these shock troops of the
"therapeutic state" rolled back time-honored restraints to free enterprise.
Atomization followed, along with dual-income households, divorce, and
the steep discounting of romantic love. Lasch counted all of this a victory
for a morally indifferent capitalist way of life.

If Lasch did not accept the progressive's search for a secular millennium, neither did he embrace the liberalism of his own day. He never made
his peace with consensus, containment, or the affluent society, nor did he
support the more radical forms of protest that guided sixties-era opposition to "the system." Like William Appleman Williams, Lasch combined an
eclectic and critical intellect with an underlying appreciation of traditional
customs and values. He appeared at times to be a man of the Left and other
times of the Right. To recover the sources of his outlook we must begin, as
we have with the other scholars in these pages, by locating personality with
place. Again, we start in the Middle West.

Christopher Lasch was born in Omaha in 1932—christening year of the new
liberalism. His father, the Pulitzer Prize–winning journalist Robert Lasch,
had grown up in neighboring Lincoln and graduated from the University
of Nebraska. There he met his wife, Zora Schaupp. Eight years Robert's
senior, Zora, a Nebraska native with a Bryn Mawr PhD, taught philosophy
and psychology, roomed with the sister of Willa Cather, and married her
best student. The old agrarian radicalism of their set left a deep impress on
the new century. Zora's father, Frederick, had won election to the Nebraska
legislature in 1912 and supported statewide internal improvements to assist
farmers; Robert worked for a decade at the Omaha *World-Herald*, formerly
edited by William Jennings Bryan. Third-party politics had a broad appeal
in the Plains states, and Lasch's parents—disciples of the old Wilsonian
progressivism, but skeptical of the patrician Franklin Roosevelt—voted
for Norman Thomas in 1932.[2]

Growing up in the house of a professor and a journalist left an enduring
mark on Lasch. He absorbed the cultural aspirations of the prewar middle
class (taking up piano and violin), served as editor of his school paper, and
displayed a preternatural capacity for critical thought that pleased his parents but occasioned bouts of adolescent isolation. "I probably felt insuffer-
ably superior intellectually, and probably showed it a lot of the time," he
later recalled. "I didn't know exactly what an intellectual was, but I don't
think there has ever been a time when kids with bookish interests didn't

feel somewhat at odds with their peers." Lasch's limited prairie horizons opened considerably when Robert moved on to the Chicago *Sun-Times*. The change in zip code introduced then ten-year-old Christopher to a rich urbanscape far from the provincial plains communities of Omaha. "My father would take me around Chicago and explore the city. . . . It was beyond anything I had experienced."[3]

Graduating from suburban Barrington High School in 1950, Lasch—winner of a statewide Latin contest—received a scholarship from the University of Chicago. Confident of his talents, he turned down the local school and held out for the Ivy League. That fall he matriculated to Harvard. While there, he maintained with his family a remarkably consistent correspondence, topically spiced with baseball, politics, and local news—local now meaning St. Louis, where Robert wrote for the *Post-Dispatch*. Lasch received thirty letters from his parents that freshman autumn, slightly more than two communications per week. Despite a heavy workload, he replied at a rate of about half that and apologized for failing to write more often. One is tempted to see a connection between these dozens of letters—added to the many dozens more preserved in Lasch's papers—and the passionate profamily arguments in his later books.[4]

At Harvard, Lasch encountered a number of distinguished scholars and tutors, including Frederick Merk, Perry Miller, and Donald Meyer, who awoke in him a latent interest in history. After receiving discouraging news from his father regarding opportunities in journalism, he began to think seriously about a career in the academy. This inclination grew stronger when Lasch, teased by the desire to write the great American novel, met a young man with literary designs of his own: "My roomie's name is John Updike, and he comes from Reading, PA. His father is a public school teacher. He was accompanied by his mother and an aunt who drove him up, and this embarrassed him somewhat, but he is a very nice guy. He wants to be either a writer or a cartoonist." Witness to his classmate's conspicuous talents—recognized in forums (*The Advocate, The Lampoon*) closed to him—Lasch later acknowledged that Updike "was a lot better at this than I was, which may have had something to do with the fact that I didn't pursue it."[5]

Within a few short weeks Lasch had sized up the social coding essential to Harvard's residence hall culture. "I find Hollis the best place on the campus to live," he informed his parents. "The rooms here are cheaper than most of the other halls, and there are a number of scholarship students. As far as I know, there are no private school students here. . . . The rich boys live down in Wigglesworth and Straus . . . and are held in much contempt." Lasch's scorn for the blue bloods connected him to a long line of interior thinkers put off by Harvard's privileged. The literary historian Vernon Parrington, for one, loathed his college years in the East. A prodigy from the provincial village of Americus, Kansas, he encountered in Cambridge a petty caste snobbery he never breached. "I could have made friends had I tried," he later observed, "but I didn't try, being as proud and independent as I was poor." In the 1920s, the Nebraskan Merle Curti experienced an amiable if telling hazing from his Harvard professors. He described Edward Channing as "a good Yankee and . . . Boston Brahmin, [who] denigrated the West and the South and tried to convert us to the belief that New England was the only part of the country that really counted." Establishing a calculated distance, Channing corrected his midwestern students' callow habit of addressing their instructors as "Professor" when the Harvard way was to call them "Mr."[6]

In the early 1950s, Lasch's period in Cambridge, the Harvard historians heard their critics' whispers of intellectual parochialism and set their sights on collecting a new colleague from the provinces. Frank Freidel, a Wisconsin PhD formerly on the faculties at Maryland, Penn State, the University of Illinois, and Stanford, fit the bill. There is evidence that Freidel—an industrious scholar who turned out a critically acclaimed multivolume study of Franklin Roosevelt and his era—encountered early turbulence in his new post. Some status-minded Ivy handicappers ranked him no better than third or fourth among historians of his generation. One student familiar with the department at this time remembers that "many on the Harvard faculty treated Freidel badly because they didn't think he was as smart as they were." For his part, Lasch seemed never to lack confidence while in the East. Yet after watching Cambridge work on some of his more sensitive classmates, he came to the following conclusion: "Insecurity [is] often found in people who are from the Midwest but seem ashamed to admit it."[7]

After graduating in 1954, Lasch headed to Columbia University, where again he encountered a stellar constellation of academic stars. Among the most influential were William Leuchtenburg ("an enormously devoted teacher"), David Donald ("very rigorous, very professional"), and Richard Hofstadter ("his ruthless but gentle criticism . . . taught me a lot"). In many respects, however, the chilly academic climate at Columbia disappointed Lasch. "I had expected graduate school to be a continuation of the exciting intellectual life that we were leading as undergraduates. It was nothing of the kind." Characterizing his doctoral training as "heavily professional," he got on with the lonely business of becoming an historian. After a year at Morningside, he took successive jobs at Williams College and

Roosevelt University in Chicago while searching for a dissertation topic ("Allan Nevins wanted me to write on the logging industry of the Pacific Northwest. . . . I didn't touch that").[8] Finally, Lasch discovered a subject that combined contemporary intellectual and political history and led to his first book—*The American Liberals and the Russian Revolution* (1962).

Described by its author as "a study of ideas more than of men and movements," the work critically assessed the Wilsonian generation's plans to reshape the world in accord with its post-Victorian notions of progress. Importantly, it prefaced Lasch's career-long conversation with liberalism and its legacy. As a twenty-year-old undergraduate, he had mourned Adlai Stevenson's 1952 defeat as the end of a great political era: "For me the hardest thing to realize is that the Democrats will no longer be in the White House, that the long journey is at last finished, that the last of the New Dealers are passing from the scene." But as a thirty-year-old historian, he was far more skeptical about the naked idealism that animated reform politics. "Liberalism in America," his revised dissertation observed, "no less than communism in Russia, has always been a messianic creed, which staked everything on the ultimate triumph of liberalism throughout the world."[9]

Lasch's growing disenchantment with the liberal tradition sprang from a number of sources. Most important, he sensed that the New Deal coalition of the 1930s had matured into a party dominated by elites and that the series of postwar foreign policy alarms associated with the influential "realist" school—punctuated by the recent Cuban Missile Crisis—could be traced to a torpid political culture. Heartened by Stevenson's "uncommon mind" and seduced by John Kennedy's wit, charisma, and style, American thinkers, Lasch argued, had too easily accepted the welfare-warfare state as a permanent fixture in national life.[10]

By the early 1960s, the co-opting of supposedly detached social critics into a "power elite" struck Lasch as a problem worth exploring. Kennedy had surrounded himself with the "best and the brightest" of his generation, while Johnson's landslide victory in 1964 and subsequent reliance on narrowly trained specialists to construct a Great Society and manage a war in Vietnam marked the high tide of the action-intellectual. Lasch was not impressed. In return for presidential pats on the back, the professors had failed, he argued, to offer reflective and searching criticism. They became, rather, invested in the programs and policies that in some sense bore their imprint.

Complicitous intellectuals swallowed their dissent. The postwar cosmopolitans agreed on a few key articles of faith: the new Keynesian capitalism worked, nation-building advanced the country's cold war agenda, and the American political system operated in an unusually democratic manner. Lasch questioned all of these suppositions. He questioned too the intellectuals who swore by this thin tissue of truths. The more he thought about the expert culture of his own day, the more interested he became in its origins and evolution. The result was Lasch's first major work.

The New Radicalism in America: The Intellectual as a Social Type appeared in 1965. More than a survey of influential or eccentric thinkers, it stands as a bracing critique of twentieth-century liberalism's efforts to accrue power, govern the lower classes, and transform the culture. The Columbia School had emphasized the "suffering" of gifted thinkers under the rule of the par-venus, but Lasch argued just the opposite. The intellectuals, he countered, coveted a "sense of separateness" and entitlement as essential to their ef-forts to restructure society in their image. And they had enjoyed consider-able success. Within a generation the thinking class rose from the ranks of bohemian marginality to ingratiate itself firmly within the nation's power structure. It advised the government and the corporations and made its expertise available for the maintenance of the American consensus. Its ef-forts were now a matter of record, and Lasch weighed in. He decried the evolution of 1930s radicalism to 1950s liberalism as a disappointing feature in intellectual life. With the help of gifted minds, a cold war state resistant to fundamental change had failed to follow up on the promise of the early New Deal. Poverty, racial divisions, and war still threatened the nation. Lasch had given liberalism no quarter.

The old guard took note. In an approving review, Alfred Kazin accepted with equanimity the generational comeuppance implicit in the book.

> I have been awaiting for some time a rejoinder to the veterans of the Thir-ties by a young historian born in the Thirties—and here it is, cool as you please. . . . It was about time that someone made a categorical definition of the stake that so many intellectuals now have in the inequalities of our society, in the perpetuation of the cold war, in the often trivial but pro-tected differentiation of professional functions; about time that someone held the mirror up to American intellectuals and showed us the extent to which we are implicated in our wars as in our prosperity.

Richard Hofstadter—who also valued *The New Radicalism* and provided a rare blurb for it—good-naturedly chided Lasch for bearing down par-ticularly hard on Manhattan's thinking class. Lasch, at this time an as-sociate professor at the University of Iowa, replied playfully: "It hurts to be accused of lining up with the anti–New York feeling. I admit it has become a fashionable attitude. . . . I didn't mean to make invidious comparisons between New York intellectuals and the intellectuals of Dubuque."[11]

Arthur Schlesinger Jr., on the other hand, was in no mood to play. The former Stevenson speechwriter and special assistant to President Kennedy proved to be an inviting target for Lasch, who described him in *The New Radicalism* as "the most representative spokesman of the new liberal orthodoxy." Combining a "career as a historian and as a Democratic polemicist," Schlesinger typified in Lasch's mind the dangers of the intellectual in politics. His shots apparently hit the mark. "You will be interested to know that a smart aleck Kid named Christopher Lasch exposes us both in a new book," the aggrieved Schlesinger apprised Richard Rovere. "I wish you would review it." In fact, Schlesinger performed the autopsy himself. In the pages of the London *Sunday Times* he described the monograph as "poor and pretentious" and accused its author of romanticizing the "democratic" radicalism of the 1930s while excoriating the "elitist" radicalism practiced by the progressive and postwar generations.[12] Certainly the book touched a nerve. Liberals had always presumed that an "irrational" radical Right threatened their hard-won political stationing—they were its potential victims. Yet Lasch's study offered a completely different appraisal. The coming eclipse of men like Schlesinger, it argued, followed years of aggressive, tradition-upending social engineering on the part of high liberalism. The average American had been the real victim.

In the opening pages of his book, Lasch described the new radicalism as a reaction to "the estrangement of intellectuals, as a class, from the dominant values of American culture." These values, emblematic of the small towns that produced Hull House founder Jane Addams (Freeport, IL), rested on the cultural power of Protestantism, laissez faire, and conventional social and sexual relations. Once unquestioned, their dominance did not last. By the 1890s the rise of an urban-ethnic dynamic led to sharp demographic shifts in American life celebrated by Greenwich Village modernists and their allies. In Lasch's words, "the exhaustion of the cultural tradition of the middle class" gave birth to the new radicalism.[13]

Looking to slip a prudish era's leash, progressives succeeded principally in eroding conventional moral constraints against commercial activity. The century's early feminists may have hoped to leave as their legacy advanced ideas about sexuality and domestic relations, Lasch argued, but their greatest—if unintended—accomplishment was the emancipation of the market. Economic rights were democratized, but rather than winning equality in gender relations, women had more significantly contributed to the expansion of an amoral capitalism. In the struggle between the sexes,

Lasch contended, the industrial system had clearly won. Hopes for social uplift through the promotion of female power collapsed before the blunt logic of the market: "the new woman began to acquire the soul of a clerk."[14]

Drawing up a fairly extensive indictment, Lasch provided numerous other examples of the progressive assault on the middle-class family. Evolution, the new psychology, child-centered education, and scientific management applied further pressures to a crumbling Puritan artifice. An army of new social theorists were on hand to give "professional" assurances that the disappearance of the old discipline need not lead to chaos and anarchy. And indeed it did not, Lasch contended, but for far different reasons than the radicals had imagined. The Hull-House trade schools, he pointed out, ably prepared young women for manufacturing work, while Dewey's educational reforms had at their heart "the socialization of the individual, not only in the general sense of adapting him to the life customs of the group into which he was born but more specifically in the sense of eliminating the selfish ambitions that presumably generated social conflict." In other words, the family, the church, and the neighborhood no longer held the moral high ground—this coveted terrain belonged now to social architects and the owners of machines.[15]

Sensitive to the social engineering of his own day—evident in the Columbia School's claims that critics of the new liberalism suffered from "status anxiety"—Lasch caught the faint but unmistakable aroma of authoritarianism in the new radicalism. "Totalitarianism was hardly the goal to which American progressives were even unconsciously striving. But the manipulative note was rarely absent from their writing: the insistence that men could best be controlled and directed not by the old, crude method of force but by 'education' in its broadest sense."[16]

Lasch contemporized his critique of "the intellectual as a social type" to address the current state of highbrow-lowbrow relations. In a final, cutting chapter, "The Anti-intellectualism of the Intellectuals," he articulated his aversion to Kennedy-era elitism by pointedly responding to Hofstadter's latest book, *Anti-intellectualism in American Life* (1963). A sweeping reevaluation of American democracy, it won its author a Pulitzer yet proved, in its unsympathetic handling of popular education, religion, and culture, to be a controversial and divisive work. As Lasch later recalled,

> The last chapter came to me only at the end, as I tried to figure out how to bring all the stuff together. By that time I had begun to read Hofstadter's books very seriously. Especially his *Anti-Intellectualism in American Life*. I was more and more dissatisfied with his approach to the problem and

I think that the title to my last chapter was in some ways a deliberate
provocation [directed at him]. It was written at a time when I was seeing
quite a lot of him because he was in England the same year and we came
back on the boat together. And then almost immediately we attended a
conference on Cape Cod, something about education. I remember getting into a number of arguments with him.[17]

If Hofstadter portrayed America's mandarins as prisoners of popular en-
thusiasms, Lasch claimed that it was intellectuals themselves who violated
the spirit of a pure idea culture. And he had a rather long and persuasive list
of offenses. The cult of containment simplified a complex cold war into a
flat "choose the West" mantra; college professors enthusiastically filled positions in a national security state known to have trafficked in secret wars
and overthrown foreign governments; Keynesian capitalism got a free pass
from social and political thinkers determined to defend the "free enterprise" system against Soviet "totalitarianism."[18]

While Hofstadter hoped to see the more distinguished universities
serve as outposts impervious to the popular will (the proverbial ivory
tower), Lasch indicted higher education for making a separate peace with
the consumer–cold war state. Both business and government, he pointed
out, relied upon the country's schools to train the engineers, managers, and
technicians necessary to their enterprises' survival. An assembly-line approach to academic life led to a constricting specialization in any number
of industrially friendly disciplines. "To the extent to which [the 'multiversities'] came to depend for support on the government and on the private
foundations," he wrote, "they lost their character as centers of independent
learning and critical thought and were swallowed up in the network of the
'national purpose.'"[19]

Three years after Lasch's book appeared, Columbia University—
Hofstadter's long-time academic home—erupted in a campuswide protest
that briefly shut the school down. The students felt, among other complaints, that Columbia had ceased to be "a center of independent learning"
because of its ties to a Department of Defense then prosecuting a long,
bloody, and unpopular war in Vietnam.

One might read *The New American Radicalism* as a cautionary tale of the
intellectuals' indiscretion. Eager (as an "embattled" minority) to evade the
cultural authority of the masses, the thinking class found relief in the arms
of the capitalists, the government, and the military—power structures that
knew how to *use* if not exactly appreciate the full range of its mental gifts.
But if Lasch anticipated the end days of the liberal intelligentsia, he kept

a calculated distance from its youthful opponents. A few months after his book appeared, he turned down a full professorship at the University of Wisconsin in favor of a post at Northwestern. Madison's reputation for student radicalism influenced his decision. "Northwestern doesn't yet have much of a loony Left," he wrote his parents at the time. "I think the loony Left at Madison may be one reason why William Appleman Williams is reportedly leaving. Northwestern's reputed conservatism, apathy, and lack of political activities turns out to be a blessing in disguise, now that so many student activists seem to have taken leave of their senses. Our campus is not graced with the likes of the Du Bois club, the Progressive Labor party, the Wobblies, Maoists, Guevaristas, etc. We don't even seem to have any Stalinists."[20]

Lasch's fragile relationship with the Left included what he regarded as the "loony"—or at least self-destructive—wing of academe. At the 1969 meeting of the American Historical Association, he sat in attendance while, as he put it, "the so-called radical caucus, although claiming to speak for the left in general, alienated practically everybody and had to abandon its ambitious plans to reform the AHA, force it to meet in Cuba (sic) until the war ends, commit the AHA to support 'guerrilla history,' etc. etc." At the business meeting, the radicals unveiled a two-pronged strategy: electing New Left candidate Staughton Lynd to the association's presidency and passing a resolution condemning U.S. involvement in Vietnam. Neither happened. "I had opposed anything to do with the caucus on the grounds that it was strictly factional," Lasch noted, "but at the same time had opposed making any open fight against them for the edification of the reactionaries, who would have liked nothing better than to see radicals attacking radicals. It seemed to me that the 'radicals' would quickly reveal their own absurdity if left to themselves. This proved to be an accurate estimate."[21]

Thinking about his country's historically uneven reaction to reform encouraged Lasch to pen a number of essays on the topic—these he compiled in *The Agony of the American Left*, a study that appeared the same year as the AHA meltdown. Lasch was clearly hoping to make sense of radicalism present by exploring radicalism past. He noticed, for example, strong connections between marginalized industrial-era protesters—Populists, migrant workers, factory laborers—and a contemporary postindustrial student movement alienated to the bone. According to Lasch, the central problem—or agony—of the Left involved a depressing lack of historical memory. While students, hippies, and black nationalists looked all over the world for radical inspiration—from Che to China—they had largely forgotten the indigenous anticapitalist traditions in America. The New Left would stand a far greater chance of advancing its programs, Lasch believed, if it abandoned the politics of cultural estrangement and committed itself to recovering the democratic principles that had fortified its radical ancestors. He shed in the process no tears for a fallen, discredited liberalism— "it is clearer than ever that radicalism is the only long-term hope for America"—and saw hope only in the Left—but one that was wise, rooted, and pragmatic. Reflecting on his own anticapitalist / cultural conservative politics, he called for "decentralization, local control, and a generally anti-bureaucratic outlook. . . . These values are the heart of radicalism."[22]

The 1969 publication of *Agony* coincided with Lasch's decision to leave Northwestern. Maybe Madison was a bit "loony," but it was never dull— and Lasch had grown bored with his suburban colleagues. "I'm not exactly overjoyed at the prospect of staying here at the kiddie corner, where the department is largely controlled by the bag-lunch and basketball set—a more obnoxious collection of young fogeys would be hard to find." Successfully recruited by the University of Rochester's Eugene Genovese, Lasch hoped to be part of a dynamic program in cultural history informed by a critical leftist perspective. His essays on the 1960s now published, and with a new decade looming, it was time to move on. "In my case," he informed his parents, "the occasion seems to call for an abandonment of political activities and occasional political writing and an effort to get down to fundamentals, and I hope to provide myself with an interval of study and reflection undistracted by political alarums and excuses." The following month he wrote of his future plans with less conviction to William Appleman Williams, a fellow sixties refugee who had recently secured his own retreat to the Oregon coast. "I seem to have come to some sort of dead end in my . . . work and am uncertain about what direction to take."[23]

The 1970s proved to be the most intellectually fertile period of Lasch's life. Tired of the sixties maelstrom, he anticipated a backing away from political affairs. Yet his scholarship had not so much abandoned its critical engagement with ideology as discovered new interpretive tools with which to assess the American Century monolith. Intensive reading in the behavioral sciences provided Lasch with fresh approaches to dissecting the liberal—now fast becoming postliberal—state. Unlike Hofstadter's assigning of social-psychological categories to cast doubt on democracy, Lasch utilized the soft sciences for frankly populistic purposes. Arranging a peculiar but potent mix of Marxism, Freudianism, and populism, he offered a compelling—and vaguely conspiratorial—critique of late twentieth-century American life. The "helping professions" and the plutocrats elevated the culture beyond older social and economic restraints into a brave new world of hyperindividualism and hypercapitalism—*The Winter of Our Discontent* surrendered before *The Fountainhead.*

Considering his Nebraska origins, Lasch wrote within a long and rich anticosmopolitan tradition. In the 1830s, a culture-changing Market Revolution had ruptured older forms of community, and the Tennessee nabob Andrew Jackson told the American public to blame the "monster" National Bank—which he summarily vetoed out of existence. Later, William Jennings Bryan thrice captured the presidential nomination of the Democratic Party by identifying railroad magnates, market middlemen, and crooked politicians as the root of all evil. And still later, Charles Beard blamed the bicoastal "big navy boys" for drawing America into World War II. Now came Lasch, lingering in this sketchy borderland of "us vs. them." In a trilogy critical of the therapeutic state—*Haven in a Heartless World* (1977), *The Culture of Narcissism* (1979), and *The Minimal Self* (1984)—he called for a revitalization of the more productive and family-affirming aspects of a bourgeois civilization then teetering on irrelevancy. Much to the surprise of intellectuals, Lasch, the left-leaning *bete noir* of sixties liberals, emerged in the 1970s as a powerful voice for a set of traditional social codes embraced by the Right.

Lasch remembered *Haven* as "the most difficult book that I ever wrote." Conceived as a preface to a larger historical study of the family, the manuscript progressed instead into an unforgiving account of the expert culture's war on "family values." Prior to publication, its author steeled himself for a rocky reception, writing to a colleague that his earlier efforts in articles and think pieces to highlight the positive aspects of bourgeois life—its resistance to anomie, rejection of the more cutthroat byways of laissez faire, and respect for the family as the primary unit for passing along moral principles—had been misunderstood: "Many readers of the things I've written about the family seem to think I'm calling for a revival of patriarchal authority." Certainly some of Lasch's statements on the women's movement gave that impression. "The trouble with the feminist program," he wrote in *Haven*, "is not that economic self-sufficiency for women is an unworthy goal but that its realization under existing economic conditions would undermine equally important values associated with the family." The proliferation of the day-care culture, combined, he argued, with the dual-income temptations of a "live for the moment" lifestyle, shortchanged the nation's children. But Lasch wasn't interested in badgering feminists, and he made it clear that capitalism stood as the real culprit of antifamilyism in America. Denouncing "the relentless demands of the job market," he counseled his readers to "ask how work can be reorganized—humanized—so as to make it possible for women to compete economically with men without sacrificing their families or even the very hope of a family."[24] *Haven's* defense of the household—rejected by much of the Left as an apology for patriarchy—won the support of an emerging cultural right that ignored the anticorporate implications it clearly advanced.

Interestingly, the old opposition between conflict and consensus that shaped much of the century's historiography made its way into *Haven*. Lasch noted that Functionalism, the dominant postwar school of sociology associated with Harvard's Talcott Parsons, provided a wide range of theories that justified the therapeutic professions' invasion of the nuclear family. Briefly, Functionalists argued that traditional community and cultural customs no longer compelled obedience in America; rather, numerous large, elite, and bureaucratic centers of socialization—justice system, national political parties, industry—served or functioned as civilization's chief acculturating components. Contextually, the heyday of Functionalism overlapped with and sustained the 1950s social and economic stasis. And this unwise investment in a defensive liberalism prefaced its fall. Incapable of accounting for the poverty, protests, and swift upswing in social change that distinguished the 1960s, Functionalism's stock collapsed in the academy. Lasch rejected Parsons's efforts to bring family life under the purview of the behavioral sciences and saw something ominous in the big academic machine that he had built at Cambridge. "When Talcott Parsons and his colleagues set up the Department of Social Relations at Harvard in 1950, they institutionalized the dominant drives in American social science: its ambition to displace the humanities as the center of the academic curriculum, its heady sense of itself as an important component (and beneficiary) of the welfare state, its crusading zeal to harmonize the world" by combining sociology, psychology, and anthropology.[25]

According to Lasch, Parsons's pioneering efforts in the behavioral sciences were part of a broader historical movement toward increased social centralization. During America's industrial revolution, he noted, production had migrated from the home to the factory, where various tools—or panoptics—of managerial surveillance gave the capitalists once unimaginable control over their workers. Shortly thereafter, the time and motion studies of the owners diminished traditional craft skills while imposing a new ethic of effort on artisans. Its domination of the external laboring life complete, it was only a matter of time, Lasch argued, before the industrial class invaded the private sphere of its employees, seeking even broader and more intimate means of management. The rise in importance of "doctors, psychiatrists, teachers, child guidance experts, officers of the juvenile courts, and other specialists" intruded upon the once sacred sovereignty of the family.[26]

Following World War II, progressive paternalism gave way to liberal paternalism. The old rugged individualism seemed out of place in a "co-operative" culture of corporations and unions. The rise of Nazism abroad and McCarthyism at home, moreover, encouraged many in the American social scientific community to see—particularly among elements of the Far Right—an "authoritarian personality" wedded to local cultures, lore, and traditions that stood in the way of an enlightened, prejudice-free future. Again, the state responded by seeking to incorporate and homogenize public life, whether through a nationalized war on poverty, support for civil rights, or determination to build a "great society."

One might have expected the "revolutionary" leaders of the 1960s—the rebel critics of the military-industrial complex—to soundly denounce the centralization of the American state. Not so, Lasch contended. In its quest for "alternative lifestyles," the New Left repeated the progressive and liberal preference for rejecting localized sources of authority. Critical of the repressive attitudes of mainstream Americans, the counterculture condoned practices of sexual liberation—homosexuality, multiple partners, uncommitted coupling—that recalled Progressive-era social experimentation at the cost of more traditional, "loving," and lasting relationships. And in its war on monogamy, its "search for sex without emotion," the new morality repeated progressivism's alliance with a capitalism indifferent to the inner life. Lasch closed this pessimistic book with a grim pronouncement that revealed his debt to the iconic French philosopher of social institutions, Michel Foucault: "Today the state controls not merely the individual's body but as much of his spirit as it can preempt; not merely his outer but his inner life as well; not merely the public realm but the darkest corners of private life, formerly inaccessible to political domination."[27]

Not everyone bought his argument. Marshall Berman insisted in the *New York Times Book Review* that *Haven* expressed "a generalized hatred for modern life," a hatred that curiously, in light of Lasch's leftist credentials, had much "in common . . . with the radical right." If this appraisal exaggerated the book's relationship to ultraconservatism, David Brion Davis more cogently described its author's current ideological leanings. "Lasch writes like a neo-Populist who has merely substituted social scientists and the 'helping professions' for Wall Street bankers and railroad magnates. . . . If Lasch stops short of indulging in fantasies of conspiracy, which in this case would veer perilously close to those of the extreme right, he does obscurely equate his homogenized enemy with the 'state,' with 'capitalists,' and with the 'same forces' for most of the misery of modern Americans."[28]

One is (lightly) reminded in these sharp assessments of Charles Beard's fate. Like Lasch, Beard had once been the darling of reform-minded intellectuals, only to be recast as a conservative (and in some quarters a crank). Beard claimed that big business sought liberation and self-expression in the open door. Lasch believed that the therapeutic state aimed to free "people from old constrictions only to expose them to more subtle forms of control." Lasch's earlier criticisms of liberalism had won a respectful hearing within the academy, but many intellectuals soured on his post-1960s work for its conservative implications. This mattered little to Lasch. By this point, he later recalled, "I had in a sense liberated myself from the professionalism I had learned at Columbia. It had never ceased to be part of my mental equipment, but I wasn't any longer under any obligation to impress a body of historians." Like Beard, Thorstein Veblen, and the sociologist Willard Wallace—fellow middle-western thinkers who also cut against the dominant intellectual trends of their times—Lasch cultivated a healthy sense of marginality that informed his work.[29]

Ironic, then, that his ideas should suddenly enter the mainstream. Lasch's surprise 1979 best seller, *The Culture of Narcissism,* captured the negative zeitgeist that followed the failed social crusades of the 1960s. A bleak book (once tentatively titled *Life without a Future*), it recorded the psychological passage of American society from the puritanical and paternalistic to the ego-ridden and ultraindividualistic. The narcissist, Lasch argued, constituted a new cultural spirit rising from the ashes of the old bourgeois prerogatives once central to Western civilization. The ascent of multinational corporations, the emergence of megabureaucratic welfare states, the decolonization of the third world, and a series of horrifically destructive global wars had bled the West of its faith in competitive (rather than managerial) capitalism, and even in its own superiority. Lasch took it all in. "This book," he wrote, "describes a way of life that is dying." In place of the "economic man" that had dominated Euro-America since the eighteenth century—a shorthand for the explosive growth of a dynamic, vibrant Atlantic world economy—stood the "psychological man," symbol of the new narcissist's anxious, uncertain social interactions. Freedom from sexual taboos "brings him no sexual peace," surplus income leads him to crave "immediate gratification," and the toleration he prizes as a symbol of his "liberation" from old dogmas ("I'm O.K., you're O.K.") fails to provide a meaningful philosophy of life.[30]

Out with the old Victorianism, Lasch argued, went traditional conceptions of love, marriage, and child rearing. The church, too, had seen its authority recede, cashiered by a mixture of medicine, therapy, and psychiatry that rejected the stern trinity of sin, guilt, and sacrifice. A new cultural investment in reassurance appeared on the horizon—remedies committed to the rejection of aging, ill-health, unattractiveness, and the psychological "anguish" that accompanies each. Cultural authority had shifted, in other words, from achievable communal needs and standards to often unrealistic and frequently superficial individual preferences. The trivial, restless, and unfulfilling lives of Americans fell under Lasch's critical gaze as he counseled a return to more conventional patterns of living:

> The best defenses against the terrors of existence are the homely comforts of love, work, and family life, which connect us to a world that is independent of our wishes yet responsible to our needs. It is through love and work, as Freud noted in a characteristically pungent remark, that we exchange crippling emotional conflict for ordinary unhappiness. Love and work enable each of us to explore a small corner of the world and to come to accept it on its own terms. But our society tends either to devalue small comforts or to expect too much of them. Our standards of "creative, meaningful work" are too exalted to survive disappointment. Our ideal of "true romance" puts an impossible burden on personal relationships. We demand too much of life, too little of ourselves.[31]

Lasch's depressing book about a "dying" way of life, a hard-hitting jeremiad that conceded virtually nothing to the "superficial" lifestyles of Americans, made its author into a minor public celebrity. Imagine Cotton Mather clambering up the best-seller list. Within two months of *Narcissism*'s release, the paperback rights were auctioned to Warner Publications and Lasch made a quick $84,000 off the deal. Northwestern hoped to lure this suddenly hot property back to Chicago, but Rochester came through with an attractive package—an endowed chair and a salary hike from $37,000 to $58,000.[32]

All this, and *People* magazine too. The 9 July 1979 copy—featuring a toothy, cowgirl-hatted Olivia Newton John in ebullient "Roller Mania" cover pose—included an interview with Lasch accompanied by a photo spread of his family in their backyard. He seized the opportunity to poke at the sixties radicals whose protests he had always regarded as indulgent and self-centered. "It is clear that the counterculture celebrated many of the values of narcissism—living for the moment, immediate gratification, and opposition to the work ethic. What is remarkable is the ease with which society co-opted the counterculture. What yesterday were gestures of re-

Figure 6. Postwar Populist: Christopher Lasch. Courtesy of the Department of
Rare Books and Special Collections, University of Rochester Library.

bellion and protest are today the stock-in-trade of advertising." Love beads and tie dyes had come to Kmart. And how, *People* wanted to know, had Lasch himself managed to sidestep the temptations of a narcissistic society? "Maybe," he replied, falling back on the ancient magic of the frontier, "I have a stable life and family because we live here in the provinces."[33]

Lasch seems not to have noticed the incongruity of appearing in a magazine that so nicely epitomized the culture of narcissism he diagnosed. Then again, that summer of 1979 was thick with irony for *Narcissism*'s author. Shortly after the book's appearance he received an invitation ("out of the blue") to dine with President Jimmy Carter. Having admonished the critical class in *The New Radicalism* for falling in love with power—"what the intellectuals admired in Kennedy was his youth, his good looks, his cultivation, his cosmopolitanism, his savoir faire"—Lasch sweated over the situation: "I wasn't sure whether I should even be there."[34] Meeting in the Diplomatic Reception Room, he and a small group that included Bill Moyers, Daniel Bell, Jesse Jackson, and Haynes Johnson took an elevator to the Carters' second-floor living area, where the president and first lady joined them for drinks on the Truman balcony. "A frugal meal consisting of a crabmeat-oyster salad, lamb chops, asparagus, and ice cream" followed. The evening concluded with an earnest if uneven discussion of what ailed the country. Obviously Carter and his aides were moving haltingly toward a redefinition of the national condition from postwar affluence to seventies sacrifice. The theme they took from the evening—a "crisis of confidence"—became a catchphrase for a tough decade. Lasch reported to his parents what transpired:

> The more formal part of the discussion began with some polls submitted . . . showing a sharp rise, since 1977, of pessimism about the country's future and about the personal prospects for individuals; of cynicism about politics and politicians; and of lack of interest in public issues. Perhaps this is where my book is thought to come in; perhaps it is read as an argument to the effect that people are too wrapped up in selfish concerns to pay any attention to politics, and a plea for more altruistic public spirit. Other people have read or misread the book in this way; but it seems to me that the attitudes reflected in the polls show a fairly realistic awareness of the economic prospects facing the country, of the failure of public policy to come to grips with the situation, of the absence of real political choices, and of the powerlessness of the ordinary citizen.[35]

Lasch resisted the easy temptation to blame "the people" for losing confidence in the nation's future. He counseled Carter that ordinary Americans were repeatedly asked to sacrifice in the 1970s—to use less gas and electricity, turn thermostats down, carpool or abstain from unnecessary driving trips—while the corporate sector continued to rake in the dollars. Hitting a populist note, Lasch put the matter this way: "The country still doesn't even believe an energy crisis exists. Does this have anything to do with the fact that the oil companies are making huge profits? or that when citizens conserve fuel in response to urgent executive demands, the utility companies raise their rates because of insufficient demand?" While conceding that Carter was "clearly a decent, honorable, and intelligent man," Lasch believed that neither he nor his administration grasped a fundamental point so clear to him—big business was in the saddle and running roughshod over the American dream. "The President does not seem terribly receptive to these suggestions."[36]

A few days after, as Lasch put it to Bell, "our curious evening at the White House," he directed a follow-up letter to Jody Powell, the president's press secretary, emphasizing the need for a revived public culture capable of keeping corporate power and influence in check.

> The polls that constituted the starting-point of our discussion show a profound reversal of values: decline of the work ethic, rising hedonism, lack of faith in the future, a desire to enjoy life in the present, political indifference and cynicism. It is important to recognize that this reorientation of values, even though it has taken a quantum leap in the late seventies, did not occur overnight. It goes back at least to the twenties, when American industry adopted two principles that have guided it ever since. Assembly-line manufacture destroyed craft skills and deprived workers of any responsibility for the design of production. Meanwhile new techniques of mass marketing and promotion broke down old habits of thrift and hard work, deliberately fostered a hedonistic mentality, and advertised the consumption of commodities as a cure-all for every form of discontent. In effect, industry held out the compensatory utopia of consumption to people who could no longer take pride and pleasure in their work.[37]

As the 1970s came to a close, Lasch grew increasingly interested in exploring possibilities for society-wide resistance to the therapeutic state and the "utopia of consumption" it promised. To do that, he commenced a wide and searching study of the American political tradition for native forms of opposition to the powerful economic and cultural forces then in command. This quest preoccupied him in the final years of his life.

Rereading *The Authoritarian Personality* in the early 1980s crystallized in Lasch's mind the risk of applying imported ideas to the American scene. Briefly, an eclectic group of émigré German intellectuals affiliated with the University of Frankfurt had creatively—if cavalierly—employed philosophy, neo-Marxism, and social research to critically dissect contemporary Western cultural and political mores. Their portrait of McCarthy-era America as a land teeming with quasi-fascist, authoritarian personality types was frightening. This unfriendly view earned not a few adherents among U.S. professors laboring in a university system that felt itself under siege during those tense loyalty-oath days. Now, thirty years later, Lasch had come to see the Frankfurt School as an antidemocratic force in modern thought. Its leading lights—including Theodor Adorno and Herbert Marcuse—had had an impact on the liberal Columbia School and later the student movement, evidence enough for Lasch of their pernicious influence. Consequently, he dropped the Marxian-Freudian framework once central to his work. He cast about for an indigenous tradition of social criticism upon which to build a fresh politics. Unsurprisingly, he summarily dismissed the Left. In the 1960s it had succumbed, he argued, to its own excesses. Inordinately infatuated with the celebrity of protest, committed to an extreme version of personal rights, and intolerant of the "squares" who refused to join them on the Haight-Ashbury barricades, radicals had failed to reconcile their protest with deeply held American customs and traditions. "It is clearer than ever," Lasch argued in a 1979 letter, "that the Left has nothing to say to the people who are worried about crime, discontinuity, disruption of the family, collapse of authority, bureaucracy, and the gospel of hedonistic self-indulgence purveyed by the mass media. It writes off concerns about these issues as evidence of the proto-fascist mentality of the working class, and then wonders why the working class remains unmoved by radical appeals."[38]

Nor did Lasch look to the Right. He rejected out of hand the neo–robber-baron ethics that accompanied the by turns free market, libertarian, and prosperity theology mantra of Reagan Republicanism. In an extended correspondence with the paleoconservative Paul Gottfried, Lasch explained his position:

> Conservatism is just as deeply compromised by its enthusiasm for capitalism, it seems to me, as the left is compromised by its enthusiasm for the Enlightenment project of building a whole new world from scratch. I can't see much value in the label. The fact is that neither the left nor the right speaks to the issues that really matter. I've just been reading John

Judis's biography of Buckley, which contains many examples of the conservative movement's tendency to identify the fate of "Western civilization" with the fortunes of capitalism, as if freedom and free enterprise were interchangeable terms. I can't accept this equation.[39]

Gottfried countered that a "managerial state" rather than multinational corporations fashioned the culture; the capitalists had no agenda other than making money, and they denounced or celebrated gay liberation, feminism, and the reconstruction of the family as the cultural pendulum dictated. Unconvinced, Lasch replied to Gottfried that "our culture is dominated by consumerist imperatives. . . . The free market subverts everything conservatives care about, or ought to care about. After a decade of Reaganism, everything is worse than before, and everything is worse not because the managers have inflicted their utopian designs on the rest of us but because old-fashioned capitalist acquisitiveness seems to have made such an unexpected comeback and won such a happy new lease on life."[40]

A great critic of the Reagan years, Lasch ironically found himself anointed a "conservative." But Lasch's conservatism was that of the prairie Populist defending local folkways from the Wall Street money managers who celebrated the Republican deregulatory impulse. Some mistook this position—combining it with Lasch's gruff remarks on feminism and the social-welfare state—as a full-scale swing to the right. He always saw this as a misapplication of his ideas. In 1980, an interviewer queried Lasch on his complicated politics: "Do you see yourself as in some sense a conservative or at least supporting conservative points of view?" Lasch: "I realize . . . that some of the arguments I put forth can be very easily put to conservative purposes. . . . It makes me very uneasy." In correspondence the following year, Lasch reaffirmed his commitment to a pluralistic, populistic radicalism. "Even though I've been critical of the left, I still consider myself in agreement with its basic objectives, and I've tried to make it clear that the underlying cause of our malaise is the power now wielded by undemocratic institutions like the multinational corporation."[41]

But for critics who had read Lasch from the left following *Haven*'s appearance, little in his subsequent work met with their sympathies. This is unfortunate, because many of the scholars engaged in fresh areas of social criticism, including cultural, gender, and postcolonial studies, shared Lasch's dim view of capitalism. In various respects, however, their work struck him as eccentric and exclusive. As defining issues, radical environmentalism, gay and lesbian liberation, and affirmative action failed to win wide support among working-class constituencies. These groups drifted from the FDR liberal center to the Reagan right. If Lasch had had his way, the conversation would have remained focused on economic and political inequality and its impact on the middle and lower middle classes. His critique of the business state shadowed the sharp birth pangs of a service economy, the painful onset of the midwestern Rustbelt, and the Reagan-era budget deficits, savings and loan crisis, and war on the poor. A frustrated Lasch watched throughout the 1980s as liberalism tilted toward irrelevancy and the Right portrayed itself as the executor of a culturally conservative heritage while advancing a culture-transforming capitalism. His response soon arrived.

In *The True and Only Heaven* (1991), Lasch produced a provocative, sprawling, and difficult analysis—a late Populist response to late capitalism. Traditional ideologies, he observed, were dangerously out of touch with reality. The Right's utopian program of ever higher standards of living and the Wilsonian Left's desire to replicate the American cornucopia throughout the world clearly failed to contend with ecological realities and nonrenewable energy resources. Lasch argued for a politics based on moral realism, a skeptical (but not pessimistic) attitude toward improvement, and a canny sense of limitations. To demonstrate the feasibility of this vision, he mined the history of American reform thought. The sheer range of his native populists is impressive if not always precise—Jonathan Edwards and Ralph Waldo Emerson ("latter-day Calvinists without a Calvinist theology"), William James (sensitive to "the morbid side of life"), Reinhold Niebuhr ("he ridiculed liberals for their trust in human nature and the power of good intentions"), and Martin Luther King Jr. ("he never ceased to believe in the reality of sin"), to name but a few.[42]

These seminal and diverse thinkers, theorists, and theologians, Lasch argued, shared an understanding of the tragic and fatalistic qualities of life that cut against the blind optimism typically regarded as something of a national creed. More important, they introduced the conduct of moderation and limitation to the pantheon of American ideas while giving the lie to the concept that Lockean liberalism monopolized the ideological landscape. Following in their wake, Lasch countered that a civic-minded republicanism—evident in the Revolutionary generation's rejection of British materialism—established a legacy of altruism, devotion, and public service much different from that of liberal individualism. "Republicanism condemned self-seeking," Lasch wrote, "when it tempted men to value the external rewards of excellence more highly than the thing itself or to bend the rules governing a given practice to their own immediate advantage. Self-seeking was objectionable because it led men to demand less of themselves than they were capable of achieving, and . . . because in measuring themselves against false standards they also injured others."[43]

Lasch had come late to the republican table. In the 1960s, Harvard historian Bernard Bailyn and his student Gordon Wood popularized the "rediscovery" of republicanism in groundbreaking studies of the Revolutionary era. The following decade, Washington University's J. G. A. Pocock enlarged the synthesis to fit into a broader Atlantic World tradition by tracing the influence of classical republican thought through the Italian Renaissance, Puritan England, and America's founding generation.[44] Lasch carried this legacy of civic paternalism into the modern era, arguing that labor's resistance to industrial proletarianization, and the Populist fight against agrarian proletarianization constituted recent skirmishes in the centuries-long struggle between a harsh liberal individualism and a humane republican communalism.

As the home of both labor and Populism, the lower middle class is clearly the hero in *The True and Only Heaven*. Having gained the least from industrial capitalism, it has the least invested in the capitalist cult of progress. And thus it is for Lasch the nation's best hope for creating political and economic attitudes independent of ever rising and unrealistic expectations.[45] Neither left nor right, after all, had managed to produce a widely accepted or satisfying politics. Each catered to specific elite and undemocratic corporate constituencies. In the wake of their failures, Lasch sought to link traditionally marginalized groups with an intellectually respectable republicanism and reform-minded Protestantism. And that effort in rehabilitation invested his book with a political angle and attitude that brought its author's own politics to the fore. Although he had repeatedly called for a hard-headed assessment of the American commitment to progress, Lasch treated the laboring poor less critically, dubiously declaring their non-consumerist lifestyle more "authentic" than others. He posited, in other words, a stark and divisive choice between a respectable working class and a predatory cosmopolitan class.

As a work of "interior" historiography, we might place *The True and Only Heaven* alongside Beard's *Economic Interpretation of the Constitution*, Williams's *Tragedy of American Diplomacy*, and Curti's *Making of an American Community*. Like Beard, who insisted that his economic approach owed more to native than European (read Marxist) sources, Lasch grounded his work in an indigenous political culture. Like Williams, Lasch saw the capitalist system as a threat to peace and stability. "Our twentieth-century experience of imperial rivalries, international competition for markets, and global wars," he wrote, "makes it hard for us to share the Enlightenment convictions that capitalism would promote world peace."[46] And like Curti in his study of Trempealeau County, Lasch fiercely defended a set of anti-cosmopolitan values that were culturally connected to a populistic middle-western frame of reference.

A brave and immense reclamation project, *The True and Only Heaven* could go only so far in bringing about the populist millennium. In a thoughtful review in the *Journal of American History,* James T. Kloppenberg identified a central problem in the book: "Much as I admire Lasch's ascetic religiosity and his vision of 'small-scale production and political decentralization,' the line of cultural criticism running from Edwards to King is difficult to connect with the historical phenomenon of petty bourgeois populism that has, by Lasch's own admission, 'generated very little in the way of an economic or political theory—its more conspicuous weakness.'" If Lasch failed to recover a consistent populistic intellectual tradition, he had nevertheless produced a major work of intellectual history that pushed beyond conventional concepts of left and right. That he did so in the hopes of recentering American politics on more economically participatory and politically egalitarian principles should be noted as well. A deeply personal study, much the product of its author's historical imagination, selective reconstruction of ideas, and mounting pessimism, it tried too hard to hold the line against "progress." One private critic who had read Lasch's work closely over the years wondered about his next move. "When you become fed up with Populism as you have with everything else," the old progressive Robert Lasch wrote his son, "where will you go?"[47]

There was nowhere else to go. Liberalism, radicalism, and Reaganism had one and all been found wanting by Lasch. He stood comfortably outside the mainstream of American politics, a muckraker on the margins.[48] He was, in other words, right where he wanted to be. In Omaha and Iowa City, Chicago and Rochester, he pursued a vision of public life both rich and rooted in democratic traditions. He fine-tuned a populistic persona that meshed more or less with his cultural tastes and exacting expectations. As defender of the lower middle class, scourge of the therapeutic state, and critic of capitalism, Lasch combined scholarship with social idealism to construct a suggestive if incomplete analysis of what ailed America. Taken as a whole, the earnest, uneven results remain exciting.

EIGHT

New Century,
Old Dreams

Even though I spent 15 years on the East Coast, in a way I never stopped feeling like a midwesterner, and never really felt that I wholly belonged to the peculiar features of northeast elite culture.

WILLIAM CRONON, 2000

The myth of the American monolith churns on. Its trust in an endless age of superpower supremacy remains seductively compelling; we long for the peace and progress it promises. History, no doubt is on *our* side—or so one side of the argument goes. For history tells us too that the imperium has never lacked for discontents. Some—Henry David Thoreau comes to mind—engaged in individual acts of civil disobedience; others—including the sweep of interior intellectuals running from Turner through Lasch—worked within a more collective framework. Among these middlewesterners, a hazy dual identity shaped their scholarship. Insiders to the localist impulses that characterized the old republic, they remained simultaneously outsiders to the metropolitan sway of contemporary life. Their distance from eastern centers of financial, military, and political decision-making offered an angle for instruction, a span of time and miles from which to record the country's uneven advance. Accordingly, they wrote in the spirit of resistance. And they do still. Place rather than personality drives this school—the Turners move on but the movement persists.

Today, *empire* is the culture's catchword, and the old dichotomy between center and periphery has again shaped the debate. Standing on one side are the new (neo) conservatives—believers, like the Wilsonians of old, in the open door's ability to redeem the world. They have received the imprimatur of "realists" like Yale scholar John Lewis Gaddis and the Scottish-born Harvard historian Niall Ferguson, whose book *Colossus: The Rise and Fall of the American Empire* (2004) encourages America's mission as global leviathan. An enlightened hegemon, Ferguson believes, can efficiently direct the flow of goods, capital, and labor around the globe, overthrow tyrannical dictators, and stop local and ethnic conflicts from disintegrating into larger, bloodier affairs. The danger of the American empire, he concludes, rests not in its hypermilitarized threat to home republican rule (a topic he glides over) but rather in the unwillingness of the Superpower's citizens to realize their special destiny—a kind of twenty-first-century white man's burden on the Euphrates.

Despite his ideological leanings, Ferguson has embraced the central theme of the old Wisconsin School: "The United States," he writes, "has always been, functionally if not self-consciously, an empire." To run from this fact, to refuse its historical role in international affairs, he continues, would render the nation "a somewhat dysfunctional entity."[1] The revisionists, of course, believed just the opposite. Civic ailing, they argued, attended the series of global engagements that shrank democracy at home while spreading military and economic power abroad. Tied to a romantic "bread and roses" approach to foreign affairs, William Appleman Williams believed the nation stood a fighting chance of breaking the bond of empire. Its real hope for global good, he concluded, lay in its ability to operate an open, demilitarized democracy at home.

Straddling these poles is the popular critic of American foreign relations Andrew Bacevich. Unlike Williams—a hard oppositionist to the American empire—Bacevich is a soft oppositionist. He is disdainful of liberal internationalism yet recognizes that the unique power, responsibilities, and history of the United States make a global retreat into a Beardian hemispheric fortress impractical, if not impossible. But unlike Ferguson, he does not think either America or the world the better for this. His books are cautionary tales; he writes of a nation imprisoned in an iron maiden of its own making—"the reality that Beard feared has come to pass: like it or not, America today *is* Rome."[2]

Bacevich was born in Normal, Illinois, in 1947; following his father's graduation from medical school, the family moved to Indiana. Unlike the other middle-westerners we have encountered in this book, he stands outside the Wasp consensus: "I am a Roman Catholic and took that Catholicism pretty seriously." In other significant respects he shares with Williams a suggestive overlap of experiences—education in one of the nation's military academies and combat experience in one of the nation's twentieth-century wars. Reared in the shadow of the armed forces (his father served as a lieutenant during the Korean War, his mother worked in the Army Nurse Corps), Bacevich attended West Point. Part of the attraction, he later recalled, involved leaving home: "I was absolutely determined as a midwest-erner to go somewhere 'out east' for school. That seemed like the definition of sophistication, 'out east.'" Bacevich served in Vietnam from the summer of 1970 to the summer of 1971 before the army sent him to Princeton, where he earned a PhD in history. After retiring in 1992 at the rank of colonel, he became an academic. "I knew I wanted to find a career in teaching or writing.... I wanted to be somewhere in that world." He landed a position at Boston University and, consistent with his "vintage" 1950s Roman Ca-tholicism and military background, sought a relationship with the coun-try's more influential conservative periodicals, placing reviews and essays in *Commentary, The Weekly Standard,* and *National Review.*[3]

A self-proclaimed "traditionalist... in the so-called culture war," Bacev-ich soon discovered that his conservative allies held what he considered to be a rather radical position in regard to America's relations with the world. They seemed intent on out-Wilsoning Wilson. That is, they urged Wilson's global plan but untethered it from the cooperative complex of interna-tional leagues and courts envisioned by the twenty-eighth president. They posited in its place an American leviathan free to crusade when and where it wished. "Foreign policy thinking on the right," he explains, "came to be imbued with a sense of hubris and confidence and a belief that we possess the power to transform the world and probably needed to transform the world for our own well-being and that of all of humankind. It was that type of thinking and the way it manifested itself in real policies that set me off in a different direction in terms of foreign policy."[4]

In *American Empire* (2002), Bacevich pays tribute to the Wisconsin School by articulating his impressions of American expansion in a Williams-like turn of phrase: "global openness." More, he writes that "the ongoing evolu-tion of U.S. policy has vindicated [Williams's] analysis of the underpinning of American statecraft." Viewing through a long lens, *American Empire* fol-lows the historiographic path plowed by *President Roosevelt and the Coming of the War* and *The Tragedy of American Diplomacy.* Bacevich's is a smoother and more balanced book, to be sure, but it is no less determined to address imperialism's ill effect on the body America. While his narrative focuses on the 1990s, Bacevich offers more than a recent gloss on foreign affairs: he makes a conscious effort to resurrect the fortunes of the middle-western thinkers who preceded him. Beard and Williams are singled out (though not uncritically) for star treatment. His book, Bacevich writes, "proposes a reconciliation with a couple of patriot-heretics whose long discredited ideas anticipated the snares and pitfalls awaiting a democracy playing the role of sole superpower."[5]

Aside from the acumen of Williams's analysis, Bacevich is drawn to the conservative foundations on which it stands. The "antidote to empire" proposed by *Tragedy*'s author "looked less to revolution than to self-restraint and restoration," he writes approvingly. As a young man Bacevich found himself in opposition to the revisionists whom he regarded as radicals, and for years he accepted the orthodox liberal position on the cold war. Yet over time his appreciation of Williams deepened, and he began to see behind the radical caricature a nuanced and complex thinker misunderstood by his critics. "I came to understand that to label him a 'Leftist' was too simplistic." A patriot, much concerned about his nation's future, Williams revived in the Vietnam era a once honorable call for limiting America's global aspirations. He thus provided Bacevich, a patriot too, with a model of historical criticism to question his country's long military engagement in the oil-rich Near East.[6]

American populism has a tendency to cut in two distinct ideological directions. Preservation of long-standing "conservative cultural values" (think Scopes Monkey Trial Bryan) is often paired with a radical opposition to libertarian free-market ethics (think "Cross of Gold" Bryan). In this latter camp Thomas Frank wields the sharpest pen. A Kansas City native educated at the Universities of Kansas and Chicago, Frank is the founding editor of the cultural-political journal *The Baffler,* which applies Mencken's go-for-the-jugular style to business culture and the culture business. In recent years he has made holy war on the promarket myths popularized by Reaganomics. It's been an uphill battle. In the 1980s, a growing reaction to welfare-state "socialism" gripped America. The nation's economic "malaise," Rustbelt slide, and stagflation standstill were the legacies, critics contended, of Depression-era overreliance on big government's tax-and-spend fixation. Many conservatives saw the 1970s as a corrective decade in which Americans were given a painful reminder that, federal involvement or no, the free market was king. In theoretical terms, this meant classical economics revisited—the withering of centralized planning. In practical terms, taxes were trimmed and social programs shrunk while calls for deregulation and the privatization of social security became more voluble and more respectable. "We who live in free market societies," Reagan said, putting his philosophical stamp on the era, "believe that . . . only when the human spirit is allowed to invent and create, only when individuals are given a personal stake in deciding economic policies and benefiting from their success—only then can societies remain economically alive, dynamic, progressive, and free."[7]

Laissez faire's late twentieth-century defenders—one thinks of the Nobel laureate economist Milton Friedman, the political philosopher Robert Nozick, and the controversial libertarian Charles Murray—share an
interesting utopian perspective worthy of the Keynesians (and Marxists)
of old. They presumed to have identified a system of statecraft and wealth-
making sufficient, under the auspices of a magic market, to eradicate all
of our ills. Problems in education? health care? the environment? Simply
allow the free market to seize upon these issues and privatize them, and
demand will create a steady supply of creative solutions. "By removing the
organization of economic activity from the control of political authority,"
Friedman wrote, "the market eliminates this source of coercive power."[8]

Frank thinks this is all a lot of nonsense. What about the market itself
as a source of coercive power? Can't unfettered capitalism impose its own
logic, expectations, and authority on the public? And can't it, in the form of
monopolies, become as centralized and corruptible as political bodies? In
his book *One Market under God* (2000), Frank takes loving shots at the "extreme capitalism" that has made rock stars out of the market astrologists
who dole out stock tips on television. As the Wisconsin School once contested foreign-policy "realists" who spent much of the nation's goodwill
battling Soviet interests in Guatemala, Iran, and Vietnam, Frank is critical
of a "realist" approach to economics that considers social welfare programs
synonymous with cultural suicide and looks to ride the free-enterprise es-
calator to the true and only heaven. In both cases, the populist position
argues for complexity and nuance while the conservative claim is anchored
in orthodoxy. We know the mixed legacy of the foreign-policy realists; we
await word on its economic doppelgänger.

Frank is not optimistic. He notes that the new economy plays the democracy card (the market will elevate all) even as it moves against popular
calls for higher minimum-wage laws, crackdowns on illegal immigration,
and protection of the environment. More troubling, there seems to be precious little democratic oversight in the system. The defenders of modern
multinational laissez faire, he reminds us, make up no wide or representative cross-section of the nation but consist rather of a fairly small cohort
of elites.

Frank is particularly adept at exposing the new money titans' ersatz populism. In *The Conquest of Cool* (1997), he argues that today's entrepreneurs
fancy themselves capitalist hipsters, different in temperament and taste
from the organization men of old. They ride the bull market for the thrill of
it—outsiders who have beaten "the man" at his own monopoly game. This
blurring of the counterculture with the cultural elite sends out confus-

ing signals. On one hand, the new rich pitch their profits in a Jeffersonian cadence, worshiping at the shrine of the software wonder boy who rose through the lucrative ranks of the Internet revolution (and then bought a professional sports franchise). On the other hand, to identify dotcom billionaires—or any billionaires for that matter—as bona fide populists seems paradoxical to say the least. And even more ironic, the precarious economy that these populist posers rode to wealth is the very same market that over the last quarter-century has created a startling gap between the rich (now often referred to as the "super rich") and poor in America.

Huey Long, an authentic radical voice, never bought into the market populism paradise. When he observed in his autobiography, *Every Man a King*, that money enough existed in America to end poverty, he relied not upon the munificence of laissez faire—certainly not on the bankers whom he blamed for the Depression, or on the Standard Oil executives who tried to impeach the then-governor for raising a special oil tax in Louisiana to pay for school textbooks. He hoped, rather, to create a community of commoners to "limit the size of the big man" and redistribute income along more equitable lines. "There are thousands of share our wealth societies organized in the United States now," he dubiously informed the Senate in 1935. "We want a hundred thousand such societies formed for every nook and corner of this country. . . . Unless . . . we give something to the little man, we can never have a happy or free people. God said so! He ordered it."[9] Rather than wait for the millionaire millennium to come, Long actively used the state government in his native Louisiana to build hospitals and schools, lay down some nine thousand miles of new road, reduce utility rates, and engage in a massive public-works program that included the construction of the Louisiana state capitol—at that time the tallest building in the South. Long's homespun radicalism seems far more deserving of the designation "populist" than the contemporary "people's capitalism" that has appropriated its democratic vibe but sports—in a day of downsizing, outsourcing, and benefitless service jobs—a predatory underside.

This struggle over the definition and distortion of populism runs through Frank's popular 2004 book, *What's the Matter with Kansas?* The title is an ironic reply to William Allen White's famous 1896 editorial of the same name. White, the longtime editor of the *Emporium Gazette*, portrayed his native state as a dying land peopled by "clodhoppers," "harpies," and "old mossback Jacksonians." A Roosevelt Republican in a land of Bryan Democrats, he insisted that his fellow Kansans had been bitten by the Populist bug and gone mad. "We don't need population," he acerbically wrote, "we don't need wealth, we don't need well-dressed men on the streets, we don't need cities on the fertile prairies; you bet we don't! What we are after is the money power. Because we have become poorer and ornerier and meaner than a spavined, distempered mule, we, the people of Kansas, propose to kick; we don't care to build up, we wish to tear down."[10] A century and some later, Frank found that indeed Kansans of his generation had "become poorer" but not, as White had complained, because of their resistance to the fruits of the capitalist system. Rather, he argued, it was precisely their openness to the new economics that failed them.

What's the Matter with Kansas? is particularly adept at drawing out distinctions between the old left-wing populism and its modern right-wing successor. As Frank observes, Bryan's brand of politics responded in the main to an industrial crisis that threatened democracy. The current strain of populism, by contrast, is primarily a cultural movement—opposition to gun control, abortion, and gay rights, combined with a bristling commitment to "family values." The business class, he notes, allies with the evangelicals by cynically playing up moral politics in order to win elections. Who got the better end of this deal? Well, the economic conservatives get tax cuts, deregulation, and laissez faire while the moral conservatives get . . . nothing. At least nothing very tangible. While there may be a kind of therapeutic satisfaction in having the party in power declare allegiance to their cause, at the end of the day abortion is still legal, violence is pervasive on television, and the secularization of American life marches on—even in the red states.

The real culprits in Kansas, Frank claims, are the high priests of laissez faire. Suburban blight? Declining property values? Shrinking social services? Point the finger no further than the author's native Johnson County and its plutocrats with their toxic prosperity theology of one part Jesus, two parts Adam Smith. "The villain that did this to my home state," writes Frank,

> wasn't the Supreme Court or Lyndon Johnson, showering dollars on the poor or putting criminals back on the street. The culprit is the conservatives' beloved free-market capitalism, a system that, at its most unrestrained, has little use for small town merchants or the agricultural system that supported the small towns in the first place. Deregulated capitalism is what has allowed Wal-Mart to crush local businesses across Kansas, and, even more important, what has driven agriculture, the state's raison d'etre, to a state of near collapse.[11]

The moralists have made a deal with the devil.

Frank makes of Kansas a metaphor of American conservatism (and in fact the book appeared in England as *What's the Matter with America?*). The unusual marriage of Christian conservatives (the old Bryan constituency) and the plutocrats (the enemies of Bryan) have galvanized the business sector's efforts to privatize America—with disastrous economic repercussions on a lower middle class that helped put them in power. Reagan emoted a pious heartland sentimentality but reigned over a decade famed for yuppie hedonism, a far-reaching savings and loan scandal, and more children living in poverty at the end of his presidency than at its beginning. Closer to our own day, George W. Bush promised "compassionate conservatism" but leaned toward a compassionless private-enterprise system that revealed his more specific growth goals. This one-sided relationship is thick with irony. Moral conservatives vote for the capitalists to help them preserve "traditional values," yet it is the capitalists that bankroll the movies, the music, and the unofficial Gay Days at Disneyland that antagonize their political partners.

Where in this scrum are the heirs of FDR? To their great discredit, Frank argues, Democrats have in recent decades turned their backs on the "little guy"—once the party's bread and butter. The Democratic Leadership Council, he writes,

> has long been pushing the party to forget blue-collar voters and concentrate instead on recruiting affluent, white-collar professionals who are liberal on social issues. The larger interests that the DLC wants desperately to court are corporations, capable of generating campaign contributions far outweighing anything raised by organized labor. The way to collect the votes—and more important—the money of these coveted constituencies, "New Democrats" think, is to stand rock-solid on, say the pro-choice position while making endless concessions on economic issues, on welfare, NAFTA, Social Security, labor law, privatization, deregulation, and the rest of it. Such Democrats explicitly rule out what they deride as "class warfare" and take great pains to emphasize their friendliness to business interests.[12]

And it is precisely this sense of class conflict/consciousness that Frank would like to see reenter public debate. A jolt of good old-fashioned anger on the part of privatization's discontents might replace the off-center moral arguments that dominate political commentary. Minus a populist revival, a rediscovery of the values that had once informed the interior's principled opposition to the more extreme proposals of the coastal capitalists, Frank has little hope. "As you cast your eyes back over this vanished Midwest, this landscape of lost brotherhood and forgotten pride, you can't help but wonder how much farther it's all going to go."[13]

It seems appropriate to conclude this book, focused as it is on the impact of place on the historical imagination, by exploring the work of William Cronon. Reared in an academic family (the son of David Cronon—PhD, historian, chair, and dean all at Wisconsin), he absorbed Madison lore at the dinner table. Its impress can be traced among the parcel of provocative and transformative books and essays he has authored in the fields of western and environmental history. His work and its very personal underpinnings reinforce the notion that it matters where historians come from, particularly so when they openly identify with a specific regional tradition or way of looking at the world.

Born in New Haven in 1954, Bill Cronon moved to Madison in 1962. This was something of a cross-generational returning. "My families on both sides actually go back in Wisconsin to the middle of the nineteenth century," Cronon explains, "so there are very deep roots." Closer to the surface, living with a scholar literally in residence may have suggested certain professional possibilities: "My father's book-lined study, and the historical research and writing he did in it, is undoubtedly one of the most powerfully evocative memories of my childhood."[14]

Following high school, Cronon attended Wisconsin, his first and only choice. Dropping out early in his sophomore year, he worked at the university bookstore while laboring on a novel. Finding the experience "exhausting," he dropped back in, reasoning that a career in the academy offered a lifestyle conducive to writing. He majored in English—briefly. "As late as my junior year," Cronon smiles, "if you told me I was going to become an American historian like my father, I would have told you you were crazy." Up to that time his primary interest had been medieval studies; it may have been a conscious turning away from the American field—"you couldn't grow up in my father's household without learning a lot about the history and traditions of the University of Wisconsin"—or his devotion to the distinguished medievalist Richard Ringler. In any case, Cronon recalls with clarity the circumstances that opened his eyes to the possibilities of writing about the American past:

> In my senior year by accident I took a course on the history of the American West taught by Allan Bogue; it had a very small environmental component to it, and that course persuaded me that I could look at the American landscape and American culture in the multifaceted way, the way that . . . Ringler had looked at medieval England or medieval Iceland, and that I would actually have freer play for my imagination to wander around a long sweep of time and space for the kind of stories I wanted to

tell and write. . . . From my senior year forward I knew doing the American West or the American frontier from an environmental point of view was going to be the focus of my work.[15]

Following graduation, Cronon studied at Yale, after which he spent two Rhodes Scholarship years at Jesus College, Oxford. There he took an accidental doctorate. Embarking on an ambitious master's thesis—he researched Coventry's energy consumption over a ninety-year period—Cronon found that his essay kept expanding, to the point that his adviser suggested submitting it for a doctorate in British urban-economic history. It was accepted, and the twenty-seven-year-old scholar left England with a DPhil. In fact, his most rigorous and sustained graduate work still lay ahead of him. Having planned only to take an MPhil. in England, Cronon had already accepted a Danforth Fellowship. Back to Yale he went, "to do," as he later put it, "my real PhD."[16]

His timing proved felicitous. Tacking in Turner's shadow, scholars of the West had long suffered under the public's impression that they dabbled in antiquarianism, the Zane Grey stuff of cowpokes and cactuses. Now, a generation of scholars influenced by the Vietnam War and the energy crisis began to discover in what would come to be called the "new western history" approaches to environmentalism and anti-imperialism that countered the "victory culture" narrative familiar to the country since World War II. A striking number of talented ones—including Donald Worster, John Mack Faragher, and Patrician Nelson Limerick—studied under Howard Lamar at Yale. Their work emphasized conquest as the central theme of western history (and American history too, some have claimed). They swapped the old mythical march of progress west (from Indian primitivism to Anglo civilization) for one attuned to the hardships of competition and capitalist development in a vast, contested region peopled with traditional (Natives and whites) as well as nontraditional (Asians, Hispanics, and blacks) actors. Turner's simple Wasp frontier appeared inadequate by comparison—cartoonish at best, racist at worst. Here, in the hands of the Yale revisionists, rose a richer and far more complex rendering of the western past, one alert to recent insights in gender, ethnic, and environmental history.

Cronon's return to New England proved important on two accounts—it gave him a genial academic home for several years while offering perspective on the differing eastern and midwestern academic traditions he had come to know firsthand. "The UW is in and of Wisconsin," he once observed, "in a way that Yale will never be in and of Connecticut." In New Haven, Cronon joined an academic community devoted principally to undergraduate education in the humanities. The Wisconsin Idea, by contrast, stressed graduate work and privileged the sciences. Its basic philosophy— improving the lives of the state's citizens—contained a conservationist component. And this continues to have a strong influence on those living and teaching in Madison. "When I consider the Wisconsin tradition that I'm interested in," Cronon explains, "it's not the Wisconsin School of History, it is broader and rooted in narratives in the American landscape that you can see in the scholarship of those working in agriculture, law, economics, and botany. They are all interested in people on the land. And you can see this [Aldo] Leopoldian tradition working not just in this university but everywhere in this town."[17]

The lure of this legacy helped to bring Cronon back to Madison— after a memorable New Haven run. Lamar left teaching in 1982 to become dean of Yale College, and Cronon, armed with an Oxford doctorate, took over his classes. He received tenure in 1988, two years before completing his dissertation. The 1991 retirement of Allan Bogue, the Frederick Jackson Turner Professor of History, opened the door for Cronon's return to Wisconsin the following year. "I'm sure a lot of my colleagues still don't get it, why you move from a Yale to a Wisconsin," Cronon later remarked. "Some people perceived what I was doing as a step down. I didn't experience it that way. . . . In the end it turned out to be a much easer decision than I had imagined it might be." Fully in Madison's favor stood the classic state school appendages that make UW such a vibrant center for intellectual engagement across a wide stretch of disciplines. "For what I do, environmental history, there are many ways in which Wisconsin is one of the strongest, maybe *the* strongest place in the world to do this kind of work," Cronon insists. "It helps me to be at a land grant institution, it helps me to have an agricultural school and an engineering school on the same campus as a liberal arts faculty, and Yale didn't have those things."[18]

Like any scholar of the American West, Cronon has wrestled with Turner's ghost. This would be the case even if he and Turner did not grow up in Wisconsin or take their baccalaureate degrees at UW; even if he was not the Turner Professor of History or if his office didn't sit across the street from the building where Turner held his seminars; and even if his home was not within walking distance of Turner's old Van Hise Avenue house. Still, one cannot call Cronon a "Turnerian" per se, for the last of that genus—in its purest strain—died off many years ago. It is too easy today, after all, to point out the rather large problems with the frontier paradigm. Following Turner's lead, Cronon has written, Americans took to "defining [Indian] land as savage land. . . . From an Indian point of view that land didn't get savage until the white folks arrived. So there's something deeply racist about this way of thinking of the frontier, which is very much of a piece with the end of the nineteenth century. Turner is very much a man of his time in thinking this way."[19] Sifting for the salvageable, Cronon has jettisoned the frontier thesis which famously if falsely prophesized the end days of American democracy with the peopling of the last free lands. In its place he has accentuated those Turnerian themes that transcend the nineteenth-century context which gave them such power but quickly dated the paradigm.

Rethinking Turner has underscored the need for a new nomenclature, and Cronon has sought to replace the problematic *frontier* with the less freighted *abundance*. In America, after all, frontiers close but the standard of living keeps escalating. In referencing abundance, one is really talking about resources, and it seems a truism as much (or more) in our twenty-first century as it did in Turner's nineteenth century that the ready availability (or scarcity) of commodities has played a powerful role shaping political culture, muting class discord, and, in broader terms, making Americans feel either secure or shaky about the future. And observers watch, sniff, and survey this psychological state in order to register the general health of the republic. When we *have*, we believe democracy works; when we don't (or feel as though we don't), we are more likely to question the prospects of popular government.[20]

Such creative recasting of the frontier thesis also offers a way to re-think the meaning of the West. Its opening to Anglos resulted not in a democracy-eclipsing 1890s census finale but rather its opposite. The region's plenty became part of the vast apparatus that allowed the nation to absorb twenty million immigrants between 1890 and 1920, helped man, equip, and feed the large democratic armies of the 1940s, and has played an important role in the postwar consumer state. In this sense, abundance reaffirms the old Turnerian idea of a safety valve. And it all seems self-evident today. The Sunbelt booms, the major parties court support (and often hold their national conventions) in the major western cities, and government dollars are distributed to dozens of military bases and suppliers from Lincoln to Los Angeles. To be sure, this "federalized" landscape bears little resemblance to Turner's romantic frontier individualism—except in one crucial sense. The West attracts and thrives; it has a role to play in the way Americans perceive themselves, their nation, and their democracy. This self-conception did not grind to a halt in 1890; it was only beginning. The conservative political realignment predicted in Kevin Phillips's influential *The Emerging Republican Majority* (1969) was shaped in part by the rise of a new Wasp West that in many respects held to the ideal of the old Wasp West as a land open to those alienated from an urban, multiethnic East. These new pioneers became a people of suburban plenty. "Turner's notion of the 'frontier' may be so muddled as to be useless," Cronon has written, "but if Turner's 'free land' is a special case of . . . American abundance, then the general direction of Turner's approach remains sound."[21]

A discussion of resources—abundance and scarcity—leads naturally to issues of environmentalism, and here too Cronon has retooled Turner for a modern audience. Like many contemporary ecologists, Turner presumed that identity came from the land. And in his own day, such thinking gave currency to the budding conservationist movement associated with John Muir and Theodore Roosevelt. To discard Turner today would be to give away a potentially valuable voice in the struggle to secure the nation's rural places. The author of the frontier thesis, after all, regarded nature as something grander than a bankable commodity for exploitation. It represented, rather, room for individual encounter, change, and self-definition—the purposeful interplay between "man" and "land." To care for the one means caring for the other. "It is no accident that much of what we today call 'environmental history' has been written in this country under the guise of *western* history," Cronon argues. "No other academic field, historical geography excluded, has proven to be a better home for those interested in studying human uses of the earth. This is Turner's doing."[22]

A commitment to environmental history may have influenced Cronon's decision to leave the academic gold coast for Wisconsin. There he discovered colleagues receptive to the kind of books he hoped to write. In the East, as well as in England, environmental history languished outside the established research lines. To the metropolitans, "place" meant palaces, cathedrals, and parliaments. And apparently it always has. Recall Turner's 1881 statement to William Allen comparing education in the East with that in the Midwest:

> The difference which I note in the plans regarding American history both here [Johns Hopkins], at Boston, and at Harvard, as compared with Wisconsin is the closer connection of the studies in English Constitutional, American History, and American Constitution. . . . It is in short, the development of the American nation *politically* that is emphasized. The great lack of it all is in getting any proper conception of the Great West. Not a man here that I know of is either studying, or hardly aware of the country beyond the Alleghenies—except two.[23]

Cronon experienced a similar prejudice:

> Imagine my surprise . . . when I discovered that the communities I joined in Oxford and Yale were not nearly so permeated with [the] landscape tradition as I was. For them, environmental history was an interesting but rather eccentric subject well outside the mainstream of their concerns. A sense of place didn't seem nearly so important to them, or had mainly to do with buildings and the things that had happened inside them. What one of my colleagues calls "outdoor history," just wasn't the Oxford or Yale way of doing things.[24]

Wisconsin, by contrast, offered a rich tradition of environmentally minded thinkers and a great state university well arranged to reflect on the relationship between people and the land. "Everything I now do," Cronon has claimed, "is a product of this place and this past."[25]

One can trace the influence of Turnerian, Leopoldian, and Muirian traditions on Cronon's major works. His first book, *Changes in the Land: Indians, Colonists, and the Ecology of New England* (1983), earned favorable reviews as a synthetic study that made the landscape an historical actor on a par with the people who altered it and were in turn altered by it. Discussing the book's origins, Cronon evoked the Midwest.

> When I wrote an environmental history of colonial New England, people thought me quite original to have taken such an unusual approach. I was happy they liked what I had written, of course, but I knew full well that there was nothing very original about it. I was simply writing history as I had learned to do back home, telling New England's story as if it had been Wisconsin's. . . . Although I certainly did not fully appreciate this as a child, I grew up in a community where "changes in the land" were topics of daily conversation. This book began not in New Haven, but in Madison: what I found in the New England landscape was what I had learned to look for in the Middle West.

And to whom could Cronon count as a model for his reading of the New England frontier? Why Turner, of course—the progenitor, he pointed out, who "first offered a land-centered interpretation of the American frontier."[26]

Changes emphasizes the agency of northern and southern New England Natives, highlighting the ways they affected the environment. Accordingly, Cronon mercifully knocks the eastern Indians off their Anglo-placed pedestal as the tenants of virgin territory, and he does so by effectively exploring the ways that these affiliated tribal communities lived and used the earth. Thus, the title-descriptor "changes in the land" refers not merely to the relatively recent European fishing, farming, and foresting habits that customarily receive textbook treatment but also to the far older hunting and harvesting practices employed by the region's original inhabitants. Long before Myles Standish set foot in Plymouth, the Wampanoag had modified their surroundings many times over. Consequently, Cronon rejects the false dichotomy of technologically advanced Europeans versus a pristine seventeenth-century garden. The real locus of conflict was varying ecological attitudes. The book's major question is delightfully straightforward: How do different peoples respond to abundance? How, that is, did the Anglo imagining of land as a Lockean "private commodity" clash with the traditional Native recognition of property as part of the "public commons"?[27]

The coming of Anglo colonization, Cronon argues, intensified the old New England economy beyond recognition. The fur trade brought European prestige goods into Native hands, which encouraged overhunting. This in turn had a devastating impact on the region's beaver, turkey, and white-tailed deer populations. "The commercialization of the Indians' early material culture," Cronon writes, "thus brought with it a disintegration of their earlier ecological practices." The culprit was capitalism. In ways different, but no less direct, than Beard, Williams, and Lasch, Cronon has tried to make his readers aware of the crippling, even deadly, cost of their economic choices. In this sense, the past he writes about is not the past at all. "By interpreting New England ecosystems into an ultimately global capitalist economy," he maintains, we see that "colonists and Indians together began a dynamic and unstable process of ecological change which had in no way ended by 1800. We live with their legacy today."[28] While Cronon refuses to recognize the Natives as "morally correct" colonial-era conservationists, his is clearly a story of heroes and villains: Anglo economic power spoiled an ecosystem more or less balanced by comparatively uncommercialized Indian peoples. At times Cronon edges close to the Virgin land myth that he is determined to write against.

In 1991 Cronon published the Bancroft Prize–winning *Nature's Metropolis: Chicago and the Great West,* a far more ambitious assessment of the American environmental record. If his first book emphasizes cultural differences in ecological thinking, his second argues the opposite—that disparate cultural traditions (the urban "center" and the rural "periphery") actually share a common responsibility in regard to caring for the soil. The rise of Chicago radically reshaped America, Cronon observes, and did so at an exceedingly high price that included "large-scale deforestation, threats of species extinction, unsustainable exploitation of natural resources [and] widespread destruction of the habitat." Yet nineteenth-century Chicago-ans seemed stunningly oblivious to the impact of their many sins against the land. Is there a message here for us moderns? Cronon does express hope that his story of the "Great West" might serve to awaken the conscience of his reader—"to take political and moral responsibility for . . . the ecological consequences of our own lives."[29]

As with *Changes,* Cronon is quick to note the midwestern roots of his second book, which he calls "a personal journey." It began in childhood, in the back of his parents' green and white station wagon over a series of lazy summer crossings from New Haven to Wisconsin. Along the way loomed Chicagoland, an alien, menacing sprawl, "a place in which," he writes, "I had no wish to linger." Cronon's descriptive editorial about entering the city (a noxious "orange cloud of smoke" gave welcome) and making his escape (a billboard hawking Budweiser beer appeared near the end of the trail) recalls Henry David Thoreau during his Walden days. Walking through Concord suggested to Thoreau the serpentine path of "digestive organs" that "cracked" and "emptied" residents and visitors alike. It culminated in a kind of village bowel movement: "I was let out through the rear avenues, and so escaped to the woods again."[30]

Thoreau clearly drew a distinction between settlement and pastoral. Cronon, on the other hand, has overcome his habit of dividing places into separate "urban" and "rural" spaces; he makes Chicago a medium for con-necting the two. Farmers, loggers, pelters, and petty merchants needed the city in order to sell their goods, after all, and the city relied upon this grand multistate coalition of producers and middlemen to build, feed, and sustain it. The fates of provincials and metropolitans converged in this "Great West," as an indivisible codependency ruled the region. As a result, Cronon's reading of the middle-western record leads him to dismiss the tidy old Turnerian dichotomy of "savagery" and "civilization"—imagining an isolated range of "free land" far from "corrupting" cities—for a more inclusive, messy, and multifaceted understanding of human geography.

Turner's frontier thesis also takes a drubbing in *Nature's Metropolis.* Hoping to bring "nature" to the city, Cronon's call for center-periphery reconciliation means that urban populations can regard their rural breth-ren as "other" only by ignoring their own vital connections to the country-side. William Jennings Bryan made this point in his famous Cross of Gold address, ironically in the Chicago Coliseum. "You come to us," he warned business-district America, "to tell us that the great cities are in favor of the gold standard; we reply that the great cities rest upon our broad and fertile prairies. Burn down your cities and leave our farms, and your cities will spring up again as if by magic; but destroy our farms and the grass will grow in the streets of every city in the country." More contemporaneously, Cronon points out that segregation from nature is not really possible; all live on the land. Thus the ecological investment marshaled in the name of conserving the soil, the water, and the air should be shared evenly by the sodbuster, the suburbanite, and the city folk. The latter have long resisted this notion, regarding the countryside as so many distant canyon-geyser-redwood acres to be sampled and trampled on holiday as a counterpoint to "real" life. *Nature's Metropolis* rejects this vacation approach to living. As Cronon puts it, "If the urban garden is part of nature, then so are its gardeners."[31]

The ominous pattern of market commodification introduced in *Changes* plays an even more visible role in *Nature's Metropolis*. The rapid growth of the railroad connected formerly distended communities with Chicago, creating an immense and complex web of reciprocity. "More and more of western nature," Cronon observes, "would become priced, capitalized, and mortgaged as the new capitalist geography proliferated."[32] And this meant the systematic destruction of certain plant, animal, and human ecologies. The near extinction of the buffalo, the shrinking north woods, and the removal of indigenous peoples were all part of a large-scale shifting of resources, culminating in the platting of a new market oasis in the new West.

In Turner's hands, the frontier symbolized the meeting place between primitive and progressive space; for Cronon, Chicago holds that honor. Here, in a sense, the frontier never really died but rather transferred its treasures to the metropolis. Wyoming cattle, Kansas corn, and northern Michigan timber converged as critical commodities that built and sustained the city. With linkages so tight, the end of the frontier would seem to mean the end of Chicago—but the city swells on. What does this suggest? Perhaps, above all, that the Turnerian ideal of the rugged individualist fails to account for the interconnections and contributions of countless middle-westerners who labored to supply Chicago with its daily needs. The cowboy was a wage earner, professional hunters picked off bison from trains, and merchants near and far relied on distant Michigan Avenue markets. Cronon records this intricate "type" mixing even as he understands the impulse of his fellow Americans to adopt an identity either "on" or "off" the land: "If I am honest about the childhood emotions that have defined my adult passions and given a sense of direction to my life, I have to admit that I am still—like many if not most Americans who care about 'the environment'—a captive of the pastoral myth. I still prefer the country to the city." His family's annual summer retreat, after all, represented an unconscious effort to leave urban life behind and reclaim the "natural" life that one associates with emerald and blue spaces. It is a relationship with the countryside that Cronon has long since rejected. "We fool ourselves if we think we can choose between . . . the green lake and the orange cloud [for they] are creatures of the same landscape. Each is our responsibility."[33]

In recent years, Cronon has been at work on a study larger than Chicago, greater even than the making of the "Great West." He is telling the story of Portage, Wisconsin (population 9,728). "My books are responses to what I felt was lacking in the previous ones," he explains. The urban-capitalist framework that drives *Nature's Metropolis* replies to *Changes'* less intricate narrative. In both volumes, Cronon points out, personalities are largely absent: "There are no flesh-and-blood living human beings in these works, and this is a generic weakness of environmental history." To Portage he has gone to recover this people-place dimension—and tell an epic tale. "I wanted to do a Michener-scale book, a really large book about the history of the Midwest from the glaciers to now, and one that would be tied to individuals. I'm investigating how an abstract geographical space becomes a human place, and doing so through a very close reading of a small town in rural America. By understanding the landscape of Portage, you can learn to read the American landscape."[34]

One cannot help but note the irony of such an ambitious enterprise. It was Turner, after all, the Portage product, who first drew upon the backcountry's ambience to draft a distinct, romantic, and personal vision of American history. The same impulse informs Cronon's current book project, and what he once wrote of Turner—that his scholarship "became a model for telling the story not just of Wisconsin, but the nation as a whole"—may one day be written of him.[35]

Thinking back on his formal education, Turner believed that his most useful courses were the ones he never took. "I had a lack of general American historical training which was an advantage in that I hadn't been fitted into the mould of the teachers. . . . I had to work out my own salvation."[36] Like Hawthorne's New England and Faulkner's Mississippi, Turner's native land proved to be his greatest influence. Allegiance to the particular culture and past of the Middle West gave his work an original frame of reference from which to rethink the national experience. "Salvation" came in a local color.

Turner's place-based way of understanding the world was shared by a cluster of distinguished historians writing within an interior tradition.

Their collective concerns about the centrality of power and politics in eastern hands shaped their rejection of liberalism in the years following Turner's death. No doubt a certain narrowness of vision informed their work, yet it sprang from a legitimate concern about the compression of democracy in an increasingly incorporated welfare-warfare state. For all its real and good achievements, the liberal moment ultimately presented Americans with a false consensus that left the country ill prepared to address the complex of issues that threatened to overwhelm it in the 1960s. Pressures built which had to search beyond the mainstream for expression, and our two-party system had made few such avenues available.

As a result, both the Left (if only briefly) and the Right experienced a revival. The latter has come, of course, to dominate political dialogue in recent decades—its brand of conservatism is the reigning consensus. Consequently, much in our civic philosophy has changed since, say, 1970, though its primary article of faith remains firmly in place. Like liberalism, the modern Right has readily embraced the broad contours of American Century exceptionalism. It invests heavily in a military-consumption culture that measures the country's strength primarily in terms of economic growth and war-making capability. More, it has little use for a midwestern historical imagination whose populistic sensibilities and imperial regrets cut uncompromisingly against the country's status as monolith.

And that is too bad. Moved by a separate American identity, a self-protective regional consciousness took root in the frontier's dying days. Born of Bryanism, Beardianism, and Turner's idealization of the open land, it abandoned the bureaucratic liberalism coming from FDR's New Deal in favor of a respectable farm and industry radicalism. Concerned with losing a way of life to an emerging way of life, it reacted to the dynamic, erratic energy that pulled the nation forward, into the maelstrom of the modern age. Bowed but unvanquished, the heart of this persuasion beats on—as it must. Our sense of place, after all, has always illuminated our sense of past.

Notes

Introduction

1. Evidence that the Midwest really is "a state of mind" can be gleaned from a 1980 survey conducted by University of Kansas cultural geographer James R. Shortridge. Based on nearly two thousand "cognitive maps," Shortridge's findings indicated that definitions of the Midwest shifted depending upon the identifier's place of residence. Respondents from Michigan tended to locate the Middle West in what used to be called the Old Northwest (Ohio, Michigan, Indiana, Illinois, Wisconsin, as well as Iowa, Missouri, and part of Minnesota); respondents from North Dakota presumed the Midwest encompassed the Dakotas, Nebraska, and eastern Minnesota, while New Yorkers "imagined" a Midwest farther to the south, with Kansas as its center and Oklahoma, Missouri, Iowa, and Nebraska its appendages. James R. Shortridge, *The Middle West: Its Meaning in American Culture* (Lawrence, 1989), 67–96.

2. John D. Hicks, "The Development of Civilization in the Middle West, 1860–1900," in *The Sources of Culture in the Middle West: Backgrounds versus Frontier,* ed. Dixon Ryan Fox (New York, 1934), 97–98.

3. "West and New East," *Independent* 72 (1912): 322.

4. Henry Luce, *The American Century* (New York, 1941), 10–11, italics in original. It was John Hay, of course, who wrote to his friend Theodore Roosevelt that the Spanish conflict had been "a splendid little war."

5. Jeremi Suri, *Henry Kissinger and the American Century* (Cambridge, 2007), 9.

6. Parkman to Turner, 2 May 1889, b1, f20, FJTPH.

7. The distinguished American foreign policy scholar Walter LaFeber matriculated in Madison for doctoral work after studying with a Merle Curti student at tiny Hanover College in Indiana. While Paul Buhle was considering graduate school options in the late 1960s, his honors professor at the University of Illinois—a Wisconsin graduate—said to him, "It's time to go home." This could mean only one thing, Buhle later recalled: "for a Progressive historian, home is always Madison." LaFeber and Buhle interviews with author.

8. George Mosse, *Confronting History: A Memoir* (Madison, 2000), 156–57.

Prologue

1. Known during the Columbian Exposition as the World's Congress Auxiliary Building, the structure was later renamed the Art Institute of Chicago. Turner's letter to Wilson is cited in Ray Allen Billington, *Frederick Jackson Turner: Historian, Scholar, Teacher* (Oxford, 1973), 126.

2. Ibid., 129; Frederick Jackson Turner, *The Frontier in American History* (New York, 1920), 38.

3. Mulji Devji Vedant, "A Brahmin's Impressions at the Chicago World's Fair," *Littell's Living Age*, 17 February 1894, 435–41; Rudyard Kipling, *From Sea to Sea: Letters of Travel*, pt. 2 (New York, 1906), 238–40. Both of these works are cited in Bessie Louise Pierce, ed., *As Others See Chicago: Impressions of Visitors, 1673–1933* (Chicago, 2004 ed.), 340–50; 250–61.

4. Robert W. Rydell, *All the World's a Fair: Visions of Empire at American International Expositions, 1876–1916* (Chicago, 1984), 47; Henry Adams, *The Education of Henry Adams: An Autobiography* (New York, 1999 ed.), 343, 345.

5. *New York Times*, 13 July 1893.

6. Ibid.; Turner, *Frontier in American History*, 37.

Chapter One

1. William B. Hesseltine and Louis Kaplan, "Doctors of Philosophy in History," *American Historical Review*, July 1942, 784. Most published lives of historians gloss over the impact of region in favor of grander narratives. This preference can be gleaned in the titles of recent autobiographies by John Hope Franklin (*Mirror to America*), John Morton Blum (*A Life with History*), and Forrest McDonald (*Recovering the Past*). Exceptions to the rule (again evident in the titles) are the biographical studies of two southern scholars—John Herbert Roper's *C. Vann Woodward: Southerner* and Merton Dillon's *Ulrich Bonnell Phillips: Historian of the Old South*.

2. Henry Cabot Lodge, *Early Memories* (New York, 1920), 205.

3. Alfred Kazin, *An American Procession: Major American Writers, 1830–1930* (New York, 1984), 254.

4. William E. Gienapp, ed., *This Fiery Trial: The Speeches and Writings of Abraham Lincoln* (Oxford, 2002), 144–45; James M. McPherson, "The Bloody Partnership," *New York Review of Books*, 15 December 2005, 46. Following the Vicksburg victory, Lincoln exulted that "the father of Waters again goes unvexed to the sea. Thanks to the great Northwest for it" (quoted in Turner, *Frontier in American History*, 142).

5. F. Scott Fitzgerald, *Tender Is the Night* (New York, 1995 ed.), 118. Of his own Brown County, Ohio, boyhood Grant wrote, "My life in Georgetown was uneventful." Attending subscription schools and working on the family farm filled up his days. Ulysses S. Grant, *Personal Memoirs of U. S. Grant* (New York, 1999 ed.), 10.

6. H. W. Brands, *T. R.: The Last of the Romantics* (New York, 1997), 168.

7. Adams, *Education of Henry Adams*, 265.

8. James Brewer Steward, *Holy Warriors: The Abolitionists and American Slavery* (New York, 1996 rev. ed.), 200.

9. Edward Pollard, *The Lost Cause: A New Southern History of the War of the Confederates* (New York, 1970 rep. ed.), 738.

10. Michael Kraus and Davis D. Joyce, *The Writing of American History* (Norman, OK, 1985 rev. ed.), 297.

11. Jesup Scott, "A Presentation of Causes Tending to Fix the Position of the Future Great City of the World in the Central Plain of North America: Showing that the Centre of the World's Commerce, Now Represented by the City of London, Is Moving Westward to the City of New York, and Thence, within One Hundred Years, to the Best Position on the Great Lakes" (Toledo, 1876), 5–6, emphasis in original.

12. Bernard Mayo, *Jefferson Himself: The Personal Narrative of a Many-Sided American* (Charlottesville, 1970 ed.), 265.

13. Booth Tarkington, "The Middle West," *Harper's Monthly*, December 1902, 76.

14. Shortridge, *Middle West*, 101–11.

15. Carl Sandburg, *Harvest Poems, 1910–1960* (New York, 1960), 35; Ronald Weber, *The Midwestern Ascendancy in American Writing* (Bloomington, 1992), 9.

16. Kazin, *American Procession*, 254.

17. Carl Van Doren, *The American Novel, 1789–1939* (New York, 1940), 299; Sinclair Lewis, *Main Street* (New York, 1998 ed.), 39–40.

18. Eugene Victor Debs, speech at Girard, Kansas, May 23, 1908, cited in Harry R. Warfel et al., *The American Mind: Selections from the Literature of the United States* (New York, 1937), 1020.

19. Thorstein Veblen, *The Theory of the Leisure Class* (New York, 1967 ed.), 17.

20. Ron Chernow, *Titan: The Life of John D. Rockefeller Sr.* (New York, 1998), 44.

21. Adams, *Education*, 500.

22. Chernow, *Titan*, 325–26.

23. "No one took Harvard College seriously," Adams singed his alma mater; "all went there because their friends went there." Adams, *Education*, 54. Fitzgerald, Ivy schooled some three generations after Adams, wrote in *This Side of Paradise* that Princeton was "the pleasantest country club in America." F. Scott Fitzgerald, *This Side of Paradise* (New York, 1986 ed.), 44. Johns Hopkins's reputation in the first decades of the twentieth century declined as it looked increasingly less like a cutting-edge, European-influenced university and more like a provincial southern school. Invited in 1940 to head the American Historical Studies program at Hopkins, Merle Curti, then at Columbia's Teachers College, turned the offer down. To a colleague he confided that "Baltimore by virtue of the color situation does not appeal to me at all. . . . It is essentially a Southern city; and in many respects more conservative than places in the South that have been touched by new currents—Chapel Hill or Vanderbilt, for instance." Curti to Bessie Louise Pierce, 13 January and 9 February 1940, b9, f6, BLPP.

24. Hugh Hawkins, *Pioneer: A History of the Johns Hopkins University, 1874–1889* (Ithaca, NY, 1960), 175, 169. Considering Adams's long and fruitful career at Hopkins, one might forget that it almost never happened. The position he filled was first offered to another Adams—Henry. But the Brahmin Adams, fresh from a seven-year stint teaching medieval history at Harvard, politely refused, as he put it, "to become again a Professor on any terms." Hopkins officials next approached the eminent German historian Herman Von Holst, hopeful that his expatriation might "legitimize" the university

and inspire an intellectual migration from Europe's brightest stars—a Berlin to Baltimore brain drain. Von Holst declined their offer, however, and remained for the time being in Freiburg (till lured to the University of Chicago in 1892). Unable to secure either of his prized peacocks—the scion of presidents or a celebrated German scholar— Gilman turned to the next best thing, an American trained in a German university. In this circumstantial way did Herbert Baxter Adams (PhD Heidelberg) begin his legendary career.

25. Richard T. Ely, *Ground under Our Feet: An Autobiography* (New York, 1938), 1, 43.

26. Ibid., 72; Richard T. Ely, *The Labor Movement in America* (New York, 1886), xi.

27. Herbert Baxter Adams, quoted in *Historical Scholarship in the United States, 1876– 1901: As Revealed in the Correspondence of Herbert B. Adams,* ed. W. Stull Holt (Baltimore, 1938), 157; Ely, *Ground under Our Feet,* 181.

28. Frank Norris, *The Octopus* (New York, 1963 ed.), 33.

29. Charles McCarthy, *The Wisconsin Idea* (New York, 1912), dedication page.

30. Turner, *Frontier in American History,* 228; Peter Novick, *That Noble Dream: The "Objectivity Question" and the American Historical Profession* (Cambridge, 1988), 26.

31. John R. Commons, *Myself* (New York, 1934), 95, 170.

32. Edward Alsworth Ross, *Seventy Years at It* (New York, 1936), 37, 66, 90.

33. McCarthy, *Wisconsin Idea,* vii, xi.

Chapter Two

1. Booth Tarkington, "The Middle West," *Harper's Monthly,* December 1902, 75.

2. John Franklin Jameson, letter, 5 January 1889, in *An Historian's World: Selections from the Correspondence of John Franklin Jameson,* ed. Elizabeth Donnan and Leo F. Stock (Philadelphia, 1956), 46. It should be noted that Jameson demonstrated an admirable capacity for growth in his attitude toward western education. He responded to a 1926 query by a Connecticut father looking to place his son in a suitable graduate program in constitutional and political history with the following comments: "On the whole, I should put Wisconsin first. . . . The library facilities at Madison are of course remarkable, and one meets there a very fine body of graduate students, from a number of different states. . . . I should also think that your son would get at [Harvard] too much of the New England point of view which ich erlaube mich zu ermelden (brought up in Boston though I was) is in respect to American history an eccentric (in the literal sense) and somewhat perverted point of view. In short, I adhere in this case to Greeley's aphorism 'Go West young man, go West'" (295–96).

3. John Higham, *History: Professional Scholarship in America* (Baltimore, 1989 rev. ed.), 6–25; Novick, *That Noble Dream,* 49.

4. Turner barely qualifies for this distinction. Following the 1910 summer session he left Wisconsin for Harvard.

5. Charles Homer Haskins to John Franklin Jameson, 15 February 1891, in *Historian's World,* 33.

6. J. Franklin Jameson to Frederick Jackson Turner, 7 June 1895, b2, f2, FJTPH.

7. Adams, *Education,* 493; Wilbur R. Jacobs, *The Historical World of Frederick Jackson Turner: With Selections from His Correspondence* (New Haven, 1968), 54.

8. J. Hector St. John de Crevecoeur, *Letters from an American Farmer and Sketches of Eighteenth-Century America* (New York, 1981 ed.), 69, 67.

9. *The Portable Thomas Jefferson*, ed. Merrill D. Peterson (New York, 1975), 496.

10. Ibid., 583.

11. Turner to Constance Lindsay Skinner, 15 March 1922, b4, FJTPW; Billington, *Frederick Jackson Turner*, 3–5.

12. Turner to Skinner, 15 March 1922, FJTPW.

13. Turner to Carl Becker, 16 December 1925, b8, CBP; Turner to Edgar E. Robinson, 12 December 1924, f10, FJTPH; *State Register*, 21, 28 September 1872; see Donald J. Berthong's "Andrew Jackson Turner: 'Work Horse' of the Republican Party," *Wisconsin Magazine of History* 38 (1954–55): 77–86.

14. Carl L. Becker, *Everyman His Own Historian: Essays on History and Politics* (Chicago, 1966 ed.), 193–94.

15. *Portage Democrati*, 12 June 1905; Turner to Max Farrand, 15 May 1907, b9, f32, FJTPH.

16. Turner to Merle Curti, 8 August 1928, b29, f69, FJTPH.

17. "Volume I, Lectures in History I," b2, FJTPW; "Medieval Institutions," b3, FJTPW. During Turner's undergraduate years, Allen prepared an essay on "The Primitive Democracy of the Germans." Read as a paper before a meeting of the Wisconsin Academy in 1881, it was published in William Francis Allen's *Essays and Monographs* (Boston, 1890), 215–30.

18. Jacobs, *Historical World of Frederick Jackson Turner*, 155.

19. Turner to Carl Becker, 16 December 1925, b8, CBP, emphasis in original.

20. Turner, *Frontier in American History*, 216.

21. Curti, University of Wisconsin Oral History Project, 1986.

22. Theodore Roosevelt, *The Winning of the West* (New York, 1889), 1:15. While researching and writing *Winning*, Roosevelt occasionally turned to the legendary Wisconsin archivist Lyman Draper for assistance and information. After one of the volumes appeared, he wrote Draper for aid in answering a competitor. The letter sheds light on the narrative type of historical recovery that men like Turner were determined to replace with a more scientific methodology. Roosevelt's plea for Draper to send him "data" would have made Turner smile. "A man named Butterfield has recently published a life of Simon Girty. In it he makes some criticisms of my *Winning of the West*, mostly of a perfectly silly character. He, however, entirely discredits the story of Girty's speech at Boonsborough and the answer made by Aaron Reynolds. In giving account of this I stated that I put it in because you had told me that the incidents had been related to you by several old men who had themselves been in the fort. Butterfield asserts that you were evidently entirely mistaken, or that the old men did not know what they were talking about. I would be much obliged therefore if you would give me some data to go by so that if necessary I may answer him." Roosevelt to Draper, 23 May 1890, b179, f54, TRP.

23. Turner to George P. Brett, 29 March 1896, b2, f13, FJTPH; Turner to Skinner, 15 March 1922, b4, FJTPW, emphasis in original.

24. Roosevelt to Turner, 10 February 1894, b1, f55, FJTPH.

25. Turner to Becker, 13 February 1926, b8, CBP.

26. Turner, *Frontier in American History*, 2, 3, 156.

27. Ibid., 204.

28. Turner to Merle Curti, 8 August 1928, b39, f69, FJTPH.

29. Jacobs, *Historical World of Frederick Jackson Turner*, 9.

30. Turner, *Frontier in American History*, 38; Becker to Beard, internal evidence suggests 1939, DC 572, f5, CMBP.

31. Turner to Becker, 21 January 1922, b7, CBP.

32. Van Tyne to Turner, 21 November 1909, b12, f56, FJTPH; Alvord to Turner, 20 November 1909, b13, f56, FJTPH.

33. Turner to Wilson, 27 November 1896, b2, f22, FJTPH.

34. Jacobs, *Historical World of Frederick Jackson Turner*, 99.

35. Turner to Charles Sumner Slichter, 14 November 1909, b12, f32, FJTPH; Turner to Homer C. Hockett, 19 October 1910, copied by Wilbur R. Jacobs and located in box 6 of the Oscar Winther Papers; Ulrich Bonnell Phillips to Carl Becker, 13 October 1925, FJTP, b34A, f51, FJTPH; Holt, ed., *Historical Scholarship in the United States*, 137.

36. Curti, University of Wisconsin Oral History Project, 1986.

37. Charles Beard, "The Frontier in American History," *New Republic*, 16 February 1921, 349.

38. Turner to Dorothy Kinsley (Turner) Main, 18 February 1921, b1, f63, FJTPH, emphasis in original.

39. Beard to Curti, 9 August 1928, DC 1021, f5, CMBP.

40. Henry Steele Commager in *New York Herald Tribune Books*, 19 May 1935, 7.

41. *The Public Papers and Addresses of Franklin D. Roosevelt*, vol. 1, *The Genesis of the New Deal* (New York, 1978), 750.

42. Richard Hofstadter, *The Progressive Historians: Turner, Beard, Parrington* (New York, 1968), 123; Turner to Skinner, 15 March 1922, FJTPW; Ray Allen Billington, "Frederick Jackson Turner Visits New England: 1887," *New England Quarterly*, September 1968, 417. Turner reported that his 1927 move to San Marino, California, "has been a real rebirth of enthusiasm to me. Incidentally, there is almost more of the New England and the best of the Middle West that I knew in my youth out here than in those regions themselves after the deluge of immigration." *"Dear Lady": The Letters of Frederick Jackson Turner and Alice Forbes Perkins Hooper*, ed. Ray Allen Billington (San Marino, 1970), 388.

43. *Chicago Record Herald*, 16 October 1901.

44. Ibid.; Turner, *Frontier in American History*, 245.

45. "Interview, Selig Perlman," 13 April 1950, UC21 A, Reel 2, WHS.

46. Perlman to Curtis Nettels, 8 October 1956, b52, f70, FJTPH, emphasis in original.

47. http://www.americanrhetoric.com/speeches/jfk1960dnc.htm, accessed 20 August 2008.

48. Frederick Logan Paxson, *When the West Is Gone* (New York, 1930), 135–36.

Chapter Three

1. Hofstadter, *Progressive Historians*, 299.

2. Charles A. Beard, "The Constitution in Cotton Wool," *New Republic*, 15 September 1937, 162; Mary Beard to Merle Curti, 2 March 1952, b5, f3, MCP.

3. Mary Ritter Beard, *The Making of Charles A. Beard* (New York, 1955), 22; Clifton J.

Phillips, "The Indiana Education of Charles A. Beard," *Indiana Magazine of History*, March 1959, 1, 2.

4. Clifton J. Phillips, ed., "Charles A. Beard's Recollections of Henry County, Indiana," *Indiana Magazine of History*, March 1929, 19.

5. Charles A. Beard, *An Economic Interpretation of the Constitution of the United* States (New York, 1986, rev. ed.), xlii; Clinton Rossiter, ed., *The Federalist Papers*, New York, 1961, rev. ed.), 79; 1926 Hanover Conference Report, Accession no. 25, Series 3, b66, f697, 492–93, SSRCP; Eric Goldman, "Charles A. Beard: An Impression," in *Charles A. Beard: An Appraisal*, ed. Howard K. Beale (Lexington, 1954), 2. "The Fathers, as you know," Beard wrote the historian Curtis Nettles, "used the economic interpretation of history. So did Calhoun and Webster. With the coming of political democracy, however, it was bad form." Beard to Nettles, 16 January 1936, b1, f15, CNP.

6. Orin G. Libby, *The Geographical Distribution of the Vote of the Thirteen States on the Federal Constitution, 1787–8* (Madison, 1894), iii.

7. Allan Bogue, *Frederick Jackson Turner: Strange Roads Going Down* (Norman, 1998), 171, 173.

8. Beard, *Economic Interpretation*, 5.

9. Charles A. Beard, *President Roosevelt and the Coming of the War* (New Haven, 1948), 582. Beard developed an acute personal distaste for Roosevelt. In one letter he declared that under FDR "we were secretly governed by our great *Fuehrer!*" Beard to Oswald Garrison Villard, 13 April 1948, OGVP, emphasis in original.

10. Novick, *That Noble Dream*, 240; Charles Beard to Max Farrand, 5 May 1913, DC 572, f21, CMBP.

11. Charles A. Beard, "A Statement by Charles A. Beard," *New Republic*, 29 December 1917, 249; *New York Times*, 9 October 1917.

12. Harry Coats to Professor Williams, internal evidence indicates October 1917, DC 572, f13, CMBP; unsigned letter to Nicholas Murray Butler, 9 October 1917, DC 572, f11, CMBP.

13. Hart to President Lowell, 13 October 1917, DC 1021, f 6, CMBP; Nicholas Murray Butler to Beard, 18 March 1940, DC 572, f11, CMBP; Carter to Beard, 9 October 1917, DC 572, f13, CMBP.

14. Beard to Oswald Garrison Villard, 26 January 1936, OGVP.

15. Ibid., 25 November 1943, OGVP.

16. Matthew Josephson, *Infidel in the Temple: A Memoir of the Nineteen-Thirties* (New York, 1967), 412.

17. Charles Beard, "War with Japan: What Shall We Get Out of It?" *Nation*, 25 March 1925, 311.

18. Charles Beard, "National Politics and the War," *Scribner's Magazine*, February 1935, 70. Among his efforts to keep the Pacific and all other wars at bay, Beard wrote the "Declaration of Policy" for American Neutrality Inc., a national organization headquartered in Washington, DC. This statement pledged the organization to "maintain a staff for the constant study of pro-war propaganda" and proposed measures to prevent "Government looking in the direction of war." "A Declaration to the American People," b5, ALCP.

19. Lindbergh to Beard, 21 August 1948, DC 1021, f18a, CMBP.

20. *New York Times Book Review,* 26 May 1940, 1; *American Historical Review,* October 1948, 382.

21. For an insightful study of Morison, see Gregory M. Pfitzer's *Samuel Eliot Morison's Historical World* (Boston, 1991).

22. Samuel Eliot Morison, "Did Roosevelt Start the War? History through a Beard," *Atlantic Monthly,* August 1948, 93. While Morison made sport of "Farmer Beard," a more sensitive appraisal of the historian's life in New Milford is offered by Detlev Vagts, Beard's grandson. "I think he had the farm because he loved it, because he felt that somebody cut off from the soil was no longer really safe and secure. There was always a feeling on his part that the people in Eastern establishment schools, who had not known the solidity of having one's own land under one's feet, really weren't all there." Vagts did, however, sustain Morison's observations on Beard's nostalgic impression of America. "The view [of New Milford] in those days was unspoiled Currier and Ives. The train used to go by and I can remember the steam whistle floating up from the valley. This would be the one note of industrialism for miles around." Detlev Vagts, remarks in *Charles A. Beard: An Observance of the Centennial of His Birth,* ed. Marvin C. Swanson (Greencastle, IN, 1976), 20.

23. Morison, "Did Roosevelt Start the War?" 96–97. Morison retired from the navy in 1951 with the rank of rear admiral (reserve); in 1979, the navy launched the *USS Samuel Eliot Morison* in honor of its favorite historian.

24. Charles Beard, "Written History as an Act of Faith," *American Historical Review,* January 1934, 220.

25. Ibid., 228.

26. Samuel Eliot Morison, "Faith of a Historian," *American Historical Review,* January 1951, 275, 262, 267.

27. Ibid., 266–67. "I thought Morison's presidential address was . . . offensive," wrote Berkeley historian Kenneth Stampp a few weeks after its delivery, "not only because of his ungracious treatment of Beard but because of his glorification of war." Stampp to Curti, 30 January 1951, b39, f8, MCP. In his 2004 essay on the Iraq War, "The Making of a Mess," Arthur Schlesinger Jr., a major critic of Beard's subjective approach, criticized pro-invasion neoconservatives for trafficking in a kind of fixed intellectual universe. He wrote in part that their putative guru, the University of Chicago political philosopher Leo Strauss, "taught his disciples a belief in absolutes [and a] contempt for relativism." *New York Review of Books,* 23 September 2004, 40.

28. Curti, University of Wisconsin Oral History Project, 1982.

29. Merle Curti, "The Democratic Theme in American Historical Writing," *Mississippi Valley Historical Review,* June 1952, 16, 25. This address may have cost Curti the opportunity to return to Harvard. Some believed that when Schlesinger Sr. retired, Curti—his first PhD student—would be a fitting replacement. After he took on Morison in such a public forum, however, any chance Curti may have had of returning to his alma mater probably disappeared.

30. Howard K. Beale, "The Professional Historian: His Theory and His Practice," *Pacific Historical Review,* August 1953, 238–39.

31. Beale to Thomas, 21 January 1941, b23, f11, HKBP; Mosse, *Confronting History,* 160.

32. Beale to Curti, 2 September 1936, b4, f11, HKBP.

33. Beale to Curti, 8 April 1950, b4, f11, MCP.

34. Richard Current wrote that Eugene Davidson, editor of the Yale University Press at the time it published Beard's Roosevelt books, "lost his job in consequence." Current to Fred Harvey Harrington, 9 July 1990, b10, FHHP. Goldman's connection to Beard began in the 1940–41 academic year, when both men were teaching at Johns Hopkins.

35. Beale to Curti, 23 November 1946, b4, f11, MCP; Schlesinger to Curti, 18 March 1948, b36, f7, MCP; Bailey to Curti, 17 March 1948, b3, f3, MCP; Bemis to Curti, 20 March 1948, 5, f8, MCP.

36. Commager to Beale, 7 November 1948, b25, f31, HKBP; Beale to Curti, 20 February 1950, b4, f11, MCP. "Mr. Knopf's declining to publish the volume when completed was a great shock," Beale reported to Hofstadter. "Mr. Knopf agreed to publish the volume and in so far as I could make it clear I thought he understood that I would not undertake the editing without assurance of publication." Beale to Hofstadter, 8 November 1949, b12, f20, HKBP. Curti presumed that the festschrift struggle severed his relations with the House of Knopf. Shortly after its conclusion, he responded to a student seeking an introduction by replying that "Knopf is the one publisher to whom I can't write. Sometime I'll tell you the story. It involves chiefly Beale and our ms. In re Beard. But I figured in it enough to be cut off the favored Knopf list, so anything I'd say would as likely as not count against you." Curti to Arthur Ekirch, 11 June 1951, Accession, M97–258, f1, MCP.

37. Memorandum to Mary Ritter Beard, internal evidence suggests 1948–50, DC 1292, f29, CMBP. After her husband's death, Beard met with the occasional historian making the New Milford pilgrimage. "Professor [Richard] Hofstadter and his wife drove up for an afternoon recently. I tried to make it clear that CAB was never a Populist or a Party Progressive disciple of Theodore Roosevelt—etc." Beard to Curti, 6 June 1951, b5, f3, MCP.

38. Eric Goldman, *Rendezvous with Destiny: A History of Modern American Reform* (New York, 1952), 296; Knopf to Mary Ritter Beard, 3 November 1952, DC 1495, f14, CMBP. For a sensitive assessment of the Beards' relationship within the broad canopy of progressive reform, see Eric Rauchway's "Mary and Charles Beard" in his study *The Refuge of Affections: Family and American Reform Politics, 1900–1920* (New York, 2001).

39. Beale to Goldman, 22 November 1952, b10, f1, HKBP.

40. Robert Dallek, *Franklin Roosevelt and American Foreign Policy, 1932–1945* (New York, 1979), 289; Warren F. Kimball, *The Most Unsordid Act: Lend Lease, 1939–1941* (Baltimore, 1969), 235.

41. Thomas C. Kennedy, *Charles A. Beard and American Foreign Policy* (Gainesville, 1975), 135; Harry Elmer Barnes, *Perpetual War for Perpetual Peace: A Critical Examination of the Foreign Policy of Franklin Delano Roosevelt and Its Aftermath* (New York, 1953), viii.

Chapter Four

1. The push to make history "scientific" may have gained momentum, as a young Carl Becker observed, because many in the academy refused to take the discipline seriously. "It is a noticeable fact that most Ethnologists, Anthropologists, Philologists and professors of kindred sciences and ever many philosophers consider . . . History as little above contempt. As one noted philosopher says of it, 'The gossip of Kings and Queens.'" Becker, "Wild Thoughts Notebook #2," 16 November 1894, b7, CBP.

2. Kraus and Joyce, *Writing of American History*, 30.

3. Paul Buhle, introduction to *History and the New Left: Madison, Wisconsin, 1950–1970*, ed. Buhle (Philadelphia, 1990), 14.

4. In the 1948 election, Truman swept the Midwest excepting Indiana and Michigan. On McCarthy's tepid Ohio Valley support, see Michael Paul Rogin's *The Intellectuals and McCarthy: The Radical Specter* (Cambridge, 1967). Saloutos is an interesting case—the son of Greek immigrants *and* an affiliate of the Midwestern School. While searching for a job in 1941, he thought his ethnicity a distinct handicap in a largely Wasp profession. Hicks tried to convince him otherwise: "Where do you get this stuff about being 'non-Aryan?' You're a Greek, not a Jew, and no one even thinks of a Greek as a non-Aryan. Don't use that term unless you want people to think you're just out of the synagogue." Hicks to Saloutos, 8 August 1941, b1, f3, TSP. Many years later, during the 1960s push for diversity in the universities, Saloutos proudly embraced his ethnic heritage, at least partly in reaction to the social radicalism of the era. "Next fall I am teaching for the first time a course on 'the Immigrant in America,'" he wrote Hicks. "I got kind of irked with all the attention being given to the Negroes, the Mexican-Americans and the likes. The assumption seems to be that they have been the only under-privileged people in the country who have encountered discrimination and cultural deprivation. Hell, my parents never spoke English, even when I was a graduate student. I did work to keep myself going that some of these punks would never do. Some day when I find the time I will sit down and write up my experiences as the oldest child in an immigrant family of six and what it was like living in two worlds. These young people have opportunities now that were non-existent when I was growing up." Saloutos to Hicks, 22 February 1969, b5, JHP.

5. Among graduate student radicals in the Wisconsin School, George Rawick belonged to the Young Communist League and Ronald Radosh to the Labor Youth League. Beale to Thomas, 21 January 1941, b23, f11, HKBP.

6. Paul Schrecker, "The Observations of a European Philosopher," *Harper's Magazine*, July 1944, 18; Curti to John Marshall, 30 July 1944, b463, f3957, Rockefeller Foundation Archives; Martha Y. Peel to Hesseltine, 12 June 1956, b18, f3, WBHP. The State Department seemed to regard Curti as politically suspect. In 1951—the year he served as president of the Mississippi Valley Historical Association—it denied him a passport. Curti never received an adequate justification from the government, but he presumed that his being listed (erroneously) as a faculty member of the communist front Abraham Lincoln School in Chicago probably precipitated the action. During these secretive McCarthy years, Curti later recalled, "the FBI . . . made no effort to evaluate the information. How easy it would have been at the time . . . had someone in the Passport Division or some other part of the cultural relations program in the State Department, asked me about this, and I could have straightened it out." Curti to H. F. Peters, 10 April 1981, Accession M96–046, b2, f5, MCP.

7. Susman to Curti and Fred Harrington, 9 April 1953, b40, f5, MCP.

8. Susman to Curti, 10 January 1954, b40, f4, MCP.

9. Merle Curti, *Probing Our Past* (New York, 1955), 158.

10. Margaret Sanger, *Pivot of Civilization* (New York, 1922), 279; Paul Elmer More, *Aristocracy and Justice* (New York, 1967 ed.), 58–59; and Norman Foerster, *The American State University: Its Relation to Democracy* (Chapel Hill, 1929), 184, quoted in J. David Hoeveler Jr., *The New Humanism: A Critique of Modern America, 1900–1940* (Charlottesville, 1977), 117.

11. Daniel Bell, ed., *The Radical Right* (New York, 1963 rev. ed.), 167, 115. The Columbia School's midcentury efforts to discover an American "authoritarian personality" made a powerful impact on the nation's intellectual community. Daniel Aaron declared in a *Political Science Quarterly* review that *The New American Right* offered a "provocative and convincing diagnosis of the McCarthyite mentality and the conditions that foster it." Rudolf Heberle wrote in the *American Sociological Review* that the book represented "a fine example of sociological analysis.... [Its] authors manage to maintain as much detachment as possible in dealing with a project of this kind." See *Political Science Quarterly,* March 1956, 128,l and *American Sociological Review,* August 1956, 517.

12. Merle Curti, *The Making of an American Community: A Case Study of Democracy in a Frontier County* (Stanford, 1959), 1, 443, 444, 447, 448; Curti to Paul Knaplund, 3 March 1957, b4, f1, PKP. Nearly a decade after the Trempealeau volume appeared, Hofstadter replied to Curti. In a book on middle-western historical writing, he noted that "Merle Curti's study of Trempealeau County ... finds some support for the Turnerian view of the frontier and democracy, but ... the site was chosen not for its representativeness but for its convenience and ... the findings are in some respects qualified." Hofstadter, *Progressive Historians,* 474.

13. Curti, University of Wisconsin Oral History Project, 1982.

14. "Merle Curti: Historian and University Professor," Accession, M96–046, b3, f4, MCP, emphasis added.

15. William Hesseltine, *The Rise of Third Parties: From Anti-Masonry to Wallace* (Washington, 1948), 74–75.

16. Gutman, "Learning about History," in *History and the New Left,* ed. Buhle, 48. Columbia had once, of course, been a vibrant center of progressive thought, the home of Beard, Dewey, and James Harvey Robinson. Then, following World War II, the university—deeply involved in providing ideas and arguments strong enough to sustain the new liberalism—grew noticeably less "oppositional."

17. Richard Hofstadter, "Democracy and Anti-intellectualism in America," *Michigan Alumnus Quarterly Review,* 8 August 1953, 281.

18. Ibid., 296.

19. Curti to Hofstadter, 20 November 1953, b34, RHP; Curti to Arthur Ekirch, 29 November 1953, Accession M97–258, f1, MCP. Considering their ideological differences in the 1950s, it is interesting to note that a generation earlier, a young Hofstadter looked to Curti for political guidance. "During the summer," Curti wrote a friend in 1983, "I read Susan Baker's ms. [published two years later as *Radical Beginnings: Richard Hofstadter and the 1930s*], a much documented biography of Hofstadter. From her research it seems I had a lot of influence on Dick, perhaps not for the best. He saw me as a Marxist historian at a time he was edging toward Communism (though we often lunched together I did not know he was briefly a member of the Party). According to Baker, he kept from his Marxist dallying, to which he expressed much appreciation to me, a dialectical method of presenting paradoxes and contradictions in all his work. I hadn't thought of myself as a Marxist historian." Curti to Ekirch, 14 September 1983, Accession M97–258, f1, MCP.

20. Curti, "Intellectuals and Other People," *American Historical Review,* January 1955, 27.

21. Ibid., 279.

22. Ibid., 277.

23. Ibid., 278, 280, 282.

24. For a recent assessment of the association's early years, see Ian Tyrrell, "Public at the Creation: Place, Memory, and Historical Practice in the Mississippi Valley Historical Association, 1907–1950," *Journal of American History*, June 2007, 19–46.

25. James B. Sellers, "Before We Were Members—The Mississippi Valley Historical Association," *Mississippi Valley Historical Review*, June 1953, 10.

26. "News and Comments," *Mississippi Valley Historical Review*, June 1914, 158.

27. Sellers, "Before We Were Members," 19.

28. Paine, quoted in William D. Aeschbacher, "The Mississippi Valley Historical Association, 1907–1965," *Journal of American History*, September 1967, 343.

29. Curti to Beale, 24 April 1946, b6, f23, HKBP. Reforming the MVHA would have to be a largely "inside" job. As Curti remarked to Beale of the 1946 Bloomington conference, "no one from Yale, Columbia, or Harvard attended."

30. Beale to Paine, 10 April 1951, b33, f17, OAHR; Gates to Curti, 20 February 1951, b26, f16, MCP; Pierce to Curti, 18 May 1951, b9, f7, BLPP; Ray Allen Billington, "From Association to Organization: The OAH in the Bad Old Days," *Journal of American History*, June 1978, 83. Aside from encouraging an end to Paine's rule, Curti's presidency unleashed momentum to drop the association's name for one that more accurately reflected the composition of the organization. One petition made the case for the change as follows: the MVHA no longer reflected a merely regional perspective; an increasing number of its members lived outside the valley; the articles published in the *Review* were national in scope; some budget-conscious libraries mistook the *Review* for a sectional journal and declined to purchase it. A number of alternative titles were proposed (Curti preferred "Association of American History"), and in October 1951—the midmark of Curti's presidency—the reformers forced an association-wide election on whether to change the name of both the *Review* and the MVHA. Tradition carried the day. The proposal was decisively defeated 530 (70%) to 236 (30%). Yet the point should not be lost that Curti's presidency encouraged a rethinking of association mores that eventually bore fruit. In 1965, 80 percent of its membership voted in the affirmative for a new name—the Organization of American Historians. Aeschbacher, "Mississippi Valley Historical Association," 339.

31. Shannon to Curti, 10 February 1951, b26, f17, MCP.

32. Gates to Curti, 20 February 1951, b26, f16, MCP; Beale, "Motion before the MVHA," b33, f17, OAHR.

33. Dwight Dumond to Clarence S. Paine, 27 November 1953, b34, f5, OAHR.

34. Oldfather to Becker, 29 October 1935, b10, CBP.

35. Curti to Gates, 19 November 1943, b11, f1, MCP. Seven years earlier, job candidate Curti experienced a religious litmus test of his own. American University wanted to offer him a post but only if he could testify to sufficient personal involvement in church activities. "I've had a talk with [the] Chancellor," one AU official informed Curti. "He wishes the definite offer to you to be withheld until he learns whether you are a member of a church. . . . Although to some persons the case might seem unusual, it is a very simple one. The school has a Christian tradition, which it would like to sustain and a constituency proud of that tradition. It believes that religion is as much a part of life as food or entertainment or scholarship. It wants its members to recognize the fact by belonging to some church and respecting the place of religion in life. I realize that it would be easy for

a person to imagine witch-hunters behind these words." What Curti imagined is not on record; what we do know is that soon after receiving this letter he accepted a position at Columbia University's Teachers College. Eugene Anderson to Curti, 2 February 1937, b2, f14, MCP.

36. Goldman to Curti, 25 January 1949, b17, f23, MCP.

37. Hesseltine to Joe Matthews, 28 October 1938, b4, f5, WBHP; E. David Cronon and John W. Jenkins, *The University of Wisconsin: A History, 1945–1917, Renewal to Revolution* (Madison, 1999), 4:17, 19.

38. Curti, University of Wisconsin Oral History Project, 1975; LaFeber interview with author.

39. George Rawick, "I Dissent," in *History and the New Left,* ed. Buhle, 54; Rawick to Curti, 30 October 1956, b34, f24, MCP. As things turned out, Beale later came to Rawick's aid when he was "viciously red-baited" by a member of his doctoral committee. "I want you to know," he wrote Beale, "how deeply I appreciate what you did for me at the examination. Although I do not know exactly what went on when I left the room, I am fairly certain that you were instrumental in having the committee grant me the degree." Rawick to Beale, 15 June 1957, b20, f9, WBHP. For an "insider" appraisal of Beale's motives for defending Rawick—one emphasizing the intricate personal dynamics of the department—see Michael Fellman's "Madison Daze," *Labour/Le Travail,* Spring 1992, 221–27.

40. Rawick to Curti, 16 July 1956, b34, f24, MCP.

41. Curti to J. D. Bright, 31 May 1955, b11, f3, MCP; Rawick, "I Dissent," 54, 55–56. In touting the job candidacy of one Protestant student, Curti wrote, "McKee grew up in a Presbyterian parsonage in Pennsylvania and . . . has continued to have and to try to exemplify the Christian virtues." Curti to Dwight E. Lee, 30 April 1957, b11, f3, MCP.

42. Perlman to Curti, 6 May 1950, b29, f19, MCP, emphasis in original.

43. Curti to Selig, 7 June 1950, b11, f1, MCP. John Hope Franklin accepted an invitation to teach the 1953 spring semester at the University of Wisconsin as a visiting professor. In 1964 he left Brooklyn College for the University of Chicago, seeing the move as "an opportunity never before extended to me, one that I had struggled and aimed for since the start of my academic career as a Harvard graduate student. . . . To be sure, several major institutions had invited me to visit for a summer or a semester, but the emphasis was always on visiting, after which I was to return from whence I came." John Hope Franklin, *Mirror to America: The Autobiography of John Hope Franklin* (New York, 2005), 207. Women's history first came to the University of Wisconsin through the Extension Division—and it was not pioneered at Madison. Jane Schulenburg, a medievalist and student of David Herlihy (his wife had a PhD in Russian history and he accepted women graduate students), began teaching "women from the Ancient World to the Renaissance" on the Milwaukee campus. The 1971 hire of Lindstrom led to the first course on women's history taught at Madison— HI 392. The section's 390 designation ("special topics") came about because many in the department dismissed the class as a fad and believed it might disappear. "At Madison," Schulenburg explains, "there was Turner, the frontier, and political history. These were all sacred cows affirmed by the department's curriculum. Women's history, by comparison, was something both alien and alienating." Schulenburg interview with author.

44. Susman to Curti, 17 March 1959, b40, f5, MCP.

45. "The Challenges and Rewards of Textbook Writing: An Interview with Alan Brin-

kley," *Journal of American History*, March 2005, 1391. In the early 1990s, Brinkley engaged in a revealing cross-generational conversation with William Leuchtenburg concerning the relative contributions of progressivism and liberalism. After reading an early draft of Brinkley's *The End of Reform: New Deal Liberalism in Recession and War*, Leuchtenburg thought his younger colleague had been perhaps too critical of liberal politics. "Is the situation really so bleak?" he wrote. "I think for example of the way that the postwar liberals starting in the Truman era moved civil rights to the forefront as it was not earlier, of the many changes wrought by liberals on the Warren Court, of the program of the Great Society. . . . One also wonders whether there is an implication in saying that liberalism does not have the answers that there is some other creed that does." Brinkley replied in part: "I do not mean to sound as censorious about postwar liberalism as I apparently do. I still consider the liberal achievements of the 1960s among the most important of this century. I do feel, though, that by the 1980s that form of liberalism had in some ways exhausted itself." Leuchtenburg to Brinkley, 1 August 1994, b3, WLP; Brinkley to Leuchtenburg, 4 August 1994, b3, WLP.

Chapter Five

1. Carl D. Weiner to Harold Baron, 4 August 1959, SOLP; Thomas Bailey, *America Faces Russia: Russian American Relations From Early Times to Our Day* (Ithaca, 1950), 355. Wisconsin historian David Shannon was an early Nevins critic. He wrote to a colleague (who also happened to be his uncle) in 1951 that "Wall Street has grown several miles to include Fayerweather [the hall housing Columbia University's historians]. Did you read Nevins' speech on the writing of business history and the proper treatment of business figures? It seems that a critical attitude toward the Robber Barons (banish the phrase!) is now 'effeminate.' I'll bet that speech will get him a several thousand dollar grant from the National Association of Manufacturers." David Shannon to Fred Shannon, 4 September 1951, b3, FSP.

2. Irving Howe and Diana Trilling in *Arguing the World: The New York Intellectuals in Their Own Words*, ed. Joseph Dorman (New York, 2000), 60.

3. "Our Country and Our Culture," *Partisan Review*, May-June 1952, 282, 319.

4. Ibid., 591.

5. John Kenneth Galbraith, *The Affluent Society* (New York, 1958), 4.

6. William Appleman Williams, *The Great Evasion: An Essay on the Contemporary Relevance of Karl Marx and on the Wisdom of Admitting the Heretic into the Dialogue about America's Future* (Chicago, 1964), 23, 83.

7. Richard Hofstadter, *The American Political Tradition: And the Men Who Made It* (New York, 1948), 55–56; Galbraith, *Affluent Society*, 7.

8. Weinstein interview with author.

9. Louis Hartz, *The Liberal Tradition in America: An Interpretation of American Political Thought since the Revolution* (New York, 1955), 11.

10. Godfrey Hodgson, *America in Our Time* (New York, 1976), 94.

11. Jeffry Kaplow, "Parenthesis: 1952–1956," and Richard Schickel, "A Journalist among Historians," in *History and the New Left*, ed. Buhle, 65, 95.

12. Perlman, interview, 13 April 1950, WHS.

13. Paul Buhle, "Madison: An Introduction," in *History and the New Left*, ed. Buhle, 6, 120; Gilbert interview with author.

14. Landau and Gilbert interviews with author.

15. Mosse, *Confronting History*, 157; Gilbert interview with author. "We were all Protestants raised in a tradition of suspicion of centralized power," write Lloyd C. Gardner and Thomas J. McCormick in "Walter LaFeber: The Making of a Wisconsin School Revisionist," *Diplomatic History*, November 2004, 616.

16. LaFeber interview with author.

17. Gilbert interview with author.

18. Ibid. *Studies'* circle included the documentary filmmaker Saul Landau, the long-time editor of the progressive magazine *In These Times* James Weinstein, and the playwright Eleanor Hakim.

19. Bank Records, b14, f2, SOLP; Subscriptions and Addresses Lists, 7 December 1962, b14, f1, SOLP.

20. Andrew Hacker, "The Rebelling Young Scholars," *Commentary*, November 1960, 412.

21. Sklar to "Dear Studiers," 14 November 1960, b9, f5, SOLP.

22. Weinstein to Saul Landau, internal evidence suggests 1959, b5, f18, SOLP; Hakim to George Rawick, 23 January 1961, b8, f3, SOLP.

23. Eleanor Hakim to Genovese, 30 April 1961, b3, f6, SOLP.

24. Rawick to Eleanor Hakim, 21 January 1961, b8, f3, SOLP; Hakim to Rawick, 23 January 1961, b8, f3, SOLP.

25. "A Statement by the Editors: The Radicalism of Disclosure," *Studies on the Left*, Fall 1959, 2.

26. Boorstin's testimony can be found in Eric Bentley, ed., *Thirty Years of Treason: Excerpts from Hearings before the House Committee on Un-American Activities* (New York, 2002 ed.), 601–12; Arthur Schlesinger Jr., *A Thousand Days: John F. Kennedy in the White House* (Boston, 1965), 266.

27. "From the Editors," *Studies on the Left* 2, no. 3 (1962): 4.

28. Vander Zanden to Sklar, 18 December 1959, b9, f5, SOLP.

29. "From the Editors: The Ultra Right and Cold War Liberalism," *Studies on the Left* 3, no. 1 (1962): 8.

30. Carl Weiner to Weinstein, 22 May 1963, b10, f9, SOLP.

31. "With the Movement," *Studies on the Left* 5, no. 2 (1965): 61; Evan Stark, "Theory on the Left," *Studies on the Left* 5, no. 4 (1965): 82. *Studies'* movement toward an increasingly activist agenda can be glimpsed in a 1964 letter from Weinstein to Todd Gitlin proposing a kind of working relationship between SOL and Students for a Democratic Society. "Since we are now orienting ourselves a little more directly toward analyses of current American problems, we would be particularly interested in anything that underlies the strategic plans for S.D.S.—that is your analysis of the various movements for social reform, the role of radical (left liberal, if you prefer) students in the general society, the problem of the influence from within or from without the system, etc." Weinstein to Gitlin, 18 March 1964, b3, f21, SOLP.

32. Jonathan M. Wiener, "Radical Historians and the Crisis in American History, 1959–1980," *Journal of American History*, September 1989, 408–9.

33. James Weinstein, *The Corporate Ideal in the Liberal State, 1900-1918* (Boston, 1968), ix.

34. Arthur Schlesinger Jr., *The Age of Jackson* (Boston, 1945), 505.

35. Weinstein, *Corporate Ideal in the Liberal State*, xi.

36. John Higham, "Changing Paradigms: The Collapse of Consensus," *Journal of American History*, September 1989, 463.

Chapter Six

1. Harrington, University of Wisconsin Oral History Project, 1982, 144; Harrington to Richard Current, 6 November 1991, b12, FHHP.

2. Cole to Walter LaFeber, 6 January 1985, b4, WSCP. Gardner and McCormick wrote of one 1956-57 seminar session that the students' "collective failure to engage Beard's arguments led Harrington to suggest, at Seminar's end that we reread Beard's *The Idea of National Interest* and make him the focus of our next meeting." Gardner and McCormick, "Walter LaFeber," 615.

3. Charles A Beard with the collaboration of George H. E. Smith, *The Idea of a National Interest: An Analytical Study in American Foreign Policy* (New York, 1934), 167.

4. Andrew J. Bacevich, *American Empire: The Realities and Consequences of U.S. Diplomacy* (Cambridge, 2002), 18-19.

5. Samuel Flagg Bemis, *A Diplomatic History of the United States* (New York, 1965 rev. ed.), 475.

6. Ibid., 907.

7. Bailey, *America Faces Russia*, 336, 331, 330, 338, 353.

8. After completing the dissertation, Cole sent the manuscript to Yale University Press, but not before Harrington advised him to erase all Wisconsin connections from his cover letter. "In writing Yale, use your Arkansas stationery. . . . No need to mention me . . . just submit it with your own letter. Bemis is at Yale." After Yale passed on the manuscript, the University of Wisconsin Press published it. Harrington to Cole, 2 March 1949 and 9 July 1951, b4, WSCP.

9. Harrington, University of Wisconsin Oral History Project, 1982, 2-22.

10. Harrington to LaFeber, 30 May 1984, b10, FHHP.

11. Harrington, University of Wisconsin Oral History Project, 1982, 144-45; Harrington to Cole, 31 March 1991, b4, WSCP. Robert Freeman Smith recently observed that "if there is such a thing as a Wisconsin School of Diplomatic History it has to be an ecumenical school. There is not one party line because Fred had a number of different students, both liberal and conservative." Smith interview with author.

12. David Cronon interview with author; Gardner to Darod Wax, 5 March 1986, b2, WAWP; LaFeber to Bill Robbins, 22 February 1986, b5, f7, WAWP; Paul Buhle and Edward Rice-Maximin, *William Appleman Williams: The Tragedy of Empire* (New York, 1995), 97.

13. Harrington, University of Wisconsin Oral History Project, 1982, 150-51.

14. William Appleman Williams, *The Roots of the Modern American Empire: A Study of the Growth and Shaping of Social Consciousness in a Marketplace Society* (New York, 1969), xxii. On the influence of radical farming movements on Williams, Wayne Cole (himself an Iowa native) believed that "in some respects [Williams] may have been more of a western popu-

list than a Marxist." Cole to Harrington, 21 May 1991, b4, WSCP. For Williams's dissent from the Hofstadter and Pollack views of Populism, see Williams to Weinstein, internal evidence suggests early 1960s, b10, f3, SOLP, emphasis in original.

15. Gardner interview with author. In New England, Schlesinger Jr. took his precollegiate training at Exeter Academy. There, in 1932, for the first (but not the last) time, he spoke against Herbert Hoover—a man Williams would come to admire. "I am a member of the debating society here," Schlesinger reported to University of Chicago historian Bessie Louise Pierce, his onetime babysitter and a former student and colleague of his father, "and we have held several meetings at which the various merits of the three presidential candidates were argued. The school is pro-Hoover by a tremendous majority; the ratio is about 16–1 over Roosevelt and 10–1 over Thomas. I am, however, a strong supporter of Roosevelt. I have had a lot of fun trying to speak to ardent Republicans and make myself heard over their boos." Arthur M. Schlesinger Jr. to Bessie Louise Pierce, 22 October 1932, b2, f7, BLPP.

16. Williams, "An Interview with William Appleman Williams," by Michael Wallace, *Radical History Review,* Winter 1979–80, 65–66.

17. William Appleman Williams, "A Good Life and a Good Death: A Memoir of an Independent Lady," manuscript, b3, f4, WAWP; Buhle and Rice-Maximin, *Williams Appleman Williams,* 22–23.

18. Williams to James Groshong, 22 July 1989, b1, f10, WAWP.

19. Turner, *Frontier in American History,* 219; William Appleman Williams, "Foreign Policy of the Mind," *Commentary,* February 1962, 157.

20. William Appleman Williams, *The Contours of American History* (New York, 1973 rev. ed.), 454.

21. Williams to Frank Unger, 7 June 1985, b1, f5, WAWP.

22. Patricia Nelson Limerick, "Dilemmas in Forgiveness: William Appleman Williams and Western American History," *Diplomatic History,* Spring 2001, 294.

23. Williams, "Interview with Williams Appleman Williams," 85.

24. Mosse, *Confronting History,* 158.

25. Williams, "Interview with William Appleman Williams," 76, 78; Williams, *Tragedy,* 206.

26. Williams, *Tragedy,* 207.

27. Williams, "Production for Peace," *Nation,* 21 February 1959, 151.

28. Buhle and Rice-Maximin, *William Appleman Williams,* 126; Williams, *Contours,* 183, 239, 409, 455, 210, 221, 485.

29. *Mississippi Valley Historical Review,* March 1962, 743–44, and September 1962, 407–8. Williams was by this time no doubt accustomed to harsh reviews. One unsympathetic commentator wrote of *Tragedy* that "measured against the normal standards of historiography, this book cannot be taken seriously as history" (*American Political Science Review,* December 1958, 1195). Handlin's "bullying"—or at least his criticism—of Williams continued throughout the 1960s, recalling the previous decade's contest between Morison and Curti. In both instances, two sharply defined points of view squared off. On the one side stood Harvard—elite, proconsensus, and proestablishment; on the other side was Wisconsin—egalitarian, progressive, and antiestablishment. This dispute forces a rethinking of common historiographical convictions. There is a tendency to regard the

contrast between the generation of Morison and the generation of Handlin—from patrician Brahmin to working-class Jewish immigrant, from New England history to urban, immigrant, and social history—as definitive. But their ideological positions reveal a great degree of continuity. As in other respects, it does for the Harvard-taught Curti and the Annapolis-trained Williams. I'm indebted to Wilfred McClay for this observation.

30. Arthur Schlesinger Jr., "Origins of the Cold War," *Foreign Affairs,* October 1967, 23.

31. Robert James Maddox, *The New Left and the Origins of the Cold War* (Princeton, 1973), 20. For Williams's defense of seriated quotations and other matters, see his response to Francis Loewenheim's "The New Left and the Origins of the Cold War" in the *New York Times Book Review,* 17 June 1973, 7; Hesseltine to Elmer Ellis, 12 July 1960, b22, f6, WBHP.

32. Maddox, *The New Left and Origins of the Cold War,* 10, italics in original; Handlin, "The Failure of the Historians," *Freedom at Issue,* September-October 1975, 3.

33. LaFeber interview with author; Williams to Mosse, 13 January 1969, GMP. Allen Davis thought Williams's move to a less distinguished university odd and asked him about it. "I am not moving to Oregon State University," came the reply; "I am moving to the state of Oregon." Quoted in Davis interview with author.

34. Harrington to Cole, 31 March 1991, b4, WCP.

35. William Appleman Williams, *Empire as a Way of Life: An Essay on the Causes and Character of America's Present Predicament along with a Few Thoughts about an Alternative* (New York, 1980), xi, italics in original.

Chapter Seven

1. Jensen to John Hicks, 28 April 1971, b28, JHPB.

2. For information on Lasch's early life I have consulted Christopher Lasch, "History as Social Criticism: Conversations with Christopher Lasch," interview by Casey Blake and Christopher Phelps, *Journal of American History,* March 1994, 1310–32; Christopher Lasch, "An Interview with Christopher Lasch" by Richard Wightman Fox, *Intellectual History Newsletter* 16 (1994): 3–14; and a draft of Eric Miller's 2002 University of Delaware dissertation "American Sojourn: A Life of Christopher Lasch," in possession of author.

3. Lasch, "Interview with Christopher Lasch," 4, 3.

4. Ibid., 4; Kit to Mom and Dad, 11 October 1950, b0, f2, CLP. The Christopher Lasch Papers include some twenty files containing almost exclusively letters between Lasch and his parents, with some thirty additional files containing such communications interspersed with other correspondence.

5. Kit to Mom and Dad, 23 September 1950, b0, f2, CLP; Lasch, "Interview with Christopher Lasch," 5. Lasch did write an unpublished novel on Watergate.

6. Kit to Mom and Dad, 23 September 1950, b0, f2, CLP. Former Hollis residents include Ralph Waldo Emerson, Charles Sumner, Wendell Phillips, Charles Francis Adams, Henry David Thoreau, George Santayana, and Horatio Alger. As the twenty-fifth anniversary of his graduation approached, Parrington caustically informed the class secretary of his recent labors: "The past five years I have spent in study and writing, up to my ears in the economic interpretation of American history and literature, getting the last lingering Harvard prejudices out of my system." Secretary's Sixth Report, Harvard College Class of

1893 (1918), 220–21, as quoted in Hofstadter, *Progressive Historians*, 364. On Curti's encounter with Channing, see Curti, University of Wisconsin Oral History Project, 1982.

7. Morton Keller and Phyllis Keller, *Making Harvard Modern: The Rise of America's University* (Oxford, 2001), 224; David Burner correspondence with author; Kit to Mom and Dad, 27 March 1953, b0, f10, CLP, as quoted in Miller, "American Sojourn," 51.

8. Lasch, "Interview with Christopher Lasch," 6, 7, 8.

9. Kit to Mom and Dad, 5 November 1952, b0, f8, CLP, as quoted in Miller, "American Sojourn," 56; Christopher Lasch, *The American Liberals and the Russian Revolution* (New York, 1962), xiii, xvi.

10. Richard Hofstadter, *Anti-intellectualism in American Life* (New York, 1963), 3.

11. Alfred Kazin, "Radicals and Intellectuals," *New York Review of Books*, 20 May 1965, 3; Hofstadter to Lasch, 27 September 1964, and Lasch to Hofstadter, 3 October 1964, both in b9, f26, CLP.

12. Lasch, *The New Radicalism: The Intellectual as a Social Type* (New York, 1965), 308; Schlesinger Jr. to Rovere, 10 April 1965, bP-38, ASJP, Harvard University; and "Intellectuals under Fire," *Sunday Times*, 27 February 1966, as quoted in Miller, "American Sojourn," 205–6.

13. Lasch, *New Radicalism*, xv, 146.

14. Ibid., 159.

15. Ibid.

16. Ibid., 146.

17. Lasch, "Interview with Christopher Lasch," 9.

18. Robert B. Westbrook, "Christopher Lasch, *The New Radicalism*, and the Vocation of Intellectuals," *Reviews in American History*, March 1995, 186.

19. Lasch, *New Radicalism*, 316.

20. Kit to Mom and Dad, 16 January 1968, b0, f38, CLP.

21. Kit to Mom and Dad, 2 January 1970, b2, f21, CLP.

22. Christopher Lasch, *The Agony of the American Left* (New York, 1969), 208, 211.

23. Kit to Mom and Dad, 2 January and 26 March 1970, b2, f21 and b0, f38, CLP; Lasch to Williams, 30 April 1970, b3, f1, CLP. For a few brief years it might be said that a "Rochester School" became the heir of the Wisconsin School. Consider the following remarks by Steven Hahn on the origins of his influential study *The Roots of Southern Populism:* "This book has . . . its . . . roots in a senior honors essay completed at the University of Rochester under the direction of Christopher Lasch, whose penetrating criticisms forced much fruitful re-thinking. Rochester was quite a splendid place to learn history, for I had the unusual opportunity of also working with Eugene Genovese, Herbert Gutman, Leon Fink, Bruce Palmer, and Bruce Levine. All taught me a great deal, not only about history but about the relationship of scholarship and political commitment." Steven Hahn, *The Roots of Southern Populism: Yeoman Farmers and the Transformation of the Georgia Upcountry, 1850–1890* (New York, 1983), ix.

24. Lasch, "Interview with Christopher Lasch," 11; Lasch to Michael Rogin, 26 May 1976, b19, f23, CLP; Christopher Lasch, *Haven in a Heartless World: The Family Besieged* (New York, 1977), xvi, xvii.

25. Lasch, *Haven*, 111.

26. Ibid., xx.

27. Ibid., 183, 189.

28. Marshall Berman, "Family Affairs," *New York Times Book Review,* 15 January 1978, 20; David Brion Davis, "The Invasion of the Family," *New York Review of Books,* 23 February 1978, 38.

29. Lasch, "Interview with Christopher Lasch," 12. Lasch devoted several pages of *Haven* to Wallace, a sociologist teaching in the 1930s, like Zora Schaupp, at the University of Nebraska. Though conceding that Wallace was "a lesser Veblen," Lasch seemed to identify with this man from the provinces and certainly agreed with his criticism of Progressive-era family sociology "from a leftist position that harked back to . . . the best of populism." Lasch, *Haven,* 20, 51, 50.

30. Lasch to Jonathan Galassi, 8 June 1977, b18, f31, CLP; Christopher Lasch, *The Culture of Narcissism: American Life in an Age of Diminishing Expectations* (New York, 1991 ed.), xv, xvi.

31. Ibid., 248.

32. Kit to Mom and Dad, 6 March and 30 August 1979, b30, f40, CLP.

33. *People,* 9 July 1979.

34. Lasch, "Interview with Christopher Lasch," 12; Lasch, *New Radicalism,* 331.

35. Kit to Mom and Dad, 11 June 1979, b5, f8, CLP.

36. Ibid.

37. Lasch to Bell, 8 November 1979, b20, f6, CLP; Lasch to Powell, 10 June 1979, b20, f6, CLP. Lasch later noted that he "wrote a couple of letters to [presidential adviser Pat] Caddell, who had invited further commentary, [in which I maintained] that this interest in cultural renewal, renewal of family values, work ethic, and so on, had to be set in the context of a quite different kind of politics than the kind of politics that they obviously had in mind, whereas I [argued for] a populistic politics." Lasch, "Interview with Christopher Lasch," 13.

38. Lasch, "Interview with Christopher Lasch," 13; Lasch to Ed and Cheryl, 3 August 1979, b5, f5, CLP.

39. Lasch to Gottfried, 28 August 1989, b7a, f21, CLP.

40. Lasch to Gottfried, 17 October 1989, b7a, f21, CLP.

41. *The Antaeus Report: From the Center for the Study of Education and Society,* Fall 1980, b6, f8, CLP; Lasch to Glenn Van Warreby, 20 July 1981, b6, f9, CLP.

42. Christopher Lasch, *The True and Only Heaven: Progress and Its Critics* (New York, 1991), 17, 15, 282, 379, 389.

43. Ibid., 174.

44. On republicanism see Bernard Bailyn's *The Ideological Origins of the American Revolution* (Cambridge, 1967); Gordon Wood's *The Creation of the American Republic, 1776–1787* (Chapel Hill, 1969), and J. G. A. Pocock's *The Machiavellian Moment: Florentine Political Thought and the Atlantic Republican Tradition* (Princeton, 1975). An excellent overview of the literature can be found in Daniel T. Rogers's "Republicanism: The Career of a Concept," *Journal of American History,* June 1992, 11–38.

45. *True and Only Heaven,* 17.

46. Ibid., 122.

47. James T. Kloppenberg, review of *True and Only Heaven, Journal of American History,*

March 1992, 1402; Robert Lasch to Christopher Lasch, 16 February 1991, b7b, f12, CLP. To Merle Curti, another "old progressive," Lasch's attempts to revive the Populist persuasion struck a false note. "The Lasch book in the first chapters interested me a lot," wrote a ninety-four-year-old Curti of *The True and Only Heaven*. "But I gave up on it long before coming to the end. . . . His high esteem for all the old pieties seemed sentimental and romantic." Curti to Arthur Ekirch, 18 September 1991, f1, MCP, Ascension, M97−258.

48. On his alienation from popular politics, Lasch wrote his parents days before the 1980 general election that "the whole system, now run by the media, is effectively rigged against any third party in any foreseeable elections. Yet I am still persuaded a third party is just about the only hope of bringing about any real change, and I cling to the faint hope that [John] Anderson's candidacy, and the wide-spread disaffection from both Carter and Regan, may somehow create a little elbow room for dissident movements and parties in the future." Kit to Mom and Dad, 30 October 1980, b0, f40, CLP.

Chapter Eight

1. Niall Ferguson, *Colossus: The Rise and Fall of the American Empire* (New York, 2004), viii.

2. Andrew Bacevich, *American Empire: The Realities and Consequences* (Cambridge, 2002), 244, italics in original.

3. "The Military and U.S. Foreign Policy: Conversation with Andrew J. Bacevich," interview by Harry Kreisler, http://globetrotter.berkeley.edu/people5/Bacevich/bacevich-con2.html, accessed 19 August 2008.

4. Ibid.

5. Bacevich, *American Empire*, ix.

6. Andrew Bacevich, introduction to William Appleman Williams, *Empire as a Way of Life: An Essay on the Causes and Character of America's Present Predicament Along with a Few Thoughts About an Alternative* (New York, 2007 ed.), v, x. On Bacevich's belief that the United States is engaged in an unwinnable war in Iraq, see his "The Islamic Way of War," *American Conservative*, 11 September 2006; on parallels between the Vietnam and Iraq wars, see his "Vietnam's Real lessons," *Los Angeles Times*, 25 August 2007.

7. http://www.quotedb.com/quotes/3258, accessed 19 August 2008.

8. Milton Friedman, *Capitalism and Freedom* (Chicago, 1962), 15.

9. Huey Long, "1935 Senate Speech and Radio Address," *Congressional Record*, January 14, 1935, http://www.voxygen.net/cpa/speeches/longtxt.htm.

10. William Allen White, "What's the Matter with Kansas?" in *Great Issues in American History*, ed. Richard Hofstadter and Beatrice K. Hofstadter, rev. ed. (New York, 1982), 3:168.

11. Thomas Frank, *What's the Matter with Kansas? How Conservatives Won the Heart of America* (New York, 2004), 29.

12. Ibid., 243.

13. Ibid., 250.

14. Cronon, University of Wisconsin Oral History Project, 2000; http://www.williamcronon.net/gallery/homeshow/gallery_home_page_slide_show.htm.

15. Cronon, University of Wisconsin Oral History Project, 2000.

16. Ibid.

17. William Cronon, "Landscape and Home: Environmental Traditions in Wisconsin," *Wisconsin Magazine of History,* Winter 1990–91, 105; Cronon interview with author.

18. Cronon, University of Wisconsin Oral History Project, 2000.

19. William Cronon, interview by New River Media for PBS, http://www.pbs.org/fmc/interviews/cronon.htm.

20. Lizabeth Cohen's *A Consumers' Republic: The Politics of Mass Consumption in Postwar America* (2003) and Daniel Horowitz's *The Anxieties of Affluence: Critiques of American Consumer Culture, 1939–1979* (2004) are but two important recent statements on the uses of abundance to advance social equality and democratize the "American Dream." Both operate within a general analytical framework anticipated by Turner.

21. William Cronon, "Revisiting the Vanishing Frontier: The Legacy of Frederick Jackson Turner," *Western Historical Quarterly,* April 1987, 176. I borrow the phrase "people of plenty" from David Potter's provocative 1954 book *People of Plenty: Economic Abundance and the American Character.*

22. Cronon, "Revisiting the Vanishing Frontier," 171.

23. Turner to Allen, 31 October 1881, b1, f4, FJTPH.

24. Cronon, "Landscape and Home," 92.

25. Ibid., 92.

26. Cronon, "Landscape and Home," 92–93; William Cronon, *Changes in the Land: Indians, Colonists, and the Ecology of New England* (New York, 2003 ed.), 173–74. University of Colorado historian Gloria L. Main, wife of Jackson Turner Main, the grandson of Frederick Jackson Turner, tendered an enthusiastic review of *Changes:* "I wholeheartedly recommend the book to everybody interested in frontier history." *Journal of Economic History,* September 1984, 887.

27. Cronon, *Changes in the Land,* 74.

28. Ibid., 99, 170.

29. William Cronon, *Nature's Metropolis: Chicago and the Great West* (New York, 1991), xv, xvii.

30. Ibid., xxiv, 6; Henry David Thoreau, *Walden and Civil Disobedience* (New York, 1965 ed.), 126.

31. Cronon, *Nature's Metropolis,* 19.

32. Ibid., 92.

33. Ibid., 266, 217–20, 384, 385.

34. Cronon interview with author.

35. William Cronon, "Why the Past Matters," *Wisconsin Magazine of History,* Autumn 2000, 10.

36. Turner to Merle Curti, 8 August 1928, b39, f69, FJTPH.

Sources

Archives, Interviews, and Correspondence

Archives

ALCP	Arthur Lyon Cross Papers, Bentley Historical Library, University of Michigan
ASJP	Arthur Schlesinger Jr. Papers, John F. Kennedy Presidential Library and Museum
BLPP	Bessie Louise Pierce Papers, Special Collections Research Center, University of Chicago Library
CALHD	College of Arts and Letters, History Department Records, University Archives, University of Wisconsin
CBP	Carl Becker Papers, Carl A. Kroch Library, Cornell University
CLP	Christopher Lasch Papers, Rush Rhees Library, University of Rochester
CLSGF	College of Letters and Science, General Files, University Archives, University of Wisconsin
CMBP	Charles and Mary Beard Papers, Roy O. West Library, DePauw University
CNP	Curtis Nettles Papers, Carl A. Kroch Library, Cornell University
DHGC	Department of History, General Correspondence, University Archives, University of Wisconsin
FHHP	Fred H. Harrington Papers, University Archives, University of Wisconsin
FJTPH	Frederick Jackson Turner Papers, Huntington Library
FJTPW	Frederick Jackson Turner Papers, Wisconsin Historical Society
FSP	Fred Shannon Papers, University of Illinois Archives
GMP	George Mosse Papers, University Archives, University of Wisconsin
HDM	History Department Minutes, University Archives, University of Wisconsin
HKBP	Howard K. Beale Papers, Wisconsin Historical Society
HWP	Harvey Wish Papers, University Archives, Case Western Reserve University
JHPB	John D. Hicks Papers, Bancroft Library, University of California at Berkeley
JHPW	John D. Hicks Papers, Wisconsin Historical Society

MCP	Merle Curti Papers, Wisconsin Historical Society
MWCP	Margaret Wooster Curti Papers, Sophia Smith Collection, Smith College
OAHR	Organization of American Historians Records, Ruth Lilly Special Collections and Archives, Indiana University—Purdue University, Indianapolis
OGVP	Oswald Garrison Villard Papers, Houghton Library, Harvard University
OWP	Oscar Winther Papers, Office of University Archives, Indiana University
PGP	Paul Gates Papers, Carl A. Kroch Library, Cornell University
PKP	Paul Knaplund Papers, University Archives, the University of Wisconsin
RGTP	Reuben Gold Thwaites Papers, Wisconsin Historical Society
RHP	Richard Hofstadter Papers, Columbia University Rare Books and Manuscript Library
SAP	Stephen Ambrose Papers, Wisconsin Historical Society
SHP	Stull Holt Papers, Special Collections Division, University of Washington Libraries
SOLP	Studies on the Left Papers, Wisconsin Historical Society
SPT	Selig Perlman Tape (three tape recordings), Wisconsin Historical Society
SSRCP	Social Science Research Council Papers, Rockefeller Archive Center
TRP	Theodore Roosevelt Papers, Wisconsin Historical Society
TSP	Theodore Saloutos Papers, Special Collections Department, Iowa State University
UWF	University of Wisconsin File, Rockefeller Archive Center
VCP	Vernon Carstensen Papers, Special Collections Division, University of Washington Libraries
VWCP	Verner Winslow Crane Papers, Bentley Historical Library, University of Michigan
WAWP	William Appleman Williams Papers, Special Collections, Oregon State University Libraries
WBHP	William B. Hesseltine Papers, Wisconsin Historical Society
WFAP	William F. Allen Papers, Wisconsin Historical Society
WHS	Wisconsin Historical Society
WLP	William Leuchtenburg Papers, Wilson Library, University of North Carolina at Chapel Hill
WSCP	Wayne S. Cole Papers, Herbert Hoover Presidential Library and Museum

University of Wisconsin–Madison Oral History Program

Paul Conkin	Merle E. Curti	Thomas McCormick
John M. Cooper	Philip Curtin	Gaines Post
E. David Cronon	Fred H. Harrington	Morton Rothstein

Interviews and Correspondence

Loren Baritz, phone interview, 26 January 2004

Allan G. Bogue, Madison, WI, 21 June 2005

Margaret Beattie Bogue, Madison, WI, 21 June 2005

Paul Buhle, Washington DC, 8 January 2004

E. David Cronon, Madison, WI, 22 June 2005

William C. Cronon, Madison, WI, 29 February 2008

Allen Davis, Philadelphia, 10 February 2004

Lloyd Gardner, Newtown, PA, 8 June 2004

James Gilbert, College Park, MD, 3 February 2004

John P. Kaminski, Madison, WI, 1 August, 2006

Richard Kirkendall, phone interview, 25 May 2005

Stanley I. Kutler, Madison, WI, 5 August 2006

Walter LaFeber, Ithaca, NY, 18 December 2003

Saul Landau, phone interview, 19 February 2004

Gerda Lerner, phone interview, 28 September 2005

William Leuchtenburg, Chapel Hill, NC, 17 June 2000

G. Don Lillibridge, phone interview, 13 February 2004

Diane Lindstrom, correspondence, 25 September 2005

Pauline Maier, phone interview, 2 June 2005

Linda Newman, Madison, WI, 22 June 2005

Stanley Rolnick, phone interview, 18 September 2003

Jane Schulenburg, Madison, WI, 24 June 2005

Robert Freeman Smith, Toledo, OH, 29 September 2006

Kenneth Stampp, Berkeley, CA, 23 August 2000

James Weinstein, phone interview, 10 December 2003

Index